The Bedside, Bathtub, and Armchair Companion to Dracula

The Bedside, Bathtub, and Armchair Companion to Dracula

Mark Dawidziak

continuum

2008

The Continuum International Publishing Group Inc
80 Maiden Lane, New York, NY 10038

The Continuum International Publishing Group Ltd
The Tower Building, 11 York Road, London SE1 7NX

www.continuumbooks.com

Printed in the United States of America

Library of Congress Cataloging-in-Publication Data
To come...

ISBN 978-0-8264-1794-7

Library of Congress Cataloging-in-Publication Data

Dawidziak, Mark, 1956-
    The bedside, bathtub, and armchair companion to Dracula / Mark Dawidziak.
        p. cm.
    Includes bibliographical references.
    ISBN-13: 978-0-8264-1794-7 (pbk. : alk. paper)
    ISBN-10: 0-8264-1794-9 (pbk. : alk. paper) 1. Stoker, Bram, 1847-1912. Dracula-
-Miscellanea. 2. Dracula, Count (Fictitious character)--Miscellanea. 3. Horror
tales, English--Miscellanea. 4. Vampires in literature--Miscellanea. 5. Vampire
films--Miscellanea. 6. Vampires in mass media--Miscellanea. I. Title.

    PR6037.T617D78227 2008
    823'.8--dc22

                                    2008019145

For my brother, Joe.

In the immortal words of Lugosi's Dracula,
"making the most out of life . . . while it lasts!"

Table of Contents

A Casket of Quotes

. . . .

Bram Stoker's Dracula *seems a remarkable achievement to me because it humanizes the outside evil concept; we grasp it in a familiar way Lovecraft never allowed, and we can feel its texture. It is an adventure story, but it never degenerates to the level of Edgar Rice Burroughs or* Varney the Vampire.
—*Stephen King,* Danse Macabre *(1981)*

Dracula is the grandfather of the modern horror tale. Like a grandfather, it should be treated with respect.
—*Richard Matheson, screen treatment for TV film* Dracula, *1972*

I think it is the very best story of diablerie which I have read for many years. It is really wonderful how with so much exciting interest over so long a book there is never an anticlimax.
—*Arthur Conan Doyle, letter to Bram Stoker, August 20, 1897*

Let me say at once that we have a complete masterpiece, flawed here and there, as the Chinese insist masterpieces should be, but nevertheless, the real thing.
—*Leonard Wolf, Introduction,* The Annotated Dracula *(1975)*

It's the yardstick, isn't it? It's not only the novel against which we measure all vampire books, it's in many ways the novel against which we measure any horror story.
—Dracula *scholar Elizabeth Miller, interview with the author, 2006*

Nobody has ever really filmed Bram Stoker's book as he wrote it. So most people don't know what a wonderful book it is.
—Christopher Lee, interview with the author, 2001

Stoker came up with one of the basic horror paradigms: the perfect stranger . . . please allow me to introduce myself, I'm a man of wealth and means. He's the seducer, bringing death and promising immortality. He embodies societal ambivalence about sex and death. That's not only remained incredibly potent, it has remained relevant.
—Wes Craven, interview with the author, 2002

How these papers have been placed in sequence will be made manifest in the reading of them.
—Bram Stoker, Preface to Dracula (1897)

The cover of the first paperback edition of Dracula depicts the chilling moment when Jonathan Harker sees the count climbing down the castle wall.

Dracula among Us, or,
The Importance of Being Dracula

. . . .

"I am Dracula; and I bid you welcome. . . ."
—**Count Dracula**, Dracula, *chapter 2*

Abbott and Costello were the ones who introduced me to Count Dracula. Although close encounters of the vampiric kind are supposed to occur at night, I'm reasonably certain this was a sunny Saturday afternoon in 1963. One of New York City's television stations was showing *Abbott and Costello Meet Frankenstein*, the 1948 Universal film that marked the second and last time Bela Lugosi played the vampire king on screen.

My twin brother, Mike, and I were somewhere between our seventh and eighth birthdays, and we never missed an opportunity to watch or rewatch an Abbott and Costello movie or TV show. We still can communicate to this day, in a kind of secret language, by quoting dialogue from Bud-and-Lou routines.

Comedy teams, you see, occupied vast stretches of what passed for children's programming in New York at that time. By the age of seven, we had spent countless hours in the company of Abbott and Costello, Laurel and Hardy, and the Three Stooges. Comedy—particularly the team variety—was king, as far as we were concerned. Maybe it was New York. Maybe it was our own distinct form of insanity. Maybe it was a twin thing.

I also saw *Room Service* (1938), my first Marx Brothers film, at the advanced age of seven, and that, too, had a profound impact. But that's a subject for another time and another book.

Abbott and Costello Meet Frankenstein opened up an entirely new world for me, largely because the monsters were played relatively true to fright form. It always was fun following Bud and Lou, of course, yet here they were, tearing along a landscape as unfamiliar to me as it was intriguing. There were coffins and capes and bats and mad experiments and dungeon lairs, and I couldn't have been more enthralled.

> . . . I could see a white face and red, gleaming eyes.
> —Mina Murray, Dracula, chapter 8

While I certainly was fascinated by the Frankenstein monster (even as robotically played by the actor Glenn Strange) and the lycanthropic Larry Talbot (Lon Chaney Jr. in his fifth go-around as the Wolf Man), it was Lugosi's portrayal of Dracula in the Abbott and Costello movie that really hooked me. Much is made in that film about the hypnotic power of the count's stare. If you looked too deeply into his eyes, you would fall under his spell. You wouldn't get any argument out of me.

Comedy now had a rival for my affections. That afternoon transformed me into a horror fan, hunting up issues of *Famous Monsters of Filmland* magazine

and scouring the weekly TV listings for any scary movie, particularly a Universal monster movie, that might show up on one of the seven New York stations (and you couldn't depend on channel 13, just relaunched as "the educa-

The well-traveled Dell Laurel Library paperback edition of Dracula *purchased by the author about forty years ago in Huntington, New York.*

tional channel," for much help in this department).

I received the Aurora monster model kit of Lugosi as Dracula for my next birthday. I caught up with the 1931 version of *Dracula* not long after that, and, by then, I was reasonably certain that my family, the Dawidziaks, must have their origins in the southeast corner of Poland touching the Carpathian Mountains. Recent genealogical research conducted by my eldest brother, Joe, appears to have driven a stake through this claim, but I'm not giving up the family castle in the Carpathians. There is great wisdom in those lines delivered by the newspaper editor near the end of director John Ford's *The Man Who Shot Liberty Valance* (1962), a film released about the time I first saw *Abbott and Costello Meet Frankenstein*: "This is the West, sir. When the legend becomes fact, print the legend."

> . . . he has a fearful hold on me.
> —Jonathan Harker, Dracula, chapter 3

So, like most Americans on the planet during the last seventy-five years, my first encounter with Dracula was through the movies. As the fascination deepened, I learned that there was this fellow named Bram Stoker, and he got this whole *Dracula* thing started with an 1897 novel. I was deeply grateful to Mr. Stoker, but I had no real interest in reading his book. There wasn't even a copy of it in our house—until, one day, with money raised from my *Long Island Press* paper

The Collier Books paperback edition of Frankenstein, *with its eerie cover promising close encounters of the Karloff kind.*

route, I proudly plunked down a dollar and twenty-five cents (plus tax) for paperback copies of Stoker's *Dracula* and Mary Shelley's *Frankenstein* (1818).

The Collier Books edition of *Frankenstein* featured a vivid, very Karloff-like drawing of the creature as I expected him to appear—with flat head, greenish face, and bolts protruding from the neck. The Dell Laurel Library edition of *Dracula* depicted its title character as a fang-bearing, red-lipped, pointy-eared (and, this is the important part) *older* gentleman with flowing white hair and a drooping white mustache, and this was not as I expected him to appear. Clearly, *Frankenstein* was going to have it all over *Dracula*. This Stoker guy didn't even seem to know how his own vampire was supposed to look. By this time, I had made allowances for Draculas who looked like John Carradine or Christopher Lee, but this drawing didn't resemble Carradine, Lee, or Lugosi.

Despite those frequent warnings about not judging a book by its cover, I decided to first tackle *Frankenstein*. Well, to paraphrase Claude Rains (not

in 1933's *The Invisible Man* or one of his other Universal horror films, but in 1942's *Casablanca*), I was *shocked*—shocked— to discover how vastly different Shelley's *Frankenstein* was from the one in the Karloff films. Hey, I was in junior high, and I was waiting for lightning bolts and spark-spewing machinery to literally shock the monster into life. More stunners awaited. Shelley's creature, despite expectations raised by the cover, was not even a close relation to the Karloff monster in looks or speech. Telling Victor Frankenstein his "life story," the creature launched into a monologue that sounded like a flowery collaboration between a philosophy student and a romantic poet. And in a paperback that was 190 pages long, this monologue lasted 37 pages. The monster rambled on for 37 pages, for crying out loud!

I was beyond baffled when the creature eloquently summed up his misery with this astounding oratorical flourish: "My sufferings were augmented also by the oppressive sense of the injustice and ingratitude of their infliction." Folks, I had to read that one a couple of times before I could bend my reeling brain around it. We were a long way from, "Bread—good! Fire—bad!"

More than just being shocked, though, I was bored. It was a long, lumbering march through *Frankenstein*, and I was in no hurry to creak open *Dracula*'s vault door. I did, however; and quicker than you can say "I bid you welcome," this hand with a jeweled ring bolted out of it, grabbed me by the throat, and never let go. This book, at least to

The film that introduced me to Dracula . . . and Frankenstein: Abbott & Costello Meet Frankenstein *(1948), with Bela Lugosi as the Count and Glenn Strange as the Frankenstein monster*

my teen sensibility, moved like a house afire. Count Dracula, I soon learned, was introduced as "a tall old man, clean shaven save for a long white moustache, and clad in black from head to foot, without a single speck of colour about him anywhere."

It wasn't Bela Lugosi, and I couldn't have cared less. Stoker's novel had the giddyap-and-go adventure appeal of one of the Sherlock Holmes mysteries I already greatly prized. It had the spookiness of an old Universal horror film. And, being structured as a series of journal entries and letters, it had the verité style of something that actually might have happened.

"Stoker was a fastidious man who was very interested in organization," comments Michael J. Barsanti, a curator who helps researchers unlock the secrets of Stoker's *Dracula* notes at the Rosenbach Museum and Library in Philadelphia. "So much of the style of the book is about bits and pieces of information put in order. There's all that emphasis on filing and assembling notes, and the use of modern devices, like the typewriter, and it grounds the book in reality. So, in essence, the reader becomes the detective and can solve the case."

For the second time, I had encountered the count and walked away with the same reaction: "I'm not completely sure what's going on here, but I sure want to be part of it."

> *I am all in a sea of wonders. I doubt; I fear; I think strange things which I dare not confess to my own soul.*
> —*Jonathan Harker,* Dracula, *chapter 2*

I reread both *Dracula* and *Frankenstein* when I was in my twenties, and this time appreciated and enjoyed the philosophical underpinnings to Shelley's novel. Again, I plead ignorance for that first time around; I was only a teenager, after all. Then again, it might be argued that Shelley was only a teenager when she wrote the book. This says a great deal about Mary Shelley as a teenager, and a little bit about me, I suppose.

What shocked me about *Frankenstein* the second time around was how much shorter it was than *Dracula*. Going into that second reading, I would have bet cash money that *Frankenstein* was the longer book, by far. It had to be. But it wasn't. Indeed, it wasn't even close. *Dracula* clocks in at a little under 161,000 words. *Frankenstein*—are you ready?—is only about 75,000 words.

The books obviously hadn't changed. I had changed and, not surprisingly, I began to see different aspects to Stoker's novel as well. I saw new and deeper metaphoric dimensions. The book was everything it had been before—and more. The same thing happened when I reread the book in my thirties. The same thing happened when I revisited it in my forties.

It never failed to be what it was at the very first: a great read. It can always be savored on the level of one terrific adventure story, complete with all the Gothic trappings and Victorian codes of chivalry. After each rereading of the novel, however, I was left grappling with a slightly different view of what Dracula represents: The seductive lure of evil? The promise of immortality? The yearning for life wrapped around our fascination with death? Freudian theory that links sex and death?

Was Dracula a creature born of xenophobia—the embodiment of a British fear and mistrust of foreigners? Was Dracula a Marxist myth created for a growing labor movement and warning of aristocratic bloodsuckers preying on the working class? Was he crafted from the Victorian era's suppression of sexual matters and its horror of venereal disease? Is the vampire kiss (bite) a sexual metaphor? Dracula, after all, has always been a sucker for a pretty neck.

Could the stake itself be a phallic symbol? Is it a book that champions the empowerment of women, or does it betray a Victorian author's mistrust of "the modern woman" and an accompanying fear of emasculation?

Are parts of the book sexist and homophobic, as well as racist and anti-Semitic? Does it subversively celebrate heterosexuality and homosexuality while, at the same time, exhibiting a lurking dread of those topics good Victorians considered taboo? Do those taboo subjects include everything from rape to (gasp!) necrophilia?

"It's a very edgy novel for the time it was written," notes J. Gordon Melton, author of *The Vampire Book: The Encyclopedia of the Undead*. "He was getting away with everything he could get away with in that book, and I think the reader perceives that."

The road to Castle Dracula is paved with all kinds of theories and countertheories. There's even debate about how much Stoker was aware of these possible subtexts. What did he know, and when did he know it? One biographer, Daniel Farson, declares that he's sure Stoker "was unaware of the sexuality in *Dracula*."

This assertion seems downright batty to another Stoker biographer, Barbara Belford, who believes that *Dracula* uses the Halloween mask of supernatural fiction to sneak into forbidden territory. And, taking issue with Farson and many scholars, she contends that Stoker, "an intelligent and insightful man," knew what he was doing: "He was many things, but naïve was not one of them; he was fully aware of the subtexts in his horror tale."

Literature professor and leading *Dracula* authority Elizabeth Miller believes the novel is simmering with subtexts, but "I don't think it was a conscious thing on his part."

And, say, what about all that Catholic imagery and ritual? The book was about confronting evil, to be sure, but was Stoker addressing the evil inside each individual, or was his symbolic target something he saw as a greater societal evil? No matter which side of the philosophical moat you end up on, redemption and salvation certainly are themes woven into this intricate tapestry of terror.

In his provocative 1993 book Horror and the Holy: Wisdom-Teachings of the Monster Tale, psychologist Kirk J. Schneider contends that "Dracula is a study of one side of infinity or the holy. It is a dizzying journey into concealment, seduction, and obliteration." For Schneider, ancient questions with biblical overtones provide the undercurrent for Dracula. He cites the book of Job, and it's a fairly convincing citation.

Religion plays a role in all this, no doubt, but does the novel reinforce traditional beliefs or merely trade on them? "Post-Darwin, this was a period of doubt in traditional Christian concepts of immortality, and the vampire offered an interesting alternative to this," Melton notes. "You weren't quite immortal, but your life could be extended. You paid a price for that, but you got to live with some kind of consciousness instead of just going into nothingness. Dracula offered that. He's a character that represents sensuality, power, and immortality. That's a formidable combination."

The interpretations and permutations seem endless. The more you read Stoker's book—and about Stoker's book—the trickier it gets. The more you talk to other fans of the novel the more your appreciation for it grows.

Here we are, more than 110 years after the publication of Dracula, still trying to get a clear image of a vampire with the ability to elude our grasp, to change shape, to slip in and out of our consciousness "on moonlight rays as elemental dust."

"There are mysteries which men can only guess at, which age by age they may solve only in part. Believe me, we are now on the verge of one."
—*Professor Van Helsing,*
Dracula, *chapter 15*

We aren't helped by the realization that Stoker was, in many ways, as shadowy and elusive a figure as Count Dracula. He was by no means a first-rate writer ranking anywhere near many of the literary figures he counted as friends and close acquaintances: George Bernard Shaw, Mark Twain, Walt Whitman, Oscar Wilde. None of his other books comes within screaming distance of Dracula. Ever read The Lair of the White Worm (1911) or The Jewel of the Seven Stars (1903)? Well, they're two of his better novels.

Yet Stoker not only caught greatness by the wolf's tail in Dracula, he produced a metaphoric masterpiece so profound that generation after generation has grafted its fears and anxieties onto its plot.

But there was no reflection of him in the mirror!
—*Jonathan Harker,* Dracula,
chapter 2

Although Dracula casts no reflection

in the mirror, the book challenges each reader to gaze into the glass and describe what is seen. What reflection is there? Is the mirror showing you something of yourself? Or is it showing an aspect of the society around you?

It is no wonder that, in the last decade of the twentieth century, *Dracula* was read as everything from an AIDS allegory to a cautionary anticult tale. It is not surprising that each generation gives us at least one screen Dracula who represents changing times and attitudes. "It's what every individual does and every generation does with this book," Miller observes. "Everyone arrives at that novel with baggage, so everyone creates his or her own Dracula."

If not a mirror, *Dracula* can be viewed as something of a literary Rorschach test. You look at the shapes on the page, and each one represents something deeply psychological to each person. Some think the ink blot looks like a bat. Some see images that are deeply sensual. Others say it looks like darkness spreading over a continent. Well, what do you see?

Was this what Stoker set out to write? You'll never convince me that it is. I believe he sat down to write nothing more than a rattling good horror yarn. Writing to W. E. Gladstone in 1897, Stoker maintained there was "nothing base" in his novel, adding that "the book is necessarily full of horrors and terrors but I trust these are calculated to cleanse the mind by pity and terror."

But Stoker couldn't help being unconsciously influenced by the amazing array of people he knew, the tur-

The man who launched a thousand impersonations, Bela Lugosi, goes for the throat in the 1931 film version of Dracula.

bulent times he lived in, his many travels, his Irish childhood, his wide reading of supernatural tales and lore. British society, like Stoker, had been shaken to its class-conscious roots, first by Charles Darwin, then by Sigmund Freud. It was a time when an internationally respected scientist could be on the Cambridge University faculty and a founding member of the Society for Psychical Research. All of these ingredients, whether the author knew it or not, went into the bubbling cauldron that is *Dracula*. And the cauldron is so big that it has the capacity to accommodate the added ingredients we've been tossing in there for more than a century.

I am in fear, in awful fear, and there is no escape for me; I am encompassed about with terrors that I dare not think of.
—Jonathan Harker, **Dracula,** *chapter 3*

I started this introduction on a personal note. I'm cashing in that note right now to underscore a few points: first, to answer why they sought out me, this particular lunatic, to write this companion to *Dracula*; second, to illustrate how few people first meet the count through Stoker's book; and third, to demonstrate how thoroughly Dracula has infiltrated the pop culture. "If you went to a local mall and showed people pictures of characters from great novels, you'd get a lot of blank stares," Miller notes. "But everybody knows Count Dracula."

They certainly do. Show pictures of nineteenth-century literary characters to a random sampling of mall shoppers, and you'll be lucky if one in a thousand can name Mr. Micawber from *David Copperfield*, Edward Rochester from *Jane Eyre*, Hester Prynne from *The Scarlet Letter*, and Mr. Darcy from *Pride and Prejudice*. And these novels are heavyweight contenders in the nineteenth-century division.

A few of Miller's mall shoppers might have a decent shot at naming Mr. Hyde, Tom Sawyer, or Long John Silver. But even those who never have read the books will come up with Sherlock Holmes, Ebenezer Scrooge, and Count Dracula. They are the truly iconic fig-

From earth box to cereal box, Count Dracula has jumped into the pop-culture consciousness.

ures who have made the pop-culture jump, instantly recognizable in commercials and cartoons. People know Sherlock, Scrooge, and Dracula (even if their image of him does look more like Lugosi than Stoker's vampire).

Dracula was the last of the nineteenth century's three major horror stories, following Shelley's *Frankenstein* and Robert Louis Stevenson's *The Strange Case of Dr. Jekyll and Mr. Hyde* (1886); yet if you take a casual look around, you'll see that Stoker's novel had the greater impact on our culture and our nightmares. Count Dracula has been called the king of the vampires, but, in truth, he is the king of all the monsters, and his influence can be seen everywhere today: in everything from the number-obsessed Count on *Sesame Street* to the vast fandom for Anne Rice's Vampire Chronicles. He is used to teach children their one-two-threes and to sell breakfast cereal (Count Chocula).

When you've been fascinated by all things Dracula since the age of seven, friends and relatives tend to be on the lookout for, well, all things Dracula. It has always made it easy for them on gift-giving occasions. If all else fails, they take the Transylvania route—through the Borgo Pass and deep into the pop-culture dungeon.

Gathered over the decades and scattered throughout my house, you'll find Dracula movie posters, Dracula action figures, Dracula books, Dracula playing cards, a replica of the Dracula Crest ring worn by Carradine and Lugosi in the Universal horror films, Dracula comic books, a Dracula air freshener, Dracula documentaries, that 1962 Aurora Dracula model, Dracula key rings, Dracula paperweights, Dracula medallions, Dracula plush dolls, Dracula bobblehead figures, a replica of the Dracula cane carried by Gary Oldman in Francis Ford Coppola's film *Bram Stoker's Dracula* (1992), Dracula movie stills by the dozens, a Dracula finger puppet, a Dracula pocket knife (shaped like a coffin, of course), a Dracula water pistol, Dracula refrigerator magnets, Dracula capes (ranging from cheap rain-poncho plastic to rich shimmering velvet), Dracula coffee mugs, Dracula puzzles (several of 'em), Dracula pens, Dracula coloring books, Dracula T-shirts, Dracula lapel pins, a Dracula mouse pad, Dracula stationery, Dracula cards, Dracula Halloween decorations (from a fang-bearing head for the front door to a four-foot plastic Lugosi statue that lights up for dark October nights), Dracula little-big-head figurines, Dracula records and cassette tapes, Dracula CDs and DVDs, a framed version of the 1997 Dracula stamp issued by the United States Postal Service, Dracula postcards, Dracula beer (um, the remaining empty bottles, at least), Dracula buttons, Dracula masks, a Dracula flashlight, Dracula coin banks, Dracula short-story anthologies, Dracula birthday cards, and . . . well, you get the general idea.

Now here's the really scary part. As extensive (and geeky) as this Dracula collection might seem to some, it's actually quite modest by fan standards. This is just the tip of the gravestone,

No crypt would be complete without a Count Dracula air freshener.

so to speak, but this sampling of items is not meant to demonstrate how deep the Dracula fascination runs in me. It's meant to show how deep a hold the vampire character has on our collective consciousness.

What manner of man is this, or what manner of creature, is it in the semblance of man?
—Jonathan Harker, **Dracula,** *chapter 3*

Stoker may not have been aware of the depth and intricacy of his book's psychological underpinnings, but he surely had a keen appreciation of how danger can attract and seduce the strongest of us. "'You may go anywhere you wish in the castle, except where the doors are locked,'" Dracula tells Harker, "'where of course you will not wish to go.'" And, of course, that's precisely where we *do* wish to go.

Psychologically, Stoker understood the power of Dracula's warning to Harker. It is, in many ways, the appeal of the entire horror genre. And whatever you do, unless you want to be scared out of your wits, *don't open that door!* We will open that door. We *will* open that book because, for some reason, we do want to be scared out of our wits.

Schneider argues that the novel's central conflict is "between the fascination with and terror of the infinitesimal." But why are we drawn to the monster and the monstrous? "Ever adaptable," writes Dracula researcher David J. Skal in his landmark book *Hollywood Gothic: The Tangled Web of Dracula from Novel to Stage to Screen*, "Dracula has been a literary Victorian sex nightmare, a stock figure of theatrical melodrama, a movie icon, a trademark, cuddle toy, swizzle stick, and breakfast cereal. Complex, contradictory, and confounding, Dracula tantalizingly begs the question put to the ghost in Hamlet: 'Be thou a spirit of health or goblin damned.'"

Skal knows better than anyone the aptness of quoting this line. References to William Shakespeare in general and this play in particular run throughout *Dracula*. So, which is it—spirit of health or goblin damned? Does he frighten you? Does he entice you? Does he frighten and entice you?

Dracula is "a creature of such symbolic force that he has become something like a culture hero whom our first duty is to hate even while we have for him a certain weird admiration," notes Leonard Wolf, author of *A Dream of Dracula* and editor of *The Annotated Dracula*. "What an elegant monster he is! How strong, how graceful, how lonely, how wise. And above all—and here is the central mystery—how deadly . . . and erotic."

And here is a central part of the Dracula mystique—he is both man and monster. "That's what allows for the vampire to be romanticized," noted the late Dan Curtis, the creator of *Dark Shadows* and the director-producer behind the 1974 TV movie *Bram Stoker's Dracula*. "He can look like you or me, so you can have the beautiful leading lady

Not Count Dracula's choice of beverage, but Cleveland's Great Lakes Brewing Company serves up a tasty Halloween choice with Nosferatu ale.

The Dracula image adorns a staggering variety of merchandise, including this puzzle marketed to children.

attracted to him. You can't do that with a mummy, Frankenstein's monster, a zombie, or a werewolf. The vampire, though, pretty much looks like us."

Viewed from this perspective, Count Dracula is almost the Transylvania equivalent of another iconic character with a license to kill: James Bond. You almost can hear the Hollywood pitch: "Women find him irresistible. Men want to be like him."

But the vampire's bloodlust knows no bounds. He is attracted to men and women, and both men and women can find him attractive. He can inflame our hidden passions. He can incite our envy, as well as our terror.

Strong and wise as he is, Count Dracula perishes at the end of the novel that set him on the path to genuine immortality. Well, of course, he does. And, of course, he must. That's the way the old vampire crumbles—to dust, in the shadow of his Transylvania castle. The vampire king also perishes at the end of almost every play, film, ballet, comedy sketch, and television program in which he appears. But you already know that. And you also know that a little thing like death isn't going to stop the bloodthirsty Count.

He comes back. Dispatch him how you choose: stake him, expose him to sunlight, drench him in holy water, force him into a movie titled *Billy the Kid versus Dracula* (1966). He just keeps coming back.

We follow Jonathan Harker (Keanu Reeves) into forbidden territory, meeting the Dracula wives and more psychological, religious, political, and sexual interpretations than you can shake a stake at.

"My revenge is just begun! I spread it over centuries, and time is on my side."
—**Count Dracula**, **Dracula,** *chapter 23*

Thus speaks the vampire king in the horror novel bearing his name. Centuries? Ah, we've caught him in a boastful mood, I'm afraid, but, still, I suspect his estimate is correct. The powerful spell cast by this endlessly fascinating character has already lasted more than a century and, if anything, his power is growing. As these undead guys go in literature, you don't get more undead than Count Dracula.

The posters for 1969's *Dracula Has Risen from the Grave* playfully proclaimed, "You just can't keep a good man down." That has been Dracula's history since Stoker launched him on his monstrous career.

Bram Stoker:
The Man behind the Vampire

· · · · · · · · · · ·

Let me begin with facts—bare, meager facts, verified by books and figures, and of which there can be no doubt.
—Jonathan Harker, Dracula, *chapter 3*

I f the name Bram Stoker is at all familiar to you, that's undoubtedly because he wrote *Dracula*. But at the height of his fame in London, Stoker not only wasn't best known as the author of *Dracula*, he wasn't even known as a writer. The tall, burly, redheaded Irishman rubbed elbows with the rich and famous as the manager of the city's Lyceum Theatre.

Bram Stoker, nearing sixty, about nine years after the publication of Dracula.

His glory was the reflected variety. He was the loyal right-hand man to Henry Irving, England's reigning superstar of the stage. Think of Laurence Olivier's stature as an actor, then wrap that around the popularity of Tom Hanks, and it will give you some idea of Irving's status in the late nineteenth century and the early years of the twentieth. Irving is chiefly known to theater students these days. In 1895, with Queen Victoria wielding the ceremonial sword, he became the first actor to be knighted. He died in 1905 and was buried in Westminster Abbey, and a nation mourned his loss. If you had suggested at the funeral that, a century later, Stoker's fame would far outlive and outshine Irving's, you would have been either laughed out or run out of the Abbey.

Bram Stoker was not knighted like his eldest brother, Thornley, a professor of anatomy and president of the Royal College of Surgeons in Ireland, and he was not the toast of two continents, as was Irving, who won acclaim in such Shakespearian roles as Hamlet, Lear, Macbeth, Othello, Richard III, and Shylock. Yet neither Sir Henry Irving nor Sir Thornley Stoker ended up with his name in the title of a major Hollywood film directed by Francis Ford Coppola.

Neither man has his name on the cover of a book available in almost any library and bookstore in the United States and Great Britain.

Stoker's fame has only grown since his death in 1912. He will survive the test of centuries because, well, he created a character capable of surviving through the centuries. During Stoker's childhood years, however, there was some question about whether he would even survive to adolescence.

Named for his father, Abraham Stoker was born on November 8, 1847. He was the third of seven children born to Abraham and Charlotte Stoker of Dublin, Ireland. He was born in Clontarf, a coastal village north of Dublin. The Stokers had temporarily gone to this seaside spot to escape the ravages of the great potato famine, and it gave the future storyteller a link to a spot celebrated in Irish lore and history (Brian Boru, high king of Ireland, defeated the invading Danes at the Battle of Clontarf in 1014). The link is a source of local pride in Clontarf, which is also home to a museum called the Bram Stoker Dracula Experience. Open Fridays, Saturdays, and Sundays, it promises a "different, most interesting, brilliantly, entertaining, interactive, educational and very scary adventure based on the life of Bram Stoker, his great vampire creation (Dracula) and horror in general."

Those who knew the strapping, athletic Bram Stoker decades later in London were surprised to learn he had been a sickly child. "I was a very strong man," Stoker wrote in his two-volume *Personal Reminisces* of *Henry Irving* (1906). "It is true that I had known weakness. In my babyhood, I used, I understand, to be often at the point of death. Certainly till I was about seven years old I never knew what it was to stand upright. I was naturally thoughtful and the leisure of long illness gave opportunity for many thoughts which were fruitful according to their kind in later years."

If anything, Stoker understates his early frailty. Although the nature of his childhood weakness is the matter of much conjecture (as is the cause of his death), it is recorded that he didn't walk until the age of seven. "While his older brother and sister ran about the house or played games in the sprawling, leafy park outside his window, he remained in bed or was carried from room to room by his mother," Barbara Belford wrote in her 1996 book, *Bram Stoker: A Biography of the Author of Dracula.*

The maxim assures us that the hand that rocks the cradle rules the world. In the case of sickly nineteenth-century children who grew up to be writers, one should look at who was rocking their world with gruesome bedtime stories. Both Charles Dickens and Robert Louis Stevenson credited the vivid, often horrifying tales told by young nursemaids with having profound influences on their imaginations. Both of Stoker's doting parents filled his evening hours with visions summoned from Irish history and mythology. Local fables and legends were, according to Belford, a rich source of "tales of ghosts, decomposing corpses, and staked bodies."

Family tradition held that the formidable Charlotte Stoker shared memories of surviving the devastating cholera epidemic of 1832. "When she told Bram her experiences of the epidemic, it is probable that she included stories of people who had been buried alive," observes Stoker's great-nephew Daniel Farson in his 1975 book, *The Man Who Wrote Dracula: A Biography of Bram Stoker.* "This must have been an early influence. And if they seem strange bedtime tales for a sick child, Bram's own collection of children's stories, *Under the Sunset,* published in London in 1882, is equally bizarre . . . a more unsuitable book for children can hardly be imagined."

And more horrific bedtime stories can hardly be imagined than Charlotte's memories of how cholera spread through her hometown, Sligo. Belford's biography relates that Charlotte told Bram of "how she heard the banshee cry when her mother died; of how some during the famine drank blood extracted from the veins of cattle, including the family cow."

So, before he could walk, Bram

A dressing-room sketch of Stoker's boss—and a possible model for Count Dracula—the great actor Henry Irving.

Stoker was traveling on the road that would lead to *Dracula.*

But Stoker's inheritance included much more than a taste for the macabre. The Protestant and conservative Stokers stressed education, stability, and diligence to their children. The family was by no means wealthy, but ambition was nurtured in the five sons of Abraham and Charlotte Stoker. A lover of books and plays, Abraham Stoker the elder was a career civil servant at Dublin Castle (not really a castle, in the Dracula sense, but a centuries-old collection of buildings).

By the time he entered Trinity College at sixteen, "Bram's recovery from his childhood sickness was absolute," Farson wrote of his great-uncle. He soon became a big man on campus, in every possible interpretation of the phrase. For one thing, the red-haired giant stood six-foot-two and weighed in at 175 pounds. For another, he was a star of both the rugby team and the Philosophical Society.

He collected first-prize silver cups and medals for foot races and walking marathons. He also developed a deep admiration for the poems of Walt Whitman—and he said so . . . out loud . . . and often . . . on the Trinity College campus. This took some courage, since the American poet was derided and denounced by many critics and most of Stoker's classmates. Stoker sent letters to Whitman, and, eventually, he would get to meet the idol of his college years.

After graduation from Trinity in 1870, Stoker followed his father into Dublin Castle and the life of a civil servant. While working as a clerk, he indulged his great love for the theater by attending plays whenever possible. Incensed by the poor level of the reviews in the city's newspapers, Stoker presented himself to Dr. Henry Maunsell, owner of the *Dublin Mail*, offering his services as a drama critic. Maunsell told him the paper could not afford the services of a drama critic. Stoker said he would gladly review plays "without fee or reward." Maunsell welcomed him aboard. "I had an absolutely free hand," Stoker recalled. "I was thus able to direct public attention, so far as my paper could effect it, where in my mind such was required."

The first review appeared in November 1871. Five years later, Henry Irving brought his production of *Hamlet* to Dublin. It was not the first time Stoker had seen Irving on an Irish stage. He had seen Irving as Captain Absolute in an August 1867 performance of *The Rivals*, and in a May 1871 production of the comedy *Two Roses*.

Irving's 1876 appearance in the title role of *Hamlet* was, however, the first time Stoker had an ability to express his opinion in print. Although not a total rave, the review of Irving's *Hamlet* was wildly enthusiastic. Was Stoker at this point under Irving's spell, the way Renfield would fall under Dracula's mesmeric power? Not yet.

The utterly delighted Irving asked to meet the young author of such a perceptive piece of criticism. They met, and Stoker was asked to Sunday dinner in his suite at the Shelbourne Hotel. The date was December 3, 1876. They talked through the night, Irving treating

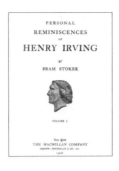

The shape of a friendship is charted in Stoker's two-volume tribute, published in 1906.

Stoker to a recitation of Thomas Hood's melodramatic narrative poem "The Dream of Eugene Aram."

"That experience I shall never—can never—forget . . . such was Irving's commanding force, so great was the magnetism of his genius, so profound was the sense of his dominance that I sat spellbound," Stoker wrote about thirty years later. "Outwardly I was as of stone. . . . As to its effect I had no adequate words. I can only say that after a few seconds of stony silence . . . I burst into something like hysterics."

Here is compelling evidence for those who claim that Irving was at least one of the models for Count Dracula. As Stoker himself tells us: "I was no hysterical subject. I was no green youth; no weak individual, yielding to a superior emotional force. I was as men go a strong man, strong in many ways." Now he had fallen under Irving's mesmeric power. He spoke with the actor until daybreak, just as Jonathan Harker, on his first night in Castle Dracula, talks with the count until the coming of the dawn.

Stoker's biographers have depicted Irving as self-centered and manipulative. The arguments are convincing, but it should be pointed out that Irving's response to Stoker was no less emotional. As tempting as it is to cast Stoker as Harker (or Renfield) and Irving as Dracula, the friendship seemed to be immediately and deeply felt on both sides. Before saying goodbye to Stoker, Irving excused himself, walked into his bedroom, and returned with an inscribed photograph for the Dublin critic. "My dear friend Stoker," he had written. "God bless you! God bless you!!! Henry Irving." Stoker noted that the ink was still wet.

"In those moments of our mutual emotion he too had found a friend and knew it," Stoker wrote. "Soul had looked into soul! From that hour began a friendship as profound, as close, as lasting as can be between two men."

Irving returned to England. Stoker returned to the life of a civil servant, continuing work on his first book. Accurately described by its author as a "dry-as-dust" volume, *The Duties of Clerks of Petty Sessions in Ireland* was published in 1879.

By then, Stoker had married Dublin beauty Florence Anne Lemon Balcombe, resigned from the civil service, and accepted Irving's invitation to manage his company. Bram and Florence were wed on December 4, 1878. The groom was thirty-one, the bride twenty. The newlyweds left Ireland five days later to join Irving's troupe in Birmingham. Their only child, Noel, was born on December 29, 1879.

Like Lucy Westenra, who, not yet twenty, receives three marriage proposals in one day (*Dracula*, chapter 5), Florence had no shortage of suitors before accepting Bram. One of the most ardent was a witty Dublin neighbor Bram knew well:

Oscar Fingal O'Flahertie Wills Wilde. The Stokers and Wilde would continue their friendship in London.

Irving had signed the lease on the 1,500-seat Lyceum Theatre in 1878. Stoker's duties as acting manager included supervising a front-of-house staff of forty-eight, handling all correspondence for "the Chief" ("and the letters were endless"), keeping the accounts, and planning company tours. The correspondence alone was a mighty task. Stoker estimated that he wrote half a million letters for "the Chief." He was at the center of London society, and, after Lyceum tours of the United States, Stoker was known and trusted by an astounding circle of celebrities on both sides of the Atlantic.

As devoted as he was to Irving, Stoker was in many ways closer to Irving's vivacious leading lady, Ellen Terry. If you're looking for some *Dracula* parallels, you'll find them in Stoker's fierce, constant, and chivalrous protection of the actress he called a "dutiful daughter." It is no great stretch to compare his idealization of Terry with the attitude adopted by the vampire-hunting men battling for Mina during the last third of the novel.

And Stoker certainly was viewed as "a man's man." His prose might not have been as muscular as the literary work of such contemporaries as Rudyard Kipling and George Bernard Shaw, but he was way ahead of them in actual muscle. Two thieves tired to rob Stoker after he delivered a lecture at Edinburgh University. He knocked down the assailants, hauling them off to the nearest police station. He also made headlines when in September

1882 he gallantly dove into the River Thames, risking his own life to rescue an elderly man who had attempted suicide. The man had jumped from a ferry, and the athletic Stoker kept him from going under, even though struggling against the tide. The man died, but Stoker's act of heroism was recognized with a bronze medal from the Royal Humane Society.

Even while taking care of "the Chief," the Lyceum, and his family, Stoker was trying to establish himself as an author. There were eighteen years and five titles between the publication of *The Duties of Clerks of Petty Sessions in Ireland* and the first edition of *Dracula*. *Under the Sunset*, a collection of eight fairy tales, appeared in 1881. It was followed in 1886 by *A Glimpse of America*, a booklet version of a lecture he delivered at the London Institution. His first novel, a romantic adventure story titled *The Snake's Pass*, hit print in 1890. Two more novels, *The Watter's Mou'* and *The Shoulder of Shasta*, were published in 1895. Then came *Dracula*.

There would be ten more books before his death on April 20, 1912. They would include the novels *The Mystery of the Sea* (1902), *The Jewel of Seven Stars* (1903), *The Lady of the Shroud* (1909), and *The Lair of the White Worm* (1911).

There are hints of what's to come in the fiction published before *Dracula*, just as there are echoes of the vampire novel in the work that followed it. None of the other work, however, even approaches the brilliance of *Dracula*. "How did the most successful horror novel in the English (and possibly in any) language come to be written by a man whose first published book was entitled *The Duties of Clerks of Petty Sessions in Ireland?*" asks Anthony Boucher in his introduction to the 1965 Heritage Press edition of *Dracula*. "One might extend the question to inquire how *Dracula* came to be written by the same man who wrote such arch fictions as *The Snake's Pass*, *The Watter's Mou'*, *The Shoulder of Shasta*, *The Mystery of the Sea*, and *The Lady of the Shroud*," adds Leonard Wolf in his introduction to *The Annotated Dracula* (1975). Boucher made no attempt to answer the question. Nor did Wolf, cautioning those who might explore the mystery that literary greatness "is easier to acknowledge than to explain."

Indeed, it is.

"Yet we acknowledge that he wrote a novel bigger than himself," *Dracula* authority Elizabeth Miller notes. "A couple of his short stories are exceptional, but the other novels are pedestrian." As much as they disagree on aspects of his personality, Stoker's biographers largely agree on the notion that this was the book where his many interests combined with his many influences to generate a perfect literary storm. It at least begins to answer the questions.

This phenomenon certainly has been known to occur in the sporting world. Consider the realm of golf, a universe often held to be more mystical and mysterious than Stoker's Transylvania. I realize that a hole in one to a vampire means a stake through the heart, but bear with me.

Consider the case of Orville Moody, a golfer no one would have confused with the legendary likes of Jack Nicklaus or Arnold Palmer. Nicknamed Sarge after spending fourteen years in the Army,

Moody caught fire in 1969 and won the U.S. Open. Mind you, this is generally acknowledged as the most difficult and demanding of the sport's four major championships. It was the only PGA tour victory of Moody's career. Bram Stoker, who no would confuse with the legendary likes of Dickens or Kipling, was the Orville Moody of English literature.

James Douglas, nicknamed Buster, was a heavyweight boxer no would have confused with Muhammad Ali or Joe Louis. But on the night of February 11, 1990, Douglas pulled off what is considered the greatest upset in ring history. He knocked out the undefeated, seemingly unbeatable Mike Tyson to claim the heavyweight championship. The Las Vegas odds were forty-two to one. Later that year, Buster made his one and only title defense, losing the championship to Evander Holyfield. He was knocked out in the third round. Greatness can be defined by a career. Or it can be defined by a moment. Submitted for your approval: Sarge, Buster, and Bram.

"At the time he died, he was considered a second-rate hack author," comments *Dracula* and vampire expert J. Gordon Melton. "And today, if it weren't for *Dracula*, none of us would know who Bram Stoker is. But Dracula, being a vampire, is immortal, and so perhaps it's fitting that he gave a kind of immortality to Bram Stoker."

Agreed. But we're back to disagreement when trying to determine just how much Stoker's home life influenced the book. Farson made some rather sensational claims in his 1975 biography. The most sensational

Bram Stoker, as one might have encountered him outside London's Lyceum Theatre in the 1880s: a tall, burly, red-headed Irishman.

was that his great-uncle had died of tertiary syphilis. "When his wife's frigidity drove him to other women, probably prostitutes among them, Bram's writing showed signs of guilt and sexual frustration," Farson writes. "He probably caught syphilis around the turn of the century, probably as early as the year of *Dracula*, 1897. (It usually takes ten to fifteen years before it kills.) By 1897 it seems that he had been celibate for more than twenty years, as far as Florence was concerned."

The death certificate listed three causes: "Locomotor Ataxy 6 months, Granular Contracted Kidney. Exhaustion." It was the last of these that held sway when the first major work on the author, Harry Ludlam's curiously titled *A Biography of Dracula: The Life Story of Bram Stoker*, appeared in 1962. It was the first of the three causes that intrigued Farson, who handed the death certificate to his doctor. He was told that Locomotor Ataxia was "the equivalent of *Tabes Dorsalis* and *General Paresis*, better known as GPI—General Paralysis of the Insane." To Farson, the medical terminology led to only one conclusion: syphilis.

It was a conclusion readily embraced by many *Dracula* scholars. How easily it could be applied to the psychosexual interpretations of Stoker's novel! It all fit: Stoker was the proper Victorian driven by sexual urges yet fearful of them, and those urges were the death of him. The vampire becomes a metaphor for venereal disease, spreading death and madness throughout the British Empire.

Farson's conclusion went largely unchallenged for about fifteen years. Leslie Ann Shephard, the founder of the Bram Stoker Society, made a strong bid to refute the syphilis diagnosis. Then Barbara Belford sided with Shephard in her 1996 biography. Although she didn't completely rule out the possibility, Belford believes that Farson leapt to conclusions on flimsy evidence. There is, after all, no conclusive proof that Florence was the frigid wife described by Farson. There also is no proof that Stoker sought comfort in the arms of prostitutes. "Stoker was never the classic demented, psychotic personality associated with syphilis," Belford writes. "We shall never know whether Stoker ever had syphilis, but the medical evidence argues against his dying from the disease." Marvin Kaye, in one of his appendixes to *Dracula: The Definitive Edition* (1996), puts it even stronger: "With no evidence other than his imagination and vague rumors that Stoker had been a 'ladies' man,' Farson decides that his great-uncle contracted the disease from Parisian prostitutes."

Other prominent *Dracula* scholars, however, have sided with Farson, and the arrival of a fourth major biography in 2004, Paul Murray's outstanding *From the Shadow of Dracula: A Life of Bram Stoker*, has not quashed the debate.

Whatever the actual cause of death, there is no doubt that the hale and athletic Stoker began to go downhill in late 1905. Within a few months, he was financially, physically, and emotionally devastated by two shattering blows: the death of Irving, and a 1906 stroke that left him unconscious for twenty-four hours. The stroke impaired his eyesight to the point that Stoker needed a magnifying glass to read and write. Farson blamed this on syphilis, noting that optic atrophy was a common symptom of the disease. Kaye countered that Charlotte Stoker also suffered from failing eyesight in her last years, and this suggested a hereditary cause.

Beset by money worries, gout, and Bright's disease, Stoker soldiered on for another six years. He died at age sixty-four, with England stunned by a tragedy not yet a week old: the unsinkable *Titanic* had struck an iceberg on its maiden voyage and sunk less than three hours later.

Ludlam records that Stoker was working to the very end, dying with "some of his early stories spread out on his bed." According to Florence, he was planning, "even as the shadow of death was over him," to publish three volumes of tales. She selected several of these short stories for the only collection to appear after his death, *Dracula's Guest, and Other Weird Stories*, in 1914. It was the last of Bram Stoker's eighteen books.

Dracula Rises:
The 1897 Publication

· · · · · · · · · · ·

I saw the manuscript in his hand, and I knew that when he read it he would realize how much I knew. . . .
—**Mina Harker,** Dracula, *chapter 17*

A newspaper sketch of Bram Stoker on the rise as a storyteller.

The first edition of *Dracula* appeared in May 1897. Published by Archibald Constable and Company, its cloth binding cover was a mustard yellow with four words— "Dracula by Bram Stoker"—in blood-red letters. Although Constable had published Stoker's two previous books, *The Watter's Mou'* and *The Shoulder of Shasta*, little care seems have been taken with this unremarkable cover. Viewed today, the only shocking thing about Constable's presentation is how incredibly ordinary it seems.

Stoker had begun outlining the story in March 1890. His first title for the book was *Count Wampyr*. He changed this to *Wampyr*, then started writing *Dracula* in his notes for the novel. But he seemed to have settled on *The Un-Dead* and (horrors!) *The Dead Un-Dead*. The title that appears on both the typescript and the May 1897 contract for the book is *The Un-Dead*. The reason for the change to *Dracula* remains a mystery.

Dracula sold for six shillings. The first print run was 3,000 copies. The first American edition, published by Doubleday, McClure and Co., appeared in 1899. The reviews were mixed. Here are some samples of the early critical response:

> The recollection of this weird and ghostly tale will doubtless haunt us for some time to come. It would be unfair to the author to divulge the plot. We therefore restrict ourselves to the statement that the eerie chapters are

written and strung together with every considerable art and cunning, and also with unmistakable literary power. Tribute must also be paid to the rich imagination of which Mr. Bram Stoker here gives liberal evidence. Persons of small courage and weak nerves should confine their reading of these gruesome pages strictly to the hours between dawn and sunset. (*Daily Mail*, June 1, 1897)

Mr. Stoker is the purveyor of so many strange wares that *Dracula* reads like a determined effort to go, as it were, "one better" than others in the same field. . . . Mr. Stoker's way of presenting his matter, and still more the matter itself, are of too direct and uncompromising a kind. They lack the essential note of awful remoteness and at the same time subtle affinity that separates while it links our humanity with unknown beings and possibilities hovering on the confines of the known world. *Dracula* is highly sensational, but it is wanting in the constructive art as well as in the higher literary sense. (*Athenaeum*, June 26, 1897)

Mr. Stoker has shown considerable ability in the use that he has made of all the available traditions of vampirology, but we think his story would have been all the more effective if he had chosen an earlier time period. The up-to-dateness of the book—the phonograph diaries, typewriters, and so on—hardly fits in with the medieval methods which ultimately secure the victory for Count Dracula's foes. (*Spectator*, July 31, 1897)

Since Wilkie Collins left us we have had no tale of mystery so liberal in matter and so closely woven. But with the intricate plot, and the methods of the narrative, the resemblance to stories of the author of *The Woman in White* ceases; for the audacity and the horror of *Dracula* are Mr. Stoker's own . . . we read nearly the whole with rapt attention. (*Bookman*, August 1897)

This weird tale is about vampires, not a single, quiet creeping vampire, but a whole band of them, governed by a vampire monarch, who is apparently a first cousin to Mephistopheles. It is a pity that Mr Bram Stoker was not content to employ such supernatural anti-vampire receipts as his wildest imagination might have invented without rashly venturing on a domain where angels fear to tread. (*Punch*, 1897)

Stoker's friend, Sherlock Holmes creator Arthur Conan Doyle, sided with the *Daily Mail* and *Bookman*, sending a wildly enthusiastic letter to the author of *Dracula*. And while mothers also aren't known as the most unprejudiced of readers, perhaps Charlotte Stoker provided the most prescient review of all. "My dear, it is splendid, a thousand miles beyond anything you have written before," she wrote her son, "and I feel certain will place you very high in the writers of the day—the story and style being deeply sensational, exciting and interesting. . . . No book since Mrs Shelley's 'Frankenstein' or indeed any other at all has come near yours in originality, or terror—Poe is nowhere. I have read much but I have never met a book like it at all. In its terrible excitement it should make a widespread reputation and much money for you."

She was wrong about the money. She was right about the book.

The Prehistory: Vampire Style—Myths and Legends around the World

· · · · · · · · · · ·

"All we have to go upon are traditions and superstitions."
—*Professor Van Helsing,* Dracula, *chapter 18*

The novel *Dracula*, like the count's Transylvania castle portrayed within it, is a vast structure rising from ancient foundations. Some of the essential building materials used by Bram Stoker were the European myths and legends about vampires.

Almost every culture has created a vampire being of some kind. Some are actual bloodsucking beings that drain away the very fluid of human vitality. Others are psychic vampires, draining away an individual's life force or will to live.

Dracula researchers Raymond T. McNally and Radu Florescu have made some questionable assertions in their books about the historical Dracula, Vlad the Impaler, but they are not overstating the case when they comment, "Vampire belief is universal; it has been documented in ancient Babylon, Egypt, Rome, Greece, and China. Vampire accounts exist in completely separate civilizations, where any direct borrowing would not have been possible."

McNally and Florescu's *In Search of Dracula* tells how vampires are found on Babylonian pottery and in ancient Peruvian rites. Chinese folklore tells of the powerful *chiang-shih*. Greek mythology gives us the bloodsucking *lamiai*. West African legends warn of the *obayifo*.

Some vampire myths are more ghoulish than others, as Gothic artist Joseph Vargo's dramatic picture, "Vampyre," makes eerily clear. (Artwork © Joseph Vargo)

The powers differ from one tradition to another, but they're all vampires of some kind. You also can find vampire traditions in Armenia, Haiti, India, Ireland, Italy, Malaysia, Mexico, the Philippines, and Thailand.

Still, vampire legends are most closely associated with eastern Europe. They run through the folklore of such Slavic countries as Bulgaria (the vampire), the Czech Republic (the *upir*), Poland (the *upier*), and Russia (the *uppyr*). But most Americans associate vampire lore with two non-Slavic countries, Hungary and Romania.

Yes, Bela Lugosi was born in a town that was then part of Hungary. And, yes, when Stoker wrote *Dracula*, Transylvania was part of Hungary. And, yes, the book begins and ends in Transylvania.

The recent work of Hungarian scholars, however, makes a strong case for there being little link between their country and the vampire. If there are or were vampire traditions in Hungary, notes vampire expert J. Gordon Melton, they probably developed from associations with Gypsies and surrounding Slavic cultures.

(Mem., *I must ask the Count about these superstitions.*)
—*Jonathan Harker*, Dracula, *chapter 1*

Romania, though, is another belfry of bats. Here there is a rich folklore concerning the undead, even though it differs greatly from the neighboring Slavic legends.

Stoker's novel was not translated into Romanian until 1992. Historians and scholars in that country considered Romania the homeland of Vlad the Impaler and *strigoi*, not Count Dracula and the vampire. "With forty-five percent of the population living and working in farm-related areas, one would expect the Romanian folklore to be very much alive, which it is, inclusive of its supernatural entities," comments Nicolae Paduraru, founder of the Transylvania Society of Dracula. "The situation is changing fast. We may witness the last generation of genuine peasants—keepers of folkloric treasures. The Romanian folklore does not know of vampires. They are proper to our Slavic neighbors, which exported them to Hungary, Germany, and Austria. The Romanians have a cousin of the vampire called the strigoi (ghost), an eternal, immaterial, malefic energy burst."

What? No vampires in Romania? In Transylvania? Strictly speaking, this is the case. While the *strigoi* shares some characteristics with the vampire, it is hardly a Stoker-like representative of the undead. "What I mean to say is that upon its arrival, in 1992, the vampire count found no vacant seat at the table of the Romanian supernatural entities," Paduraru adds. "With the strigoi fully functional, Dracula has to wait a few generations till the Romanians also loose their folklore, then welcome the Count."

Not even the word *nosferatu* is Romanian. Nor does it mean undead. It means . . . well, we're not quite sure what it means, or its precise derivation. One etymological theory is that it comes from the Greek word *nosphoros*, "plague carrier" or "disease bearing." Yet

The Count's influence can be seen at the Dracula Pub in Gniezno, a town in western Poland, a country with its share of vampire lore. (Photo by Joseph C. Dawidziak)

there's no good explanation for how a Greek word would have jumped into the Romanian language. Other theories are that it is a corruption of the Latin for "not breathing" or the Romanian words for "unclean" and "insufferable."

Stoker, who never set foot on Transylvanian soil, originally intended to set the novel in Styria, an Austrian location already used for a vampire story (Joseph Thomas Sheridan Le Fanu's "Carmilla," 1872). He switched to Transylvania (a name meaning "land beyond the forest"), making detailed notes after consulting such works as William Wilkinson's *Account of the Principalities of Wallachia and Moldavia* (1820), A. F. Crosse's *Round about the Carpathians* (1878), Charles Boner's *Transylvania* (1865), Major E. C. Johnson's *On the Track of the Crescent* (1885), and Emily de Laszkowski Gerard's *The Land Beyond the Forest* (1888).

He may have first spotted the name Dracula in Wilkinson's book. He certainly gleaned a great deal from Gerard, who lived in the area for two years. It also was in Gerard's book (or her 1885

essay, "Transylvania Superstitions") that Stoker found the word *nosferatu*, accepting her claim that it was a Romanian term for vampire. She got it wrong, and no one is really certain why or how.

Borrowing from the literary vampire traditions as well as the superstitions, Stoker took all of this research and planted it in the fertile Transylvania soil of his imagination. When an American journalist questioned the wisdom of describing a country he never saw, Stoker responded, "Trees are trees, mountains are, generally speaking, mountains, no matter in what country you find them, and one description may be made to answer for all."

This would suggest a cavalier—and, perhaps, sloppy—attitude toward research. But Stoker's notes, housed at the Rosenbach Museum and Library in Philadelphia, show how thoroughly the author investigated everything from traditions to timetables. While it's certainly true that his book is not a reliable source of Transylvanian history or folklore, *Dracula* did use a fictional version of the region to masterfully synthesize the many literary and folk tales about vampires into a rule book that, for the most part, we're still using for coping with the undead.

Les Daniels was not overstating the case when he wrote, in *Living in Fear: A History of Horror in the Mass Media* (1975), "The story is so well known that it has become the authoritative source on the care and feeding of vampires; Stoker's decisions regarding the legendary attributes of these lecherous leeches have been accepted as gospel truth."

The Prehistory: Vampire Lit 101—Lord Ruthven, Varney, and Carmilla

. . . .

"A year ago which of us would have received such a possibility, in the midst of our scientific, sceptical, matter-of-fact nineteenth century?"
—*Professor Van Helsing,* Dracula, *chapter 18*

Lord George Gordon Byron was bored. It was the night of June 15, 1816. Weary of the stormy weather hanging about the rented Villa Diodati on Lake Geneva, he read some supernatural tales to the small circle of companions driven indoors. It was the prelude to a proposal: "We will each write a ghost story."

On the receiving end of this ghostly gauntlet were the teenage Mary Wolstonecraft Godwin; her married lover (and soon-to-be husband), poet Percy Bysshe Shelley; Mary's stepsister, Claire Clairmont; and John Polidori, a young doctor and aspiring writer. It was, of course, the spark that gave birth to Mary Wollstonecraft Shelley's *Frankenstein* (1818).

While clearly the most important literary outcome of that competition, *Frankenstein* was not the only completed story to see print. There was another, and it would have a direct influence on Bram Stoker's *Dracula*. Polidori had started a story about a skull-headed

Roddy McDowall, Ione Sky, Meg Tilly and Roy Dotrice star in Showtime's 1989 cable version of horror master Joseph Sheridan Le Fanu's pre-Dracula vampire story, Carmilla.

woman; he gave it up before too long. Byron had started a story about a man encountering a friend he saw die in Greece, and he, too, gave it up before too long. Polidori, though, decided to take it up, developing the abandoned Byron story into a short story titled "The Vampyre" (1819).

Polidori took a playful shot, calling his vampire Lord Ruthven, the name a former Byron lover, Caroline Lamb, had given a Byronesque character in her novel *Glenarvon*. But Byron may have had the last laugh. The first major literary vampire tale was published in the April 1819 issue of *New Monthly Magazine*, mistakenly under Byron's name.

No less an authority than Johann Wolfgang von Goethe acclaimed it as a masterpiece. And Goethe knew from vampires, having dallied with the undead in his 1797 work "The Bride of Corinth." The German writer not only gave Byron full credit, he declared that "The Vampyre" was Byron's greatest composition. Poor Polidori again was denied authorship when the owner of *New Monthly Magazine* published the story as a booklet. Although Byron had written a letter explaining how the story developed, his more bankable name also appeared on the booklet version.

Obviously inspired by Byron, Lord Ruthven is killed by bandits in Greece. Before he dies, Ruthven makes his friend, Aubrey, "swear by all your soul reveres, by all your nature fears, swear that for a year and a day you will not impart your knowledge of my crimes or death to any living being in any way, whatever may happen, whatever you may see." Aubrey swears, only to encounter Ruthven, very much undead, in London. "Remember your oath," Ruthven keeps saying, all the time closing in on Aubrey's sister.

By the time Polidori committed suicide in 1821, Lord Ruthven was on his way to becoming a matinee idol in France. Cyprien Bérard wrote a sequel novel, *Lord Ruthven ou Les Vampires*, that was published in 1820. And Jean Charles Emmanuel Nodier turned Polidori's story into a three-act play, *Le Vampire*, that was first staged in June 1819. This first vampire drama ignited a theater craze that quickly sent Ruthven across the English Channel to the London stage. There soon would be four more plays with Ruthven, and, in 1852, Alexandre Dumas used him as a character in a play.

Lord Ruthven paved the way for *Dracula* in many ways. Polidori's story demonstrated the literary possibilities for a mysterious and powerful nobleman vampire. The stage success showed how effectively the vampire character could be transferred to another medium—one in which he could flourish as a more romantic figure. "Polidori gave us the prototype vampire, as, at least in English literature, we will get him ever after," writes *Dracula* scholar Leonard Wolf. "That is to say, as a nobleman, aloof, brilliant, chilling, fascinating to women, and coolly evil."

In a way, therefore, that stormy June night in 1816 planted the seeds for both *Frankenstein* and *Dracula*.

Other literary vampires include those in Gottfried August Burger's poem

"Lenora" (1796), British poet Robert Southey's ballad "Thalaba the Destroyer" (1801), and French author Théophile Gautier's *La Morte Amoureuse* (an 1836 story later published in English as *The Beautiful Vampire*).

A year after Polidori's "The Vampyre" hit print, Irish clergyman Charles Robert Maturin published what may or not be the first vampire novel in English—it depends on how you view the central character of *Melmoth the Wanderer* (1820). Greatly admired by H. P. Lovecraft, Maturin's convoluted story combined elements of the "wandering Jew" figure and the vampire. It tells of a somber scholar who sells his soul to the devil for 150 years of life. *Dracula* researchers Raymond T. McNally and Radu Florescu count this as a vampire tale; but indefatigable researcher J. Gordon Melton cites another book as the first English vampire novel. It has been similarly argued that a few of Edgar Allan Poe's short stories, including 1835's "Bernice" and "Morella," feature vampire characters, but this seems to be stretching a paranormal point.

There are, however, intriguing Maturin links to Stoker. An Anglo-Irish Protestant who attended Trinity College, the eccentric curate specialized in Gothic plays and novels. He was the uncle of Jane Wilde, who was the mother of Oscar Wilde, who was well acquainted with Bram and Florence Stoker.

Melton contends that the sprawling *Varney the Vampire* is the first vampire novel in English. First published in 109 weekly installments, the 220-chap-

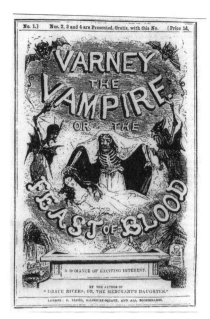

Appearing fifty years before Dracula, *the penny dreadful* Varney the Vampire *was one of three major nineteenth-century vampire stories to set the stage for Stoker's novel.*

ter story was wrongly believed to have been written by Thomas Preskett Prest, author of *The String of Pearls: A Romance* (1846), which is famous for introducing the character Sweeney Todd. Although other authors probably contributed to the sprawling work, the majority of the installments of *Varney the Vampire* appear to have been written by James Malcolm Rymer.

Varney the Vampire: or, The Feast of Blood, A Romance of Exciting Interest has no claim on being a work of serious literature. It was written for the English popular press known as "the penny dreadfuls." Indeed, Prest's *String of Pearls*, packed with sensationalism and ghastly murders, was one of the best known of the penny dreadfuls.

Influenced by Polidori's "The Vampyre," Rymer's tale presents another nosferatu nobleman, Sir Francis Varney. The tall, gaunt vampire with "fearful looking teeth" appears in chapter 1 attacking Flora Bannerworth: "With a plunge he seizes her neck in his fang-like teeth—a gush of blood, and a hideous sucking noise follows. *The girl has swooned, and the vampire is at his hideous repast.*"

This is vintage penny-dreadful stuff, turned out fast and aimed at the widest possible audience. Published over a two-year span in the mid-1840s, the chapters were collected into an 868-page book that appeared in 1847. As poorly written as much of it is, *Varney the Vampire* provides the obvious and sturdy bridge between Polidori and Stoker. Sir Francis is the transitional vampire between Lord Ruthven and Count Dracula.

The third major nineteenth-century vampire tale was extremely literary in tone and style. Joseph Thomas Sheridan Le Fanu's "Carmilla" was first published in *Dark Blue* magazine, then in the Irish author's 1872 collection, *In a Glass Darkly*. This time, the vampire is a woman: Carmilla attacks the daughter of an Austrian civil servant, providing the story with its much-discussed lesbian subtext.

A horror writer of rich imagination, the underrated Le Fanu was read and appreciated by Stoker. So perhaps the genuine native soil for a vampire is to be found in Dublin. Certainly one is at least justified in asking what it was about the city that made it the ideal breeding ground for spinners of supernatural stories. How's this for ghostly grouping? Le Fanu, Maturin, and Stoker all grew up in Dublin and attended Trinity College; that's quite a Trinity terror trio.

The spacing of the landmark nineteenth-century vampire stories also is fascinating. There's roughly a twenty-five year gap between the publication of Polidori's "The Vampyre" and the first chapters of Rymer's *Varney the Vampire*. The space of time between the publication of *Varney the Vampire* as a book and the appearance of "Carmilla" in Le Fanu's *In a Glass Darkly* is exactly

1847 was a big year for vampire literature: the undead Varney the Vampire *made his appearance in print, and Bram Stoker was born in Ireland.*

twenty-five years. And the time frame between *In a Glass Darkly* and the first edition of *Dracula* is precisely—care to guess?—twenty-five years.

The literary stage had been set for Stoker, and the time seemed more than right. It seemed like destiny.

The Prehistory:
Horror Ancestry—Shelley,
Poe, and Stevenson

· · · · · · · · · · ·

". . . in exact order all things that have been, up to this moment."
—*Professor Van Helsing,* Dracula, *chapter 18*

As we have seen, Bram Stoker was building on vampire lore and literature to construct the mighty edifice that would become *Dracula*. But he also was consciously building on and borrowing from at least three other (or at least related) literary forms. First, and most conspicuously, there was the broader and richer horror field.

The nineteenth century was a time when the modern horror tale came of age, and two novels provided a creepy climax to this rich period of fright fiction: *Dracula* in 1897 and the Henry James ghost story *The Turn of the Screw* in 1898.

Thanks to Edgar Allan Poe, Mary Wollstonecraft Shelley, and Robert Louis Stevenson, supernatural fiction made the jump from sensationalism to literature in the nineteenth century. Only a small percentage of what Stevenson wrote could be considered horror, but his 1886 best-seller *The Strange Case of Dr. Jekyll and Mr. Hyde* demonstrated to Stoker how wonderfully suited the terror tale was for plumbing great metaphoric and psychological depths. Stevenson, like Charles Dickens and Washington Irving before him, was a family author who couldn't resist a good spooker. What is Dickens's *Christmas Carol* (1843), after all, if not the story of a man haunted by ghosts? Yet *A Christmas Carol* isn't classified as horror literature. Shelley's *Frankenstein* (1818) and Stevenson's *Dr. Jekyll and Mr. Hyde* are, and, thematically, they are the two books that paved the way for Stoker. *Dracula* often is linked with the Shelley and Stevenson classics, and rightly so. They are the three seminal horror novels that few would deny a place on the literature shelf. Their descendants surround us today in bookstores, in movie theaters, and on television screens. How many eerie ideas have emerged from Victor Frankenstein's laboratory, bubbled up from Dr. Jekyll's foaming beaker, or crawled out from Count Dracula's coffin?

S stands for supernatural. S also stands for Shelley, Stevenson, and Stoker. They didn't invent the notion of monsters as metaphors, but this terror triumvirate certainly took the concept to grand and glorious heights (more on this in a later chapter; gotta keep moving).

On the short story front, Ambrose Bierce, Joseph Sheridan Le Fanu, Edgar Allan Poe, and, again, Stevenson were making acres of nineteenth-century flesh

creep with terror. The children of the night—what music they were making!

But *Dracula* also fits into a second and closely related genre, that of the Gothic. In tone, texture, and trappings, *Dracula* is as much a Gothic novel as it is a horror novel. More romantic and mysterious than terrifying, the Gothic genre got rolling with Horace Walpole's *The Castle of Otranto* (1764). Many consider this the first Gothic novel, but the genre reached a new height of popularity with the work of Ann Radcliffe (1764–1823). The daughter of a London haberdasher, Radcliffe enticed readers with seemingly supernatural events, typically providing natural explanations in her denouements. She reached a wide readership with *The Romance of the Forest* (1791),

The master of psychological terror, Edgar Allan Poe demonstrated the literary possibilities of the horror themes with his stories and poems.

The Mysteries of Udolpho (1794), and *The Italian* (1797). Some say the genteel and proper Radcliffe retired from the Gothic field when Matthew Gregory Lewis introduced elements of sensationalism, sensuality, and gore with *The Monk* (1796). Others say a nervous disposition had more to do with her withdrawal from spooky landscapes.

With Lewis picking up the Gothic torch in England, Charles Brockden Brown was trying his hand at the genre in the United States. Preceding even Irving as a professional American author, Brown turned out several novels in the Radcliffe tradition. They included *Wieland; or, The Transformation: An American Tale* (1798) and *Ormond; or, The Secret Witness* (1799). Like Radcliffe, Brown preferred scientific or pseudoscientific explanations to his romantic mysteries.

A century later, however, Stoker followed the lurid Lewis lead when plotting *Dracula*. Unlike Radcliffe and Lewis, Stoker rejected the disturbing strain of anti-Catholicism that runs through the English Gothic works of the nineteenth century. Indeed, throughout the book, Catholicism provides key weapons for battling the count. Still, *Dracula* carries on many of the traditions of the Gothic novel—the same traditions that also influenced Anne, Charlotte, and Emily Brontë; Lord George Gordon Byron; Dickens; Henry James; Poe; Shelley; and Stevenson.

Drawing literary lines can get tricky, and you can find *Frankenstein, Dr. Jekyll and Mr. Hyde*, and *Dracula* classified as Gothic works as well as horror novels. Or is *Frankenstein* early science fiction? There is no definitive answer. What is certain is that both the Gothic and horror lines met at the entrance to Castle Dracula.

The third literary path to Stoker's masterpiece provided the novel with its compelling form: diaries, letters, journals, newspaper clippings, telegrams. This was the epistolary novel, and here Stoker unquestionably was most influenced by the success of *The Woman in White*, the multivoice mystery novel by Wilkie Collins. It was serialized (1859–60) in *All the Year Round*, the weekly magazine started by the author's close friend, Dickens. A meticulous craftsman and a master of mood, Collins was ideal for the "make 'em laugh, make 'em cry, make 'em *wait*" school of serialized storytelling. *The Woman in White* (published as a book in 1860) and *The Moonstone* (1868) did much to shape the English mystery novel. And *The Woman in White* did much to provide *Dracula* with its shape as a novel.

Vlad Tidings!

• • • • • • • • • • • •

"Here I am noble; I am boyar; the common people know me, and I am master."
—**Count Dracula**, Dracula, *chapter 2*

Vlad the Impaler was not a complete unknown when Boston College professor Raymond T. McNally and Romanian historian Radu Florescu published their landmark book *In Search of Dracula* in 1972. Many with an interest in Bram Stoker's novel or European history were at least vaguely aware that there had been a fifteenth-century Romanian ruler called both Dracula and Vlad Tepes (pronounced tse-pesh, meaning "impaler").

Vlad Tepes (1431-1476), the historical Dracula, provided a name for Bram Stoker's vampire, and probably very little else.

Indeed, vampire specialist Donald F. Glut had devoted several pages to Vlad in his *True Vampires of History*, published in 1971. In the February 1966 issue of *Famous Monsters of Filmland*, editor Forrest J Ackerman captioned a picture of the staked vampire, "Dracula the Impaler at last himself impaled on a wooden stake!" Was the assumption that most fans of the magazine would get this rather pointed reference?

Still, after years of academic research, McNally and Florescu put the historical record together in a tantalizing and remarkably engaging way. And they put the historical Dracula on the pop-culture map. They also started a debate that has been raging among *Dracula* devotees ever since.

Did Stoker actually use Vlad the Impaler as the model for his vampire character? The link forged by McNally and Florescu in 1972 became stronger

and stronger over the next twenty years. By the time *Bram Stoker's Dracula* appeared on movie screens in 1992, the popular perception was that Vlad had inspired Stoker's character and the novel. So why shouldn't director Francis Ford Coppola include scenes of Gary Oldman as a prevampiric Vlad Dracula in fifteenth-century Transylvania? The connection already had been firmly established in the general public's mind. "We went from almost no one knowing about Vlad the Impaler to everyone assuming he was the inspiration for the book," comments *Dracula* expert Elizabeth Miller.

There's no question that Stoker stumbled across a mention of Vlad the Impaler when he was researching his story. The author's *Dracula* notes at Philadelphia's Rosenbach Museum and Library include two typed entries that, at first blush, seem to bolster the McNally-Florescu claim of Stoker fusing Vlad and his vampire king into one character.

By the time Gary Oldman played Dracula in director Francis Ford Coppola's 1992 film, the link between Stoker's vampire and the historical figure of Vlad the Impaler was firmly established in the mass culture.

Both entries are drawn from William Wilkinson's *Account of the Principalities of Wallachia and Moldavia.*

The first note states that Dracula "in Wallachian language means DEVIL. Wallachians were accustomed to give it as a surname to any person who rendered himself conspicuous by courage, cruel actions or cunning." This is likely where Stoker first saw the name that became the title of his vampire novel.

The second entry is a fourteen-line note about the *voivode* (warrior ruler) Dracula, a fifteenth-century Wallachian ruler who crossed the River Danube and battled Turkish troops.

Similarly, two passages in the novel seem to underscore the Vlad connection. In chapter 3, Dracula asks Harker, "'Who was it but one of my own race who as Voivode crossed the Danube and beat the Turk on his own ground?'" The count revels in memories of battle: "'This was a Dracula indeed!'" Then, in chapter 18, Professor Van Helsing tells his group of vampire hunters that their adversary "'must, indeed, have been that Voivode Dracula who won his name

against the Turk, over the great river on the very frontier of Turkeyland. If it be so, then he was no common man; for in that time, and for centuries after, he was spoken of as the cleverest and the most cunning, as well as the bravest of the sons of the "land beyond the forest." That mighty brain and that iron resolution went with him to his grave, and are even now arrayed against us.'"

It may all seem pretty convincing in a circumstantial kind of way. Yet Miller, author of the aptly titled *Dracula: Sense and Nonsense,* isn't buying it. "I have no doubt that Stoker knew diddly squat about Vlad the Impaler," remarks Miller, who has made a painstaking study of the author's notes. "He knew very, very little, and that was all from one source—Wilkinson. Some people have really gone overboard with the argument that Count Dracula is loosely based on Vlad the Impaler. Stoker borrowed the nickname, and that's pretty loose. Then you get people who say Vlad the Impaler inspired the novel, and that just drives my blood pressure up fifty points. Stoker was already writing a vampire novel before he came across references to Vlad, so how can anyone say that Vlad was the inspiration for a vampire novel?"

You might just as easily argue that the inspiration for Count Dracula was a dressed crab. Really. Noel Stoker has said that the spark for his father Bram's book was "a nightmarish dream" brought on by "a too generous helping of dressed crab at supper." The dream was of a vampire king rising from the grave. If this is true, there's a certain Shelley–Stevenson–Stoker supernatural symmetry to the nightmare scenario. Both Mary

Wollstonecraft Shelley's *Frankenstein* (1818) and Robert Louis Stevenson's *Dr. Jekyll and Mr. Hyde* (1886) were credited by their authors as starting in dreams.

Stoker made his first outline for *Dracula* on March 8, 1890, before he'd read about either Transylvania or the voivode Dracula. These earliest notes set the story in Styria, but there are basic ideas the writer would carry with him through the book's publication in 1897. There is a visit to a mysterious old castle. There is an old count. And there is the nightmarish encounter with vampire girls driven back by the old count: "rage & fury diabolical—this man belongs to me." The latter part of the line survived, suggesting to some Dracula's sexual attraction to Jonathan Harker.

By the middle of March, Stoker had completed an extensive four-part outline for his vampire novel. Each section was given a title: "Styria to London" (he later

German pamphlets about Vlad Tepes stressed atrocities, depicting the Wallachian ruler happily dining while surrounded by his impaled victims.

crossed out "Styria" and replaced it with "Transylvania"), "Tragedy," "Discovery," and "Punishment."

It's likely that Stoker found the passages on Transylvania and Dracula in a copy of Wilkinson's book borrowed from the Whitby Public Library. He was vacationing in the English seaside town during the summer of 1890, and Whitby, with its big graveyard and the ruins of Whitby Abbey, became the spot where the *Demeter*—the death ship bearing Dracula and his "earth boxes"—reaches land. Stoker probably pursued the Dracula and Transylvania research under the grand dome of the British Library's massive reading room. Stoker may well be describing his own experience when in the first chapter of *Dracula* he has Harker write, "Having some time at my disposal in London, I had visited the British Museum, and made search among the books and maps in the library regarding Transylvania; it had struck me that some foreknowledge of the country could hardly fail to have some importance in dealing with a noble of that country."

It's assumed that Stoker consulted a 1491 German pamphlet about Vlad Tepes; there was such a pamphlet in the library's collection. "Pretty much all Stoker knew was that there was this voivode named Dracula, who, in the 15th century, ruled Wallachia and crossed the Danube and fought against the Turks," Miller comments. "And according to Wilkinson, the name Dracula was the Romanian word for the devil. That's it. And there never was anything connecting Vlad to vampires."

Vampire legends, as we've already discovered, aren't even indigenous to Romania. Stoker, though, was so fascinated by the names Dracula and Transylvania that he took two huge geographical liberties that caused confusion to no end. First, he planted the vampire legend in Transylvanian soil, putting the region on the creepy path to its eventual status as international headquarters for all things horrific and supernatural. Second, he moved the historical Dracula's seat of power to the north.

Although Vlad Tepes was born in Transylvania (in the fortress town of Sighisoara in late 1431), the region he ruled was Wallachia. Those searching for a real Castle Dracula in Transylvania, therefore, are looking in the wrong area of modern-day Romania.

Vlad Dracula was the son of Vlad Dracul, so named after being initiated into the Holy Roman Emperor's Order of the Dragon. Members of the order used a dragon symbol as part of their standards, and *Dracul* was the Wallachian word for dragon (from the Latin *draco*). McNally and Florescu say that Dracul can also mean "devil" in Romanian.

Son of the dragon? Son of the devil? McNally and Florescu made much of the second interpretation of the name.

". . . we of the Dracula blood were amongst their leaders, for our spirit would not brook that we were not free."
—**Count Dracula,** Dracula, *chapter 3*

Vlad Dracula ruled Wallachia three times: October–November 1448; 1456-62; and November–December 1476. Killed in battle, he was buried in the island monastery of Snagov, near Bucharest.

German and Russian stories of Vlad Tepes depict him as a cruel tyrant and mass murderer. Several lurid pamphlets claimed to document his atrocities. It was the Turks, however, who gave him the nickname *kaziklu bey* (impaling prince), an acknowledgment of his preferred means of execution. While Tepes (impaler) was a title eventually acknowledged and accepted by Romanians, it was not one used by Vlad during his lifetime. He did, though, refer to himself as Dracula.

Impalement was meant to strike fear in enemies, and it worked. But many of the histories were written by Vlad's enemies. "There's little question that Vlad could resort to some fairly bloody and drastic methods," Miller observes. "There's also little question that many of the sources telling about his deeds are biased."

You get a far different story in Romania. Here, Vlad Tepes often is depicted as a national hero, a cunning soldier, an able administrator, or an almost-Robin Hood like figure. "No one here paid much attention to the Count until 1972 and Raymond McNally and Radu Florescu's *In Search of Dracula* confused the vampire-count with the Romanian fifteenth-century Vlad Dracula," comments Nicolae Paduraru, founder of the Transylvania Society of Dracula. "A flurry of apologetic books, in Romanian, defended the prince from vampiric associations. Vlad has always been perceived by the Romanians as an enabler and provider of competence, justice, law, and order. Applying 'tolerance zero,' Vlad turned his unruly, crime-ridden Valahia (Wallachia) into a model country—in only six years of rule."

Whichever view of Vlad you take, we're clearly a long way from Stoker's vampire king. "Yes, it is quite confusing for the Romanians to see their revered prince mixed up with a supernatural entity of malefic extraction, and equally confusing for the poorly informed western visitor to see the historic Dracula," Paduraru comments.

Even though Miller believes that *In Search of Dracula* and its sequels gave rise to the idea that Vlad Tepes was the direct inspiration for Count Dracula, she does not dismiss the book's importance to research on Stoker and the historical Dracula. "*In Search of Dracula* validated Dracula studies, and the historical aspects of that book is without significant historical error," she notes. "It was when McNally tried to graft on the argument that Vlad was the direct inspiration for the book that things got shaky. That theory has been thoroughly disproved."

J. Gordon Melton, author of *The Vampire Book: The Encyclopedia of the Undead*, echoes that thought: "The great thing that McNally and Florescu did was to create an intellectually interesting hypothesis to pursue. That made it legitimate to be interested in *Dracula* and vampires. McNally did try to push the notion that Vlad in some way could be considered a vampire, and nothing has the Romanian scholars more up in arms than that claim."

Yet while the link between Vlad Tepes and Count Dracula has been overstated, it cannot be completely dismissed. "It's wrong to think that Stoker took the historical Dracula and simply turned him into a vampire to suit the needs of his novel," notes Michael J. Barsanti, the Rosenbach Museum curator who has made a careful study of Stoker's *Dracula* notes. "But the discovery of the name, Dracula, gave this character an ethnic identity and a historical context. As slight

as that is, it is significant to the formation of the character."

It also gave him a name. "It's quite obvious the influence came in toward the end, it was nowhere near as powerful a link as McNally and Florescu projected back in 1972, and what influence was there was very indirect," Melton adds. "But the name was what was important. It changed the title of the book, and that was a stroke of genius. Would we still be reading this book if it was called *The Un-Dead* or *The Dead Un-Dead*?"

Vlad gets his own comic books, thanks to Topps.

And it appears that Stoker sent the manuscript to Archibald Constable and Company with *The Un-Dead* as the title. Whether it was changed before publication by Stoker or an editor is not known, "but the decision was fortuitous," *Dracula* authority David J. Skal has written in *Hollywood Gothic*; "the one-word title itself, the three sinister syllables that crack and undulate on the tongue, ambiguously foreign but somehow alluring, would be an undeniable component of the book's initial and continued mystique."

The German pamphlet in the British Library might also have given Stoker an idea or two on how to describe his vampire. There was a woodcut portrait of Vlad, so this could be another way the historical Dracula influenced the character. Yet speculation is a tricky game. "There's no hard evidence that Stoker used the pamphlet for his physical description of Dracula," Miller comments. "It's like the Arminius reference. Where's the proof?"

When Van Helsing is addressing the circle of friends in chapter 18 he notes, "I have asked my friend Arminius, of Buda-Pesth University, to make his record." From what Arminius has told him, Van Helsing concludes that the Transylvania vampire must be the voivode Dracula.

Van Helsing's friend unquestionably is Arminius Vambery (1832–1913), an adventurer, linguist, and professor at the University of Budapest. Vambery, who wrote in twelve languages and spoke in sixteen, dined with Henry Irving and Stoker in 1890. Since that was the year Stoker began work on the novel, it was widely assumed that Vambery was the one who introduced the author to Transylvania folklore and the historical Dracula.

Stoker's first biographer, Harry Ludlam, makes this leap when he writes that "Count Dracula began to stir in his tomb" during that 1890 dinner. The second biographer, Daniel Farson, adds, "There is good reason to assume that it

Professor Van Helsing (here played by Laurence Oliver to Frank Langella's Dracula) tells his group of vampire hunters that their adversary "must, indeed, have been that Voivode Dracula," proof to some that Stoker used the historical Vlad as a model.

was the Hungarian professor who told Bram, for the first time, of the name of Dracula." Again, we have an assumption that seems logical. "Unfortunately, no correspondence between Vambery and Stoker can be found today," McNally and Florescu write in *In Search of Dracula*. "Moreover, a search through all of the professor's published writings fails to reveal any comments on Vlad Dracul, or vampires."

Farson's biography lacks sourcing, and it's not always reliable, yet it contains a sage warning about *Dracula* speculation: "Anyone who wishes to play the Dracula game can bend the most surprising pieces of evidence to fit the puzzle." Farson does some mighty bending of his own in *The Man Who Wrote Dracula*, yet this word of caution sounds one of the truest notes in his book.

What did Stoker know, and when did he know it? It's entirely possible he didn't even know the historical Dracula's name was Vlad. It doesn't appear in his notes, and it sure doesn't appear in the book. "Everyone brings preconceptions and misconceptions to that book," Miller notes. "I've had students come to me and say, 'I could have sworn this was in the book.' I had one student absolutely certain that the name Vlad appears in the book. And I said, 'Okay, you find it and you've got your "A" right now. You don't have to go any further.'"

Did some scant knowledge of the historical Dracula color Stoker's depiction of the vampire? That seems plausible. Did Vlad Tepes serve as the model for Count Dracula? That seems like a monstrous overreach.

I Am Dracula? Other Possible Models

· · · · · · · · · · · ·

In the meantime, I must find out all I can about Count
Dracula, as it may help me to understand.
—*Jonathan Harker,* Dracula, *chapter 3*

Artist Joseph Vargo's "Dark Tower" stresses our romantic view of
vampires, and several romantic figures have been suggested as
models for Count Dracula. (Artwork © Joseph Vargo)

Count Dracula emerged from Bram Stoker's book as the model for how a vampire should act. But who was the model for this vampire? If Vlad the Impaler was not Stoker's direct inspiration for the bloodthirsty count, who was? As with the acres of speculation covering the identity of Jack the Ripper, there is no shortage of candidates. And, by the way, Jack the Ripper is one of them.

The serial killer known as Jack the Ripper had terrorized London in the second half of 1888. The last murder credited to Jack occurred just fifteen months before Stoker made his first notes on what would become *Dracula*. Hmmm . . . a relentless and elusive killer moving through the fog-shrouded London streets, preying on women. Certainly the public fascination with the slayings was not lost on Stoker.

Intriguingly, it was in 1888 that London's Lyceum Theatre staged *Macbeth*, the William Shakespeare tragedy that echoes throughout *Dracula*. It also was the year Stoker met a scene painter named Joseph Harker. Stoker biographer Barbara Belford writes that Harker "was the only name from the Lyceum family used in *Dracula*" and the "secretive Stoker never revealed why."

Still, perhaps Stoker did use the most prominent member of the Lyceum family to actually shape the book's title character. A prime suspect among *Dracula* experts remains Stoker's charismatic "governor" at the Lyceum, Henry Irving. The theory is that Stoker became entranced by Irving during that 1876 meeting, remaining the master's faithful servant. Some see Stoker as Jonathan Harker, a kept prisoner in the Lyceum forced to write letters for a cunning and manipulative ruler of a magical realm. Others toss in a bit of Stoker as Renfield, doing the master's bidding yet struggling with doubts and resentments.

Like the Vlad Tepes connection, this all seems a bit overstated. Stoker may have seen a devilish glint or two in Irving's portrayals of Mephistopheles in Johann Wolfgang von Goethe's *Faust* and Mathias in Leopold Lewis's *The Bells*. He may, as it has been suggested, even have entertained thoughts of

Irving one day playing Dracula on the stage. But his description of Dracula in the book is extremely un-Irving-like, and there's no reason to think that his expressions of affection for the great actor were less than genuine. All right, but couldn't Stoker have been using the novel to psychologically work out buried anger and repressed grudges?

David J. Skal, for one, has cautioned against making easy Freudian assumptions about Irving's impact on *Dracula*. In his revised edition of *Hollywood Gothic*, the leading expert on *Dracula*'s journey to the stage and screen conceded that the casting of Irving as "a boss literally from hell" has the trappings of "a good story and a glib, if irresistible sound bite." But he concludes that this puts us back on the tricky path of speculation.

Belford, though, has made the most of this speculation. She sees Irving as the clear and obvious model for Dracula. She also sees Harker as Stoker's alter ego and *Dracula* as "his most autobiographical novel . . . a Freudian vortex, bristling with repression and apprehension of homosexuality, devouring women, and rejecting mothers."

There will now be a brief pause for everyone to say, "Wow!" This is part of the fun of talking *Dracula*. It's worth noting that the publication of *Dracula* just preceded the rapid rise of Freudian interpretation. And the Freudians have had more of a go at Stoker and *Dracula* than all of the stake-wielding Van Helsings pressed into service by Hollywood.

Leonard Wolf raised the psychological stakes greatly with his provocative *A Dream of Dracula*, published the same year as Raymond T. McNally and Radu Florescu's *In Search of Dracula*. It was the *Dracula* daily double, kicking up unparalleled interest on two different fronts.

While Belford keeps Stoker on the couch for much of her biography, there are many leading *Dracula* authorities who endorse her view of Irving as a model for Dracula. "I'd be hesitant to draw any direct lines, but I certainly think the character of Dracula owes something to the stage presence of Henry Irving," Elizabeth Miller comments. "But I also think he owes something to Jack the Ripper and Stoker himself. I think you see bits and pieces of Stoker in many of the characters."

Irving was a commanding stage presence. He could hold an audience, or an individual, in a thrall described as mesmeric. He could suggest great power and evil. "My feeling is that Dracula is Henry Irving," says Michael J. Barsanti, an expert on Stoker's *Dracula* notes, which are collected at Philadelphia's Rosenbach Museum and Library. "Stoker describes Irving's power as being almost mesmeric. Stoker didn't leave behind an autobiography, and, ironically, much of what we know about him is from his biography of Irving. And that biography details the force of Irving's personality and the almost unnatural influence he had over Stoker. I think you find him working out complex issues with Irving in *Dracula*."

Despite Skal's doubts, Irving has emerged as the frontrunner for many *Dracula* scholars. "I'm completely convinced that Irving is one of the models," J. Gordon Melton, author of *The Vampire Book: The Encyclopedia*

of the Undead, remarks. "I'm not at all convinced that he's *the* model. I think Stoker's father probably was one model, but we don't know a lot about him. We happen to know a lot about Irving, so we see the parallels a bit more obviously. But Dracula is a very, very complex admixture of many real people and literary models."

Those literary models include titled vampires: John Polidori's Lord Ruthven in "The Vampyre" (1819) and James Malcolm Rymer's Sir Francis Varney in *Varney the Vampire* (1847). And since Lord George Gordon Byron was the inspiration for Lord Ruthven, the romantic poet must be listed as at least an indirect model for Dracula. Another fictional character influencing *Dracula* might have been serial killer Sweeney Todd, who appeared in *The String of Pearls: A Romance*, an 1846 penny-dreadful penned by none other than Thomas Preskett Prest, the writer long assumed to have been the author of *Varney the Vampire*.

Another model from the theater world might have been actor Herbert Beerbohm Tree, who created a sensation as Svengali in the London production of George du Maurier's *Trilby* (1894). Then, too, there were those dark Shakespearian characters so dear to both Stoker and Irving, from Macbeth to Richard III.

There are traces of all of them in Count Dracula: Irving and Tree, Stoker and his father, Ruthven and Varney, Jack the Ripper and Sweeney Todd, Mephistopheles and Mathias, Macbeth and Richard III. They all fit quite nicely under that cape we habitually throw around the vampire's broad shoulders.

The Verité Vampire:
Information in *Dracula*

· · · · · · · · · · ·

I must put down every detail in order.
—*Jonathan Harker*, Dracula, *chapter 4*

As tempting as it is to impose modern sensibilities on *Dracula*, the novel remains very much a product of its time. And its time was the Victorian Era—that greatly misunderstood period roughly defined by the long reign of Queen Victoria (1837–1901). Although Bram Stoker lived the last eleven years of his life in the Edwardian period, he, too, was Victorian through and through.

To some this suggests repression, prudery, imperialism, industrialization, and stiff-upper-lip British stoicism. Contradictions were rampant in British society, however, and the deeper one digs in this territory the more intriguing the paradoxes become. Charles Dickens was all but creating the traditional English Christmas at the same time that Charles Darwin was revolutionizing scientific theory. *Mrs. Beeton's Book of Household Management* continued as the

standard middle-class guide to cooking and child care at the same time that Sigmund Freud and Karl Marx were introducing radical new ideas in psychology and political economy. English society was as fascinated with the possibility of communicating by telephone as the possibility of communicating with the dead.

Being a proper Victorian gentleman, Stoker was a burly mass of contradictions. He honored traditions, yet he also shared his era's often overlooked fascination with modernity. In short, he loved gadgets. He embraced technology. And this interest runs all through his most famous novel.

Jonathan Harker keeps his diary in shorthand. Dr. John Seward keeps his by phonograph, later griping when travel forces him to make entries in handwriting. Mina Harker, who also has mastered shorthand, uses a typewriter. Jonathan uses a Kodak camera to take pictures of Carfax for Dracula. Telegrams are sent constantly, and a telephone is used once.

"We have here much data. . . ."
—*Professor Van Helsing,*
Dracula, *chapter 18*

"It's a feature of the novel that has been lost over time," comments Michael J. Barsanti, a curator at the Philadelphia resting place of Stoker's *Dracula* notes. "There is a great deal of attention given to dictaphones and typewriters. For its time, this was all very up to date and gave the book's fantastic plot a strong grounding in realism. Stoker was fascinated with this stuff, and the book almost is obsessive in explaining how information has been gathered, assembled, arranged, filed, and presented."

If writing today, Stoker probably would have his characters using BlackBerries, cell phones, text messaging, Internet searches, digital cameras, laptop computers, and digital tape recorders.

When it comes to drawing up a battle plan, Mina gets the job of assembling a file that includes telegrams, newspaper clippings, and letters. She gets out her typewriter and transcribes both Jonathan's diary and Dr. Seward's cylinder recordings.

Stoker's notes show a tremendous amount of research on everything from train schedules to tombstone inscriptions. He worked out letters and dates on the pages of an appointment calendar. For European and English locations, he consulted standard travel guides. While vacationing in Whitby during the summer of 1890, he jotted down descriptions of weather conditions, some of which were used, nearly word for word, in *Dracula*. He also recorded more than eighty tombstone inscriptions at St. Mary's churchyard in Whitby, using them for Mina and Lucy's encounter with an old sailor in chapter 6.

For the fate of the Russian schooner *Demeter*, he examined a photograph and reports of the October 1885 Whitby wreck of the *Dmitry*, a Russian schooner that had sailed from Narva (which appears as an anagram in the *Demeter's* home port, Varna). And when he wanted to describe the results of Dracula's attack on Renfield, the author wisely sought the advice of his physician brother, Sir William Thornley Stoker, president of the Royal College of Surgeons in Ireland. Thornley replied with a detailed memorandum and a diagram indicating the locations and damages of head wounds. "The research shows," notes Elizabeth Miller, author of several highly regarded books on *Dracula*. "He did take seven years with *Dracula*, while he just dashed off most of the other books."

Working from the dates given in the novel and from Stoker's notes, *Dracula* scholars have attempted to fix the year in which the story is set. Editing *The Annotated Dracula*, Leonard Wolf opted for 1887, "but a reader is cautioned not to believe in it too precisely." David J. Skal, one of the editors of the Norton Critical Edition of *Dracula*, suggests that 1893 is a good candidate, a year also recommended by *Dracula* scholars Raymond T. McNally and Radu Florescu. And 1895 also has emerged as a contender. Stoker's notes make the strongest case for 1893. "For all the research he did, Stoker got dates wrong," Miller points out. "Internally, the book can get sloppy. There are contradictions. And yet, that has become part of the book's power. In a strange sort of way, it contributes to the realism. If you keep a diary, you make mistakes. You get a date wrong. So it becomes part of the realism of the book."

The mistakes become as much a part of the fabric as the carefully presented bits of information. Both contribute to the all-important suspension of disbelief, giving you the idea, however momentary, that it might actually have happened just this way.

Mina, played by Winona Ryder in Bram Stoker's Dracula, *knows shorthand and uses a typewriter to keep information in order for the vampire fighters led by Professor Van Helsing (Anthony Hopkins).*

Rhode Island Red Headlines

· · · · · · · · · · ·

> *. . . so I shall look through the evening papers since*
> *then, and perhaps I shall get some new light.*
> —*Mina Harker,* Dracula, *chapter 17*

Tucked away in the boxes of Bram Stoker's working notes for *Dracula* is a clipping from the *New York World* of February 2, 1896. This article would have appeared about a year and four months before the publication of *Dracula*, and three years before the first American edition of the novel. This was the extended headline that topped the lengthy article:

Vampires in New England
Dead Bodies Dug Up and Their
Hearts Burned to Prevent Disease
Strange Superstition of Long Ago
The Old Belief Was that Ghostly
Monsters Sucked the Blood of Their
Living Relatives

Boy, they don't write 'em like that anymore. Oh, wait a minute. Yes, they do. For those of you who think the *Weekly World News* and the *National Enquirer* invented this sort of sensationalism, we submit for your approval

Joe Pulitzer's *New York World* of 1896. Pulitzer's paper was in a yellow journalism war with William Randolph Hearst's *New York Journal*, and blood red was the yellow journalist's favorite color.

Stoker probably saw this article about a Rhode Island vampire scare during the Lyceum Theatre's 1896 tour of the United States. How his heart must have leapt at the sight of a banner headline about hearts being burned to prevent the spread of vampirism! Here he was, working on a vampire novel; and there was the very topic making headlines in the United States. Stoker clipped the article, perhaps thinking, as any good theater manager would have, "You can't buy publicity like this."

The article described how the good citizens of Rhode Island "have been digging up the dead bodies of relatives for the purpose of burning their hearts." Now we're cooking. The reporter

Varney the Vampire couldn't have scared up better copy than the 1896 newspaper stories about a New England vampire scare.

stressed, "Not merely the out-of-the-way agricultural folk, but the more intelligent people of the urban communities are strong in their belief in vampirism."

It gets better.

"In some parts of Europe the belief still has a hold on the popular mind," the article notes for the good readers of the *World*; it continues,

On the Continent from 1727 to 1735 there prevailed an epidemic of vampires. Thousands of people died, as was supposed, from having their blood sucked by creatures that came to their bedsides at night with goggling eyes and lips eager for the life fluid of the victims. In Servia it was understood that the demon might be destroyed by digging up the body and piercing it through with a sharp instrument, after which it was decapitated and burned. . . . There was no hope for a person once chose as a prey by a vampire. Slowly but surely he or she was destined to fade and sicken, receiving meanwhile nightly visits from the monster. . . . Vampirism became a plague, more dreaded than any form of disease.

It must be true. I read it in the newspaper.

All the World's a Stage

· · · · · · · · · · · ·

*I have not yet seen the Count in the daylight. Can it be
that he sleeps when others wake, that he may be awake
whilst they sleep?*
—Jonathan Harker, Dracula, *chapter 4*

*Henry Irving as Hamlet, a play refer-
enced many times in* Dracula.

Bram Stoker also was a man of
the theater, and the impact of this
world on *Dracula* was immense.
This would seem obvious even
before any consideration of the
author's working notes for the novel.
There are, for instance, all of those
direct and indirect references to
William Shakespeare. No one in
this book seems capable of dis-
coursing for too long without dropping a quote from The Bard. It gets
so you expect the Gypsies guarding
Dracula's "earth boxes" to take a
gander at Jonathan Harker's Kukri
knife and proclaim, "As Macbeth
so famously asks, 'Art thou but a
dagger of the mind, a false creation,
proceeding from the heat-oppressed
brain?'"

Yet Stoker's deep love of the theater also informs the novel's overall
mood and its very structure. There is a sense of the theatrical pervading the characters' actions, reaction, and dialogue. Whether talking to Harker in his castle or
defying his pursuers in England, Dracula himself often seems to be aware that's he
holding center stage.

Stoker certainly saw the possibilities in transferring *Dracula* to the boards. Chicago
drama critic Frederick Donaghey recorded a conversation in which Stoker related
his attempts to convince Irving he should play the count. He envisioned Dracula
on stage as a composite of the actor's spookier roles, including Mephistopheles in

Johann Wolfgang von Goethe's *Faust* and Mathias in Leopold Lewis's *The Bells*. If Stoker was not exaggerating when he told Donaghey that Irving laughed away such suggestions, then history has proved the writer's theatrical instincts were far more prescient than those of his idolized boss.

Those instincts served Stoker well throughout the planning and writing of *Dracula*. His March 1890 outline for the novel is broken down in four books, or parts, much like a four-act play. An early programlike list of characters, Stoker's "Historiae Personae" includes many of the essential players: Count Dracula (he crossed out "Count Wampyr," also jotting "Count Dracula" at the top of the list), "lawyer Peter Hawkins," "his clerk—Jonathan Harker," "fiancée of above—Wilhelmina Murray (called Mina)," Lucy Westenra, "doctor of mad house—Seward," "mad patient" (no name given, but clearly Renfield), "a German professor—Max Windshoeffel" (he becomes Dutch and is given the more theatrical name of Professor Van Helsing), and "a Texan—Brutus M. Morris" (changed to Quincey P. Morris).

Stoker had planned to make Lucy the fiancée of Dr. Seward, so Arthur Holmwood, later Lord Godalming, is the one major character missing from the Historiae Personae. Jettisoned characters include a detective named Cotford, a painter named Frances Aytown, a psychical research agent named Alfred Singleton, two other lawyers, and a "schoolfellow" friend for Mina, Kate Reed.

A novelist, particularly one working with a three-decker Victorian structure, has no need to limit the number of characters or locations presented on the printed page. With a few strokes of the pen, the novelist can press into service hundreds of French revolutionaries to surround a guillotine or thousands of armored knights ready to do battle. By Dickensian standards, there's plenty of room in *Dracula* for Frances, Alfred, and Kate.

The man of the theater, however, reduces the character load to the essentials. So Stoker's theatrical instincts told him to take three characters—a detective, a psychical research agent, and a German professor—and combine them into one compelling individual: Professor Abraham Van Helsing.

Stoker's notes also show that he intended to begin the novel with a series of letters; a Count Dracula letter to his lawyers being among the first. This is a horror novelist's choice, and not a bad one: what better way to ground the book in everyday reality than an all-business letter? The horror novelist knows that the supernatural tale makes great demands on the readers' all-important suspension of disbelief, so the more attention that gets paid to workaday details the more the reader lowers the guard of resistance. But Stoker wisely slashed this opening, opting to get the book off to a faster start with what was first planned as the second chapter. This is the man of the theater coming to the rescue of the literary man. And the man of the theater demands a delayed stage entrance for Dracula, building the mystery and suspense as Harker travels closer and closer to Castle Dracula. Here, again, you sense Stoker's theatrical instinct kicking in and suggesting a better, more dramatic path. You don't ring up the curtain and clumsily kick your star on stage. You keep your protagonist off stage, waiting in the wings—or hanging upside-down with bat wings, as the case may be.

Stoker then gives Dracula one hell of an entrance—two of them, in fact. The count storms onto the scene, disguised as his own coach driver. Then the castle door creaks open, and we get the whole "Enter freely and of your own will" invitation. And then? Incredibly, after the opening Transylvania section, Dracula largely disappears from the book bearing his name. It's a marvelous stage effect maintained by the author. Consider this: counting his appearances as a bat and a wolf, the count, by the most liberal of estimates, appears on just under sixteen percent of the novel's pages. Yet he remains a looming presence felt in every chapter. It's a daring choice, and one suspects it's another choice informed by Stoker's experience with the stage. You can maximize the power of an effect by minimizing its use. Did Stoker learn this through the many long hours writing supernatural fiction? Maybe, but it seems more likely he learned it as a drama critic or during his years of service at the Lyceum Theatre.

"Stoker's working notes seem to show him thinking of it as a stage production," comments Michael J. Barsanti, a curator at the resting place for those notes, the Rosenbach Museum and Library in Philadelphia. "The book is very theatrical in the way it builds tension and suspense. No one knows why the original concept for the opening chapter was cut. But I think it's logical to assume Stoker learned more than a trick or two from his many years of being intimately involved with the theater."

These notes show that Stoker at one point planned a dinner party scene for thirteen (the writer loved playing with words, names, and significant numbers). It would be at the home of the "Mad Doctor" (presumably Seward, the superintendent of an asylum for the insane). One guest would start a strange story, with the other guests each adding to it. At the conclusion of this tale, "the Count comes in." Theatrical enough for you? This is a nifty little sequence, but it's difficult to think of a spot for it in the novel we know as *Dracula*. It would, however, be right at home in an English drawing-room melodrama, just as Stoker felt right at home in a theater.

SIDEBAR

Ten Shakespeare References in *Dracula*

. . . .

There is a method in his madness.
—Dr. John Seward, Dracula, *chapter 6*

Stoker uses many Shakespeare quotes to emphasize that "something wicked this way comes."

Bram Stoker was both a literary man and a man of the theater—and that theater was the Lyceum, where Henry Irving was the star and William Shakespeare the guiding light. Shakespearean echoes rumble through the chapters of *Dracula*. There are multiple references to *Hamlet*, *Macbeth*, and *Othello*. "It's amazing how many Shakespearean allusions there are, not just in the direct quotations," comments *Dracula* expert Elizabeth Miller. "And he cut several quotations from the typescript. So that's one aspect of the novel that he was very conscious of, and it's an aspect you could discuss forever."

These are just a few, most of them fully footnoted in one of the best annotated, researched, and sourced mass-market versions, the Norton Critical Edition, edited by Nina Auerbach and David J. Skal:

. . . like the ghost of Hamlet's father.

Jonathan Harker uses *Hamlet* in a simile (chapter 3).

Up to now I never quite knew what Shakespeare meant when he made Hamlet say:—

My tablets! my tablets!

'Tis meet that I put it down, etc.

Harker again cites *Hamlet*, although not accurately (chapter 3).

. . . I feared to see those weird sisters.

The three witches in *Macbeth* are repeatedly called the "weird sisters." Harker uses the term here to describe the three vampire women in Castle Dracula (chapter 4).

I sympathize with poor Desdemona. . . .

Lucy Westenra refers to the doomed character in *Othello* (chapter 5).

He evidently is the Sir Oracle of them. . . .

Mina Murray compares someone to the character in *The Merchant of Venice* (chapter 6).

This, with an iron nerve, a temper of the ice-brook. . . .

Dr. Seward paraphrases *Othello* to describe Professor Abraham Van Helsing (chapter 9).

Well, here I am tonight, hoping for sleep, and lying like Ophelia in the play, with "virgin crants and maiden strewments."

Lucy Westenra now compares herself to another doomed Shakespeare character, Ophelia in *Hamlet* (chapter 11).

. . . such a smile as would have become the face of Malvolio . . .

Dr. Seward uses this *Twelfth Night* character to describe Renfield (chapter 20).

The matter seemed to be preying on this mind, and so I determined to use it to "be cruel only to be kind."

Dr. Seward quotes *Hamlet* this time (chapter 20).

" 'Rats and mice and such small dear,' as Shakespeare has it, 'chicken feed of the larder. . . .' "

Renfield is paraphrasing from *King Lear* (chapter 20).

A Whitby Glossary

· · · · · · · · · · ·

*Here comes old Mr. Swales. He is making straight for me, and
I can see, by the way he lifts his hat, that he wants to talk.*
—**Mina Murray**, Dracula, *chapter 6*

Dear old Mr. Swales. Do you know this character? One of Bram Stoker's more
delightful areas of research was the slang of Whitby. And most of this was for
three chapter 6 monologues for the salty Swales, a talkative fellow with a face "all
gnarled and twisted like the bark of a tree." Swales doesn't make it out of chapter
7. After some chatty encounters with Mina, he is found with his neck broken (presumably by Dracula), "a look of fear and horror on his face."

But Swales leaves behind a stream of Whitby slang that would have confounded
Henry Higgins. Stoker compiled a lengthy glossary, only some of which he used
for the old sailor. Here's a sample, with the translations. Don't geck now. You're
bound to keckle:

ails: evils

arr: scar

bad lad: the devil

belly-timber: food

by-gang: bypath

cabs: sea gulls

clampers: claws

clegs: horseflies

clicker: body snatcher

comers: visitors

crowp: grumble

dwam: slight swoon

gawm: understand

geck: sneer

hutter: stammer

keckle: chuckle

kipper: nimble

knag: gnaw

lay-bed: grave

lidwake: awake

loomy: cloudy

nar: near

sauf: yellow

seeing glass: mirror

shoor: scare

skew-gobbed: wry-mouthed

slake: kiss

waft: ghost

And my personal favorite:

ugsome: ugly

The Novel

The Characters, in Order of Appearance or First Mention

· · · · · · · · · · · ·

"My friend,—Welcome to the Carpathians.
I am anxiously expecting you."
—**Count Dracula**, Dracula, *chapter 1*

Jonathan Harker—a young clerk and solicitor in the employ of an Exeter firm

Wilhelmina (Mina) Murray (later Harker)—an assistant schoolmistress and the fiancée of Jonathan Harker

Landlady—elderly wife of the innkeeper at the Golden Krone Hotel in Bistritz

Peter Hawkins—Harker's gout-ridden employer in Exeter

Count Dracula—a Transylvania nobleman welcoming Harker as his guest

Samuel F. Billington—Whitby solicitor engaged by Dracula

The three wives (also called the three sisters)—the count's three vampire brides

Lucy Westenra—Mina Murray's friend and former student, engaged to Arthur Holmwood

Arthur Holmwood (later Lord Godalming)—Lucy's fiancé, friend to Dr. John Seward and Quincey P. Morris

Mrs. Westenra—Lucy's mother

Dr. John Seward—physician, superintendent of a lunatic asylum in Purfleet

Quincey P. Morris—an adventurer from Texas, friend to Seward and Holmwood

R. M. Renfield—an inmate at Dr. Seward's lunatic asylum

Simmons—asylum attendant who reports on Renfield

Mr. Swales—an elderly and gnarled Whitby sailor

Captain of the *Demeter*—master of the doomed Russian schooner sailing from Varna

Mate—*Demeter* sailor who jumps overboard to escape Dracula

Sister Agatha—nurse and nun caring for Harker at Buda-Pesth hospital

Abraham Van Helsing—Dutch physician, metaphysician, scientist, professor, philosopher, and lawyer

Thomas Bilder—Regent's Park Zoological Grounds keeper

Patrick Hennessey—medical doctor reporting on Renfield to Seward

Thomas Snelling—laborer who helps Joseph Smollet move Dracula's "earth boxes"

Joseph "Jack" Smollet—hired to move Dracula's earth boxes to several locations

Hardy—asylum attendant who has his finger broken during struggle with Renfield

Mr. Marquand—a solicitor handling the estate of Mrs. Westenra

Mary—maid to Jonathan and Mina Harker in Exeter

Dr. Vincent—North Hospital physician consulted by Seward and Van Helsing

Samuel F. Billington, Jr.—Whitby solicitor in partnership with his father

Sam Bloxam—man who carts "earth boxes" for Dracula

House Agent—agent with the London firm of Mitchell, Sons, & Candy

Captain Donelson—master of the *Czarina Catherine*

Immanuel Hildesheim—Galatz man instructed to give Dracula's "earth box" to the Slovaks

---

The Mystery of Hommy-Beg

· · · · · · · · · · ·

I may get some light on the mystery.
—Dr. John Seward, Dracula, *chapter 15*

Almost every edition of *Dracula*—and there have been more than you can count—has included Bram Stoker's dedication, "To my dear friend Hommy-Beg." *Dracula* and Stoker researchers certainly know the identity of this dear friend, but it tends to be a puzzler for anyone without an annotated edition (say, Nina Auerbach and David J. Skal's Norton Critical Edition or Leonard Wolf's *The Essential Dracula*).

The mysterious dedication certainly confused me when I spotted it on the copyright page of the Dell Laurel Library edition of *Dracula* I purchased in the 1960s. None of the articles I read about *Dracula* or Stoker provided a clue. I didn't have a copy of the only Stoker biography published at that time (Harry Ludlam's *A Biography of Dracula: The Life Story of Bram Stoker*), and no likely candidate could be singled out from the scraps of information I had assembled on the writer. So who was this Hommy-Beg?

He was English novelist and playwright Hall Caine. That was your first guess, right? Like Henry Irving, Hall Caine is largely forgotten today. But like Henry Irving, he was an English superstar in 1897. And he was, indeed, Stoker's dear friend.

You would have recognized his name at the time *Dracula* was published. Thomas Henry Hall Caine was one of Great Britain's best-known authors. Hommy-Beg was Caine's childhood nickname. An affectionate Manx expression meaning Little Tommy, it was bestowed on him by his grandmother.

Stoker was returning an honor. Caine dedicated his 1893 work *Capt'n Davy's Honeymoon* to Stoker. Many of his stories recorded the colorful Manx speech and ways of his father's birthplace, the Isle of Man. Although born in the Cheshire town of Runcorn, where his father was working at the time, Caine always felt a strong connection to the Isle of Man.

Like Stoker, Caine was working as a drama critic when he fell under the spell of Irving's *Hamlet*. Like Stoker, Caine wrote a rave review that led to a long friendship with Irving. Incredibly popular during his lifetime, Caine was the author of such best-sellers as *The Deemster* (1887), *The Manxman* (1894), *The Christian* (1897), and *The Eternal City* (1901). "Ironic that his real name is now virtually forgotten," Daniel Farson writes of Caine in his biography of Stoker, "while thousands of new readers must be wondering who 'Hommy-Beg' could have been."

Caine bought Greeba Castle, a castellated house on the Isle of Man, the year before *Dracula* was published with its dedication to Hommy-Beg. He died there on August 31, 1931, six months after Universal Pictures insured the immortality of Stoker's novel by releasing the film version starring Bela Lugosi.

A Chapter-by-Chapter Breakdown

· · · · · · · · · · ·

. . . it was all very mysterious and not by any means comforting.
—*Jonathan Harker,* Dracula, *chapter 1*

*D*racula is an epistolary novel told through a series of journal and diary entries, letters and telegrams, newspaper clippings and memos. The material is arranged in twenty-seven chapters. The book's length is just under 161,000 words. Except for a brief epilogue, all of the events take place within a calendar year, starting with Jonathan Harker's journal entry of May 3 and ending with Mina Harker's journal entry describing the events of November 6.

Come on in and meet the wives. Dracula and his vampire brides as imagined by Gothic artist Joseph Vargo. (Artwork © Joseph Vargo)

Chapter 1

Jonathan Harker, a clerk in the employ of Peter Hawkins of Exeter, is traveling through Transylvania on business. He describes his journey, leaving Munich on May 1, proceeding east to Buda-Pesth (Budapest), across the River Danube, staying at the Hotel Royale in Klausenburgh (modern-day Clug, Romania), and arriving in Bistritz (Bistrita). He stays at the Golden Krone Hotel, where a note from Count Dracula awaits him. Jonathan has found property for Dracula to purchase in England, and he is on his way to the count's castle to make his report. The next morning, May 4, the hotel owner's elderly wife expresses concern for Jonathan's safety. She places a rosary around his neck, "For your mother's sake." Although troubled by expressions of concern for his safety, Jonathan dismisses them as fears rooted in superstitions and legends. A coach takes him to the Borgo Pass, where the carriage from Count Dracula is to meet him. The driver, a tall man with a long brown beard and eyes that seem to gleam red, stops once to drive away a pack of wolves. He does this, to Jonathan's astonishment, with a sweep of the arms and an imperious command. The carriage arrives at Castle Dracula, "a vast ruined castle . . . whose broken battlements showed a jagged line against the moonlit sky."

Chapter 2

Jonathan is left alone in front of the castle's massive door. He hears the sounds of rattling chains, bolts being drawn back, and a key grating in the lock from long disuse. The door swings open to reveal an elderly man dressed completely in black: "I am Dracula; and I bid you welcome. . . ." There are no servants on hand. The count carries Jonathan's bags, taking him to a comfortable, well-lighted bedroom warmed by a log fire. Reassured, Jonathan eats dinner, taking notice of Dracula's sharp, protruding, white teeth, his remarkably ruddy lips, and his nauseatingly bad breath. Over the next few days, Jonathan realizes there are no mirrors anywhere in sight. He tells Dracula about the estate secured for him in Purfleet, a London suburb. It is called Carfax—about twenty acres surrounded by a solid stone wall. The property includes a large medieval house, a dark pond, and an old chapel. One of the few houses near it is a private lunatic asylum. Dracula is pleased. But it also dawns on Jonathan that the count typically leaves him at dawn. One dawn encounter gives Jonathan a jolt. He is shaving, using a small traveling mirror, when the count enters behind him. But Jonathan sees no reflection of his host in the mirror, and an enraged Dracula flings the mirror onto the stones outside the window. Jonathan never sees the count eat, and never sees a servant. And, during the day, Jonathan is confined to a few rooms. He concludes that the castle is "a veritable prison" and he is its prisoner.

Chapter 3

Suspicious, Jonathan decides to learn more about Dracula by encouraging his host to talk about himself. The count speaks of the Draculas with great pride, boasting of their deeds as leaders—particularly one Dracula who crossed the Danube to battle the Turkish invaders. Dracula insists that Jonathan stay for a month, and, although greatly dismayed, Jonathan feels bound to accept the invitation. Looking out his window at night, Jonathan is horrified to see Dracula emerge from another castle window and crawl, lizardlike, down the sheer stone wall, his cloak spread around him like bat wings. After watching a repeat performance and determining that Dracula has left the castle, Jonathan decides to investigate his surroundings. He keeps trying one locked door after another until one, with a push, gives way. The furniture in this room suggests a grander part of the castle from bygone days. Jonathan pauses here to make some journal entries and falls asleep. He is approached by three young women—two dark, the other fair. Both thrilled and repulsed, Jonathan feels two sharp teeth touching his neck when the furious count suddenly appears, commanding them away: "How dare you touch him, any of you? How dare you cast eyes on him when I had forbidden it? Back, I tell you all. This man belongs to me!" When they ask if they are to having nothing this night, Dracula tosses them a bag containing an infant. Jonathan faints.

Chapter 4

Jonathan awakens in his bedroom, wondering if the encounter with the three women was a dream. He tries to get back to the room in daylight, but now it is locked. On May 19, the count asks him to write three letters: the first, dated June 12, saying he is about to leave for home; the second, dated June 19, saying he is starting for home the next morning; and the third, dated June 29, saying he has left the castle and arrived at Bistritz. Jonathan records in his journal, "I now know the span of my life." On May 28, he notices a band of Gypsies camping in the castle's courtyard. He throws letters to them from his window, but they are turned over to Dracula. On June 17, Jonathan sees the Gypsies and Slovak laborers moving great, square boxes in carts. He yells to them, but they only point at him and laugh. A woman arrives at the castle, screaming, "Monster, give me my child!" Dracula summons wolves to take care of the woman. On June 25, Jonathan makes a desperate attempt to get the key to freedom. He imitates Dracula, crawling down the wall to the count's room. He makes his way to an old, ruined chapel, where he finds the count, eyes open, on newly dug earth in one of the great boxes. On June 29, Dracula bids Jonathan farewell. Realizing he will be left to the three women, Jonathan again scales the wall in hopes of gaining the key. He again finds Dracula in the "earth box," but looking younger. Infuriated by the count's mocking smile, he picks up a shovel. As he strikes, however, the head turns, with eyes blazing full on him. Momentarily paralyzed, Jonathan only gashes the vampire's forehead, causing a scar noticed later in England. Jonathan again flees to his bedroom, but, after hearing the Gypsies and Slovaks leave, he determines to scale the castle wall to the ground and escape—or die trying.

Chapter 5

Mina Murray, an Exeter assistant schoolmistress and Jonathan Harker's fiancée, is exchanging letters with her friend and former student, Lucy Westenra, who lives in south central London. Mina tells of Jonathan being abroad on business, and of mastering both shorthand and the typewriter. Lucy responds with news of getting three proposals in one day. The three suitors are close friends: Arthur Holmwood, son of Lord Godalming; Dr. John Seward, superintendent of a lunatic asylum in Purfleet; and Quincey P. Morris, a young adventurer from Texas. Mina accepts Arthur's proposal. Seward, meanwhile, is fascinated with the case of R. M. Renfield, "a morbidly excitable" and "possibly dangerous" inmate with great physical strength. Quincey invites Arthur for a get-together with just one other guest, John: "we both want to mingle our weeps over the wine-cup, and to drink a health with all our hearts to the happiest man in all the wide world."

Chapter 6

Lucy and Mina meet in the seaside town of Whitby on July 24, two weeks after Jonathan's attempted escape from Castle Dracula. They enjoy the bench-lined walkways of the fishing port, and are befriended by the elderly Mr. Swales, a colorful and talkative old sailor. By August 3, Mina is concerned about not having received any word from Jonathan. She is also worried about Lucy's sleepwalking. Arthur wishes to join them in Whitby, but his father is very ill, and he can't get away from London. He and Lucy are planning a fall wedding. Dr. Seward, meanwhile, is charting Renfield's obsession with catching and consuming flies, at first, then spiders, then sparrows. He invents a new classification, *zoophagous*, for the life-eating inmate. A storm is about to break on August 6, and Mr. Swales tells Mina, "There's something in that wind and in that hoast beyont that sounds, and looks, and tastes, and smells like death. It's in the air. I feel it comin'." At that moment, the coast guard reports that a Russian ship is approaching Whitby, "knocking about . . . mighty strangely."

Chapter 7

The newspapers are reporting on the sudden and devastating storm that has hit Whitby. The Russian schooner *Demeter* crashes into the beach, and what's believed to be an immense dog jumps from the deck and disappears into the darkness. The *Demeter* is carrying a cargo of wooden boxes consigned to a Whitby solicitor, S. F. Billington who takes possession of the goods. An eerie scene is waiting on board. The body of the *Demeter*'s captain is found tied to the wheel, his dead hands clutching a rosary. The log of the *Demeter* charts how the ship set sail from the Black Sea port of Varna on July 6 with the captain, two mates, a cook, and a crew of five hands. It describes a hellish journey, during which the men go missing, one by one.

A tall, thin stranger is spotted on board, then disappears. On August 3, only the captain and one of the mates are left. The mate goes below decks. He jumps overboard, yelling that the sea will save him. On August 4, the captain records seeing the thin stranger. The captain ties his own hands to the wheel, "and along with them I shall tie that which He, It, dare not touch." After the *Demeter* hits shore, a coal merchant's dog, a half-breed mastiff, is found dead, its throat torn away and its belly slit open. The funeral of the *Demeter*'s captain is held on August 10, and Mr. Swales is found dead on a Whitby bench, his neck broken.

Chapter 8

Increasingly concerned about Jonathan, Mina awakens in the early hours of August 11 to find Lucy missing from her bedroom. She sees Lucy, a half-reclining figure in white, on their favorite walkway bench. She also sees a figure in black bending over Lucy. When Mina calls out to her friend, the figure lifts its head, and Mina sees a white face and gleaming red eyes. But Lucy is alone, seemingly asleep, when Mina reaches her. Mina pins her shawl around Lucy's neck, later guessing she must have been clumsy with the big safety pin, pinching up a piece of loose skin, because there are two little red wounds on Lucy's throat. Lucy's sleepwalking continues, and Mina hears her mumble in a half-dreamy state, "His red eyes again! They are just the same." By August 17, Lucy has grown weak and languid. Mina is concerned because the small throat

wounds haven't healed. On August 18, Mina happily reports that Lucy seems better. On August 19, she is overjoyed to have word of Jonathan, who, under the care of Sister Agatha at the Hospital of St. Joseph and Ste. Mary in Buda-Pesth, is recovering from "some fearful shock." The next day, Renfield escapes from the asylum. Seward finds him on the grounds of Carfax, saying, "I am here to do Your bidding, Master. I am Your slave, and You will reward me, for I shall be faithful."

Chapter 9

Mina writes to Lucy on August 24 from Buda-Pesth, where she has gone to care for Jonathan. He has no memory of his horrible ordeal. He does know that the secret is in his journal, which he gives to Mina. He also asks her to marry him that afternoon. She happily agrees. Lucy writes from Whitby on August 30 that she is better, and her wedding to Arthur will be on September 28. Seward records in his phonographic diary that Renfield again has escaped from his cell, again to be apprehended on the Carfax grounds. Renfield grows calm when an exceptionally large bat is spotted in the moonlight. Lucy, once again growing weaker, is plagued by bad dreams. Arthur, whose father also has taken a turn for the worse, asks his friend Seward for an opinion on Lucy's condition. Baffled, Seward recommends calling in his "old friend and master" Professor Abraham Van Helsing of Amsterdam. Van Helsing examines Lucy on September 3, but offers no definite conclusions. By September 6,

Lucy's condition has taken a "terrible change for the worse."

Chapter 10

Lucy is ghastly pale, and an appalled Van Helsing declares she will die without an immediate transfusion. Arthur, just arrived on September 7, becomes the first donor. Van Helsing clearly has suspicions, but he dares not voice them. On September 10, Lucy is found near death, her heart beating feebly. A second transfusion is performed immediately, this time with Seward as the donor. Lucy seems improved by this operation, and Van Helsing makes a wreath of garlic for her and rubs garlic leaves around the windows of her bedroom. He assures Lucy that it will have a beneficial effect.

Chapter 11

Lucy's mother, thinking her actions for the best, removes the garlic from her daughter's room. They discover a weakened Lucy on September 13, and Seward now performs a third transfusion, this time with Van Helsing as the donor. A few days later, a London newspaper reports on the escape of a wolf from the zoological gardens in Regent's Park. A Cockney zookeeper, Thomas Bilder, tells of how one of the wolves, Beserker, escaped on September 17 after the mysterious appearance of a tall, thin man with red eyes. The wolf smashes through the window of Lucy's room, frightening Mrs. Westenra to death and clearing the way for Count Dracula. The frightened maids fortify their shaken nerves with sherry that has been laced with laudanum. Beserker returns to the zoo, his head cut and full of broken glass. That same night, Renfield attacks Seward with a dinner knife, cutting the doctor's left wrist. While the shaken Seward attends to his wound, Renfield is lapping up the blood on the floor. He keeps repeating, "The blood is the life!"

Chapter 12

Van Helsing and Seward find the four servants unconscious, Mrs. Westenra dead, and Lucy near death. A fourth transfusion is necessary, and a just-arrived Quincey Morris volunteers to be the donor. Quincey is stunned to learn that, in ten days, Lucy "has had put in her veins" the blood of four strong men. "Man alive, her whole body wouldn't hold it," he says, then asking in a half-whisper, "What took it out?" Not knowing Lucy is barely clinging to life, Mina writes her, telling that she and Jonathan have settled in a house at Exeter. Jonathan, growing stronger, has been named a partner in the firm, now called Hawkins & Harker. She writes again on September 18 to say that Peter Hawkins has died suddenly, leaving Jonathan as his heir. The next day, Arthur's father dies. The title of Lord Godalming has passed to Arthur. Patrick Hennessey, a physician at the Purfleet sanitarium, reports to Seward on September 20 that Renfield has escaped yet again, this time attacking two hired men, Jack Smollet and Thomas Snelling, who were carting large boxes away from Carfax. One attendant, Hardy, has his finger broken during the struggle to subdue Renfield. Lucy, near death, seductively summons Arthur to her bedside. Van Helsing pushes him back, and Lucy, restored to herself, thanks him for being their "true friend." Lucy dies—the fourth death in four days. When Seward says it is the end, Van Helsing ominously replies, "Not so; alas! not so. It is only the beginning!"

Chapter 13

Van Helsing asks Arthur's permission to examine all of Lucy's papers. After the funeral for Peter Hawkins, Jonathan and Mina take the bus to London's Hyde Park Corner. Walking down Piccadilly in the middle of the day, Jonathan is aghast to see a man who surely is Count Dracula grown younger. They return to Exeter on September 22 and find a telegram from Van Helsing, whom they have not yet met. He tells them the sad news of Lucy's death. He informs them that Lucy and her mother were buried that very day in a cemetery near Hampstead Heath. On September 25, the *Westminster Gazette* reports on missing Hampstead children being found weak and emaciated with tiny wounds on their throats. Each tells of being lured away by a mysterious "bloofer" (childish term for beautiful) lady. Headlines begin referring to the bloofer lady case as the Hampstead Horror.

Chapter 14

Mina finally reads Jonathan's journal account of his ordeal at Castle Dracula.

The next day, she receives a letter from Van Helsing, asking for her help and for permission to visit her in Exeter. When he arrives, she shows him both a typewritten version of her journal entries about Lucy and Jonathan's journal. Van Helsing's belief gives Jonathan renewed strength. Jonathan no longer fears even the count, because "Van Helsing is the man to unmask him and hunt him out." Trying to prepare Seward for the horror ahead, Van Helsing points out the similarities in the wounds on Lucy's neck and those on the necks of the missing Hampstead children. But the wounds on the children's throats, he tells the perplexed Seward, "were made by Miss Lucy!"

Chapter 15

Van Helsing sets out to convince Seward that Lucy is one of the undead. They first meet with Dr. Vincent, the North Hospital physician treating victims of the bloofer lady. Afterward, they enter the Westenra tomb, and Van Helsing opens Lucy's coffin. It is empty. In the cemetery, they spot a figure in white. Near where they see the figure, the two doctors find a small child. The next afternoon, they return to the tomb and again open the coffin. Lucy is there, her body showing no signs of decay. The only explanation is that Lucy is a vampire, Van Helsing says, and the only cure is to drive a stake through her heart, cut off her head, and fill her mouth with garlic. He presents this plan to a horrified and still unconvinced Arthur, Quincey, and Seward. The notion of vampires is unbelievable to them, and Arthur refuses to allow Lucy's grave to be desecrated. But they agree when Van Helsing asks them to accompany him to the cemetery that night. It is September 28, the day Arthur and Lucy were to be married.

Chapter 16

In the Westenra tomb, Seward confirms that Lucy's body was in the coffin the previous afternoon. They open the coffin. It's empty. Van Helsing seals the tomb, using the Host he has brought from Amsterdam ("I have an Indulgence"). They soon see Lucy approaching the tomb with a small child. With blood streaming from her lips, Lucy's sweet features now are a mask of cruelty. She beckons to Arthur, but recoils when confronted by Van Helsing's little golden crucifix. Van Helsing clears a chink no wider than a knife blade, and, making herself so small as to be invisible, Lucy enters the tomb. Van Helsing then reseals the opening. The next day, they return, and Arthur drives the stake through the vampire Lucy's heart. The two doctors remain, sawing off the top of the stake, cutting off the head, and filling the mouth with garlic. Van Helsing tells them a greater task awaits them. He leaves for Amsterdam later that day, but will soon return. In two days, he tells them, the four of them will meet with two others "you know not as yet."

Chapter 17

Van Helsing gives Seward the typed versions of the journals given to him by Jonathan and Mina Harker. He then departs, and Seward meets Mina's train in London, thereby meeting Mina for the first time. Jonathan is in Whitby, consulting with, among others, Samuel F. Billington, Jr., a solicitor in the firm that handled the delivery of fifty boxes of common earth to Carfax. Seward lets Mina take the cylinders of his phonographic diaries. She also makes a typed version of these. Jonathan arrives at Purfleet on September 30. He and Mina work together to assemble a chronological record of all the gathered diaries, journals, letters, and newspaper clippings. Jonathan suggests watching Renfield as an index to Count Dracula's comings and goings. Arthur and Quincey arrive. Both are moved by Mina's expressions of sympathy and compassion.

Chapter 18

While Jonathan goes off to find the carriers employed to move Dracula's earth boxes, Arthur and Quincey read the typed record made by Mina and Jonathan. Mina asks Seward if she can see Renfield. Mina's presence seems to touch some deep memory in Renfield, who, to Seward's astonishment, speaks eloquently and philosophically. He also warns Mina to leave. Seward goes to the station to meet Van Helsing. He tells Van Helsing that they now know Dracula purchased the very estate next to the asylum. That evening Van Helsing meets with Jonathan, Mina, Seward, Arthur, and Quincey. He outlines everything they know about vampires and Count Dracula. He explains the vampire's powers and weaknesses. Quincey notices a large bat sitting on the windowsill. He takes a shot at it, but misses. Van Helsing concludes by saying they must track down Dracula's earth boxes and render them useless to him. In the early morning hours of October 1, the five men are about to set off for Carfax, but are detained by a message from Renfield. They go to the inmate, who seems remarkably calm and sane. He asks, then pleads, to be sent away. When his request is denied, Renfield says, ominously, "You will, I trust, Dr. Seward, do me the justice to bear in mind, later on, that I did what I could to convince you to-night."

Chapter 19

The five men walk to Carfax, discovering that only twenty-nine of the count's fifty earth boxes remain. A few moments later, they are surrounded by thousands of rats presumed to be commanded by Dracula. Arthur is prepared, and blows a whistle that summons his dogs. The terriers disperse the rats, and Van Helsing declares the night a success. They know that twenty-one boxes need to be traced. To that end, Jonathan resolves to find Thomas Snelling, one of the laborers hired to move the boxes. Mina records having a disturbing dream that reminds her of the red eyes and the attacks on Lucy in Whitby. She is pale and tired the next day.

Chapter 20

Jonathan finds Thomas Snelling, who is too drunk to recall anything. But his wife tells Jonathan that Snelling was only the assistant to Joseph Smollett. Jonathan finds Smollett, who consults his "wonderful dog's-eared notebook." Six boxes were taken from Carfax and left at 197 Chicksand Street, Mile End, New Town, and another six at Jamaica Lane, Bermondsey. Dracula is scattering his boxes around London. Jonathan asks Smollett if he knows if any other boxes were removed from Carfax. He only moved the twelve, but he heard of a man named Sam Bloxam taking on a "rare dusty job in a old 'ouse at Purfleet." The next day, October 2, he tracks down Sam Bloxam, who remembers making two trips between Carfax and a house in Piccadilly. Nine boxes were moved, and, with the twelve moved by Snelling, it accounts for the twenty-one missing boxes. Bloxam doesn't recall the number of the Piccadilly house, but he describes it to Jonathan. He also describes the man who employed him as "the strongest chap I ever struck, an' him a old feller, with a white moustache." Jonathan finds the house, learning that it was recently sold and that the house agents for it were Mitchell, Sons, & Candy. Jonathan returns to Purfleet and reports his findings to the others. After talking to Renfield, Seward is convinced Dracula has visited him. Mitchell, Sons, & Candy reports that the Piccadilly house was purchased by Count de Ville, a foreign nobleman who paid cash. That night, the attendant rushes in to to tell Seward that Renfield has met with a terrible accident.

Chapter 21

Seward finds Renfield lying in a pool of blood. His back is broken, and his skull fractured; he is unconscious, and dying. Van Helsing and Seward operate to reduce pressure on the brain. Arthur and Quincey arrive to hear Renfield's dying words. He tells how Dracula appeared outside his window, showing him thousands of rats and promising to give them to him—if Renfield will give him total allegiance. Renfield invites him in, providing the vampire access to Mina. The next time Dracula appears, Renfield realizes Mina is his target. He struggles with the count, who easily breaks the back of the unnaturally strong inmate. "We know the worst now," Van Helsing declares. The men rush to Jonathan and Mina's room. Breaking through the door, they find Jonathan unconscious and the count forcing Mina to drink from a vein he has opened in his chest with those long sharp nails. Dracula lunges at the men, but he's repelled by the sacred Host held by Van Helsing. The men advance, holding crucifixes. The count transforms into vapor and disappears. Van Helsing tries to calm Jonathan and Mina. The count has not only taken Mina's blood and infected her with his own but has burned the Harkers' copy of the typed manuscript and Seward's wax cylinders. There are other copies, but Dracula boasts to Mina of making her "my companion and my helper."

Chapter 22

The six friends plot a course of action. They decide to sterilize the count's earth boxes, rendering them useless to him. Before they go, Van Helsing attempts to bless Mina's forehead with the sacred Host. She screams. It leaves a red scar on her forehead, and Mina yells out, "Unclean! Unclean!" Van Helsing vows to do all in his power to forever remove the scar. The five men again enter Carfax, leaving a portion of the Host in each of the twenty-nine boxes. They proceed to Piccadilly, where they find that one of the nine boxes has been removed. They sterilize the remaining eight. Quincey and Arthur then set off to find the boxes in Dracula's houses at Walworth and Mile End. Jonathan remains with the doctors Seward and Van Helsing.

Chapter 23

Arthur and Quincey return to the house in Piccadilly, reporting that they've sterilized the twelve boxes in Dracula's other two London houses. In quick order, they have rendered forty-nine of the fifty boxes useless to Dracula. The count shows up at the Piccadilly house, Harker narrowly missing the vampire's heart with his Kukri knife. With Van Helsing advancing and holding a crucifix and the Host, Dracula escapes by crashing through a window. Before fleeing, he brags that his revenge has just begun and he will spread it over centuries. Van Helsing, though, realizes that, behind the bravado, Dracula fears them. They return to Purfleet. On October 4, Mina realizes that Van Helsing must hypnotize her. Dracula has established a link between them, and it's a link they can use to fight him. Under hypnosis, she can tap into Dracula's senses. Responding in a hypnotic state to Van Helsing's questions, Mina tells them that she can hear lapping water and the creaking of a chain. Dracula is on a ship weighing anchor in the port of London. With just one earth box left him, he is escaping, but time is on his side. He is immortal, and Mina is mortal with the mark of Dracula on her throat.

Chapter 24

The six friends meet late on October 5 to make plans. Since Mina had told, under hypnosis, of hearing sails set, an inquiry was made into sailing vessels leaving London. One sailing ship fits the date and destination for Dracula: it is the *Czarina Catherine*, which left from Doolittle's Wharf for the Black Sea port town of Varna. Sure enough, a tall, thin man dressed all in black arranged for a large box to be taken aboard. Realizing that if Mina can tell what Dracula sees and hears, perhaps the count can reverse the process, Van Helsing suggests they keep Mina ignorant of their plans. Mina comes to the same conclusion. Knowing that the *Czarina Catherine* will take three weeks at top speed to reach Varna, Van Helsing recommends beating Dracula to the Bulgarian port by traveling overland. Since the count can command wolves and other creatures,

Quincey suggests adding Winchester rifles to their weapons. The plan is for Van Helsing, Seward, Arthur, and Quincey to make the journey, but Mina argues that she and Jonathan must go, as well. Under hypnosis, she may be of use to them.

Chapter 25

Mina entreats Jonathan and their four friends that if she should die under the vampire's curse, they will set free her soul, "even as you did my poor Lucy's." They promise her that the proper steps will be taken. The six vampire hunters leave London on October 12, boarding the Orient Express in Paris and arriving in Varna on October 15. Here they wait for news of the *Czarina Catherine*. By their estimation, the ship cannot reach the port earlier than October 26. Under hypnosis, Mina can see nothing. All is dark. She can hear waves lapping against the ship, water rushing by, and wind in the shrouds. The friends hope to meet the ship as it docks, and if they can board after sunrise, Dracula will be at their mercy. Arthur keeps posted on the ship's progress with telegrams sent by Lloyd's in London. When the ship hasn't arrived in Varna by October 27, the friends grow anxious and suspicious. A telegram from Lloyd's on October 28 tells them that the *Czarina Catherine* has reached Galatz, a River Danube port to the north of Varna. It has access to the Black Sea. Van Helsing believes that Dracula has learned of their presence in Varna by reading Mina's mind.

Chapter 26

The six friends board the next train to Galatz, which leaves October 29. Mina, under hypnosis, confirms that Dracula's earth box has not yet left the ship. There still is a chance they'll make it in time to corner the vampire. They arrive in Galatz, Quincey taking Mina to their hotel, Arthur calling on the consul's office, while Jonathan, Van Helsing, and Seward head for the *Czarina Catherine*. They interview Captain Donelson, who tells them that a heavy fog prevented the scheduled docking at Varna. When the fog finally lifted, Donelson found that his ship was just in the Danube, near Galatz. After reaching the port, a man named Immanuel Hildesheim took possession of the box for a Count Dracula. The box was supposed to be shipped to Galatz from Varna, so Donelson sees their detour as fortuitous. Hildesheim tells them that he received his orders from London, instructing him to avoid customs and give the box to Pertrof Skinsky, who deals with the Slovaks trading on the river. Skinsky's body is found in a churchyard, his throat torn open. That evening, October 30, Mina calculates the advantages and difficulties of Dracula having his earth box transported to his castle by river, rail, and road. Mina concludes that the count always meant for the ship to land at Galatz, summoning the fog and favorable winds to do his bidding. She also deduces that the box is being transported by river boat. But which river? The Pruth is more easily navigated.

The Sereth, joining the Bistritza, gets Dracula closer to his castle. To increase their odds, the six friends decide to converge on Castle Dracula in three teams: Arthur and Jonathan heading upriver on a steam launch, Seward and Quincey on horseback, and Mina and Van Helsing traveling by train. At least the count is a prisoner until he reaches the castle. If he makes his presence known in any way, the Slovaks would throw the box overboard and abandon him.

Chapter 27

Mina and Van Helsing reach the Borgo Pass on November 4. Camping in view of the castle, Van Helsing builds a fire and makes a protective circle, using the sacred Host. Dracula's three vampire brides appear to them, beckoning to Mina, "Come, sister. Come to us." An accident to the launch delays Arthur and Jonathan, but, on November 5, Seward and Quincey see a group of Gypsies dashing away from the river in a wagon. They are in pursuit. "We ride to the death of some one," writes Seward. "God alone knows who." That same day, Van Helsing enters Dracula's castle and carries out the gruesome task of staking the three brides. He also fixes the entrance so Dracula may not enter it in the undead state. Late in afternoon of November 6, Mina and Van Helsing see a group of men on horseback surrounding a wagon. On the cart is a large box. They are being pursued from the south by Quincey and Seward. Then, two more riders appear from the north: Jonathan and Arthur. The Gypsies are riding toward Mina and Van Helsing, armed with revolvers. They are racing the sunset. The Gypsies' mad dash is halted short of the castle, in front of Mina and Van Helsing. They are surrounded. There is a skirmish as Quincey and Jonathan fight their way toward the box. Quincey is injured, but the Gypsies, covered by the Winchesters held by Arthur and Seward, capitulate. The lid of the box is pried open, and the look of hate in the count's eyes turn to triumph when he sees the sinking sun. At that instant, Jonathan's Kukri knife slashes through Dracula's throat and Quincey's bowie knife plunges into the heart. There is a look of peace, and then the body crumbles into dust. The gypsies flee, and the wounded Quincey collapses, dying. "'I am only too happy to have been of any service,'" he tells Mina. "'It was worth this to die! Look!'" The scar is gone from her forehead. Seven years later, Jonathan adds a note to the record. He and Mina have a son, born on the day that Quincey (and Dracula) died. He has been named for the five men of "our little band." Arthur and Seward are both happily married. There is no actual proof of their experience, but it is enough that the boy someday will "know what a brave and gallant woman his mother is" and "how some men so loved her, that they did dare much for her sake."

Castle Kept

Stoker originally planned a spectacularly cinematic end for Castle Dracula. Upon the killing of the count, there was to be "a terrible convulsion of the earth" and "a roar which seemed to shake the very heavens." The castle would be destroyed in a cataclysm resembling "one fierce volcano burst." Stoker discarded the castle collapse, perhaps thinking it would literally and figuratively overshadow the destruction of Dracula.

A Map of Romania and Locations in the Book

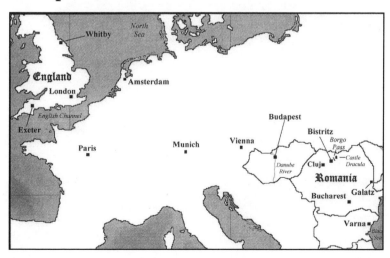

The Real Count Dracula

. . . .

His eyes were positively blazing. The red light in them was lurid, as if the flames of hell-fire blazed behind them.
—*Jonathan Harker,* Dracula, *chapter 3*

Nobody got it all, but aspects of Stoker's Count Dracula can be found in the portrayals by Louis Jourdan, John Carradine, and Jack Palance.

It's not exactly a case of one-size-cape fits all, so we have welcomed Draculas ranging from the ghoulish Max Schreck in the silent *Nosferatu* (1922) to the sensual Frank Langella in the 1979 film *Dracula*. Hollywood has given us Draculas who have looked like John Carradine, Louis Jourdan, Francis Lederer, Christopher Lee, Bela Lugosi, Michael Nouri, Gary Oldman, and Jack Palance. How do you like your Dracula?

Tall, dark, and sexy? Or bald, bug-eyed, and creepy?

No question, there are some very different looks represented by this group of "Dractors." Yet they do have something in common: not one of these ten gentlemen resembles the Count Dracula described by Stoker in the novel.

Would you recognize the real Count Dracula if he strolled by? Could you pick him out of a lineup, standing between, say, Lee and Lugosi? Jonathan Harker could. We have his eyewitness testimony for the APB (all *pints* bulletin, for you're on the plasma watch).

Harker tells us that Dracula is "a tall old man, clean shaven save for a long white moustache, and clad in black from head to foot, without a single speck of colour about him anywhere . . . excellent English, but with a strange intonation . . . a strength which made me wince, an effect which was not lessened by the fact that it seemed cold as ice, more like the hand of a dead than a living man."

That's not much to go on. What else did you notice, Mr. Harker?

I had now an opportunity of observing him, and found him of a very marked physiognomy. His face was a strong, a very strong, aquiline, with high bridge of the thin nose and peculiarly arched nostrils, with lofty domed forehead, and hair growing scantily round the temples but profusely elsewhere. His eyebrows were very massive, almost meeting over the nose, and with bushy hair that seemed to curl in its own profusion. The mouth, so far as I could see it under the heavy moustache, was fixed and rather cruel-looking, with peculiarly sharp white teeth. These protruded over the lips, whose remarkable ruddiness showed astonishing vitality in a man of his years. For the rest, his ears were pale, and at the tops extremely pointed.

The chin was broad and strong, and the cheeks firm though thin. The general effect was one of extraordinary pallor.

Extraordinary pallor? All right, got that. Any peculiar marks or physical characteristics?

I had noticed the backs of his hands as they lay on his knees in the firelight, and they had seemed rather white and fine. But seeing them now close to me, I could not but notice that they were rather coarse, broad, with squat fingers. Strange to say, there were hairs in the centre of the palm. The nails were long and fine, and cut to a sharp point. As the Count leaned over me and his hands touched me, I could not repress a shudder. It may have been that his breath was rank, but a horrible feeling of nausea came over me, which, do what I would, I could not conceal. The Count, evidently noticing it, drew back. And with a grim sort of smile, which showed more than he had yet done his protuberant teeth. . . .

Hmmm. Male . . . Caucasian . . . white hair . . . bushy eyebrows . . . pointed ears . . . high forehead . . . drooping mustache . . . beaklike face . . . nails filed to a point . . . hair in palms . . . favors black . . . really bad breath. Oh, and has been known to take the shape of a bat or a wolf. Got that?

Dracula's Powers

· · · · · · · · · · ·

"The vampire live on, and cannot die by mere passing of time; he can flourish when that he can fatten on the blood of the living."
—*Professor Van Helsing,* Dracula, *chapter 18*

Gathering his vampire hunters, Van Helsing runs down Count Dracula's formidable powers:

- He has the strength of twenty men.
- He can transform into a bat and a wolf.
- He can appear as mist or as elemental dust.
- He can grow larger or small enough to slip through "a hairbreadth space."
- He can become invisible.
- He can see in the dark.
- He can hypnotize people to do his will.
- He can utilize necromancy (divination by the dead).
- He can, within limits, command fog, thunder, and storm.
- He can command the bat, wolf, rat, owl, fox, and moth.
- He can grow younger.
- He cannot be hurt by ordinary bullets or knife wounds that do not pierce his heart.
- He can turn his victims into vampires.
- He can live forever.

Stoker tells us that Dracula can transform himself into several creatures, but the bat is the animal most strongly associated with vampires. (Artwork © Joseph Vargo)

Dracula's Weaknesses

. . . .

"Now let us see how far the general powers arrayed against us are restrict . . . let us consider the limitations of the vampire in general, and this one in particular."
—*Professor Van Helsing*, Dracula, *chapter 18*

Having outlined Dracula's considerable powers, Van Helsing gives a checklist of his weaknesses:

- He can be destroyed when his heart is staked and his head is cut from the body. (Van Helsing does not insist on a wooden stake, although this is what they use to release Lucy. The wooden stake became the prescribed method with the stage and film versions of *Dracula*. Dracula crumbles to dust after Jonathan Harker's Kukri knife slashes through the throat and Quincey Morris pierces the heart with his bowie knife.)

- His powers cease with the coming of the dawn (although sunlight is not fatal to him—this notion was introduced in the 1922 silent film, *Nosferatu*, and then becoming a fixed part of vampire lore. Stoker has Dracula move about in the daytime, but we must assume without vampiric powers).

- He cannot enter anywhere unless first invited in by one of the household.

- If he has not reached where he is bound, he can only change himself at noon or exact sunrise and sunset.

- He can only pass running water at the slack or the flood of the tide.

- His powers are diminished by garlic and the branch of the wild rose. (Wolfbane was another later addition.)

- He is repelled by sacred symbols, notably the crucifix and the sacred Host.

- He must sleep on the soil of his native land.

- The branch of the wild rose placed on his coffin will keep him a prisoner.

- A sacred bullet fired into his coffin will destroy him. (Silver was considered a talisman against evil things, so later stories added that he could be killed by a silver bullet fired through the heart, particularly one that had been blessed, or made from a melted down holy object.)

- He can be detected among the living because he throws no shadow and casts no reflection in a mirror.

The cross and the crucifix are powerful weapons against Stoker's Dracula (here played in a TV production by Michael Nouri).

So does Count Dracula die at the end of the book? Well, this is a matter of some debate. It has been suggested that Stoker considered a sequel. If so, had he left himself an out in the novel's final chapter? Dracula is not dispatched by methods advocated by Van Helsing. "Dracula is described as crumbling into dust," David J. Skal writes in *Hollywood Gothic*, "though we already know that he has the ability to take the form of dust motes." Is this the reason for the look of triumph Mina notices in Dracula's eyes? Maybe, then, he escaped his pursuers. Maybe, then, he's still out there. On the other side of the destruction debate, the mark of the unclean leaves Mina's forehead when Dracula crumbles into dust. There is the final look of peace in Dracula's eyes. And Stoker seems pretty clear about the count being dispatched. Then again, proponents of the Dracula escapes theory point to Stoker's last-minute deletion of the castle's volcanic destruction. Is this proof that a sequel was in the back of Stoker's mind? It doesn't really matter. Either way, the count lives on, attaining immortality as a character.

The Cape, the Bat, and the Sunlight

· · · · · · · · · · ·

*I went to the window and looked out, but could see
nothing, except a big bat, which had evidently been
buffeting its wings against the window.*
—**Lucy Westenra,** Dracula, *chapter 11*

*Any place you hang
your bat is...*

Right off the bat, even those just casually familiar with Count Dracula can tell you the significance of the cape, the bat, and the sunlight. Count Dracula wears a cape. He can turn into a bat. And sunlight will kill him.

But a careful reading of Stoker's novel reveals that only the second of these statements is inarguably certain.

The cape? Well, maybe. Illustrations for *Varney the Vampire* depict the undead Sir Francis Varney in a black cape that gives him a distinctly batlike appearance. And, clearly, Varney had an influence on *Dracula.* But the word *cape* only appears in Stoker's novel twice, referring not to a garment, but to Cape Farewell and Cape Matapan. Stoker describes Dracula as being dressed all in black, never specifying the cape. The closest we get is the unsettling scene of Harker observing Dracula as he crawls down the side of his castle, "his cloak spreading out around him like great wings." Is the cloak a cape? Could be. What we know for certain is that the classic vampire cape really became fully associated with Count Dracula in the authorized 1920s stage productions starring Edmund Blake, Raymond Huntley, and Bela Lugosi. This allowed for the stage trick of Dracula's disappearance (men holding an empty cape after the actor playing Dracula has dropped through a trap door), yet it also gave him a more batlike appearance. The cape went with Lugosi into the 1931 film, making it a permanent part of the vampire's wardrobe.

The bat? This is an association strongly embraced by Stoker, and the wall-crawling scene, while not offering a definitive answer on the cape question, does provide the first strong batlike image. Indeed, the 1901 cover illustration for Archibald Constable and Company's first paperback edition of *Dracula* depicts this scene complete with bat "wings" for the barefoot count. The cover for the 1912 W. Rider and Company popular edition shows the same moment, making the cloak wings even more impressive. Dracula is first seen in the actual form of a bat by Mina in chapter 8. He appears in five more chapters as a bat (being fired at by Quincey Morris in chapter 18 for eavesdropping on Van Helsing's talk on vampires). Stoker's choice of native soil for Dracula led to another long-standing misconception about Transylvania: that vampire bats can be found soaring through the night skies of the Carpathians. In chapter 14, Van Helsing rightly talks about bats in the pampas that "come at night and open the veins of cattle and horses." In chapter 12, Quincey recalls a time in the pampas when a favorite horse was attacked in the night by one of "those big bats that they call Vampires." Vampire bats are found in Mexico, Central America, and South America (although both Quincey and Van Helsing greatly exaggerate the amount of blood these bats can drink).

But the power of the *Dracula* myth is so strong that it created an enduring pop-culture bond that planted the vampire and the vampire bat in Transylvania.

The sunlight? As previously noted, Stoker had no reason to believe that the dawn's rays would destroy a vampire. This wasn't in any of the superstitions or major vampire stories that preceded Dracula in the nineteenth century. Director F. W. Murnau killed off his vampire this way in his unauthorized silent-screen version, *Nosferatu* (1922). Intriguingly, later filmmakers accepted this as part of the rule book. Lon Chaney Jr. dies at dawn in *Son of Dracula* (1943). John Carradine's count is destroyed by the sun's rays in both Erle C. Kenton's *House of Frankenstein* (1944) and *House of Dracula* (1945). Peter Cushing's Van Helsing reduces Christopher Lee's Dracula to dust by forcing him into sunlight at the conclusion of Terence Fisher's *Horror of Dracula* (1958). Even more intriguingly, writers of landmark vampire novels, including Richard Matheson (*I Am Legend*, 1954), Stephen King ('*Salem's Lot*, 1975) and Anne Rice (*Interview with the Vampire*, 1976), have followed the *Nosferatu* lead. Both Matheson and Rice rejected the notion of transformation into a bat, which is very much a part of *Dracula*. Rice rejected the idea of vampires being repelled by sacred objects, also a part of *Dracula*. But post-*Nosferatu*, just about everyone has fallen under the spell of the vampire being forever cut off from a sunlit world. The cape may be in question, but sunlight is a burden Stoker never put on Dracula's shoulders.

Ten Great Lines from
Bram Stoker's *Dracula*

· · · · · · · · · · ·

These classic quotations are pure Stoker, although you probably first encountered most of them in film versions of the novel. *Dracula* is the *Laugh-In* of horror novels, responsible for launching several widely quoted and often-imitated phrases and lines. How many lines from Mary Wollstonecraft Shelley's *Frankenstein* (1818) or Robert Louis Stevenson's *The Strange Case of Dr. Jekyll and Mr. Hyde* (1886) can you quote? Anyone? *Anyone?* Right off the bat, I'm guessing you know at least a couple of these:

"For your mother's sake."
—**Elderly Transylvanian land-lady putting a rosary around the neck of Jonathan Harker (chapter 1)**

"Welcome to my house! Enter freely and of your own free will!"
—**Count Dracula's first words to Jonathan Harker (chapter 2)**

"I am Dracula, and I bid you welcome."
—**Count Dracula at the door of his castle (chapter 2)**

"Listen to them, the children of the night. What music they make!"
—**Count Dracula's review of the wolf chorus howling outside his castle (chapter 2)**

"How dare you touch him, any of you? How dare you cast eyes on him when I had forbidden it? Back, I tell you all! This man belongs to me!"
—**Count Dracula halting the attack on Harker by the three vampire sisters (chapter 3)**

This was the being I was helping to transfer to London, where, perhaps, for centuries to come he might, amongst its teeming millions, satiate his lust for blood. . . .
—**Jonathan Harker (chapter 4)**

"I have learned not to think little of anyone's belief, no matter how strange it may be."
—*Professor Abraham Van Helsing (chapter 14)*

"There are mysteries which men can only guess at, which age by age they may solve only in part. Believe me, we are now on the verge of one."
—*Professor Abraham Van Helsing (chapter 15)*

"There are such beings as vampires."
—*Professor Abraham Van Helsing (chapter 18)*

"Then he began to whisper. 'Rats, rats, rats! Hundreds, thousands, millions of them. . . . A dark mass spread over the grass, coming on like the shape of a flame of fire . . . and I could see that there were thousands of rats with their eyes blazing red, like His only smaller. He held up his hand, and they all stopped, and I thought he seemed to be saying, 'All these lives will I give you, ay, and many more and greater, through countless ages, if you will fall down and worship me!'"
—*R. M. Renfield (chapter 21)*

Professor Van Helsing (played by Edward Van Sloan) knows there "are such beings as vampires," and he knows how to fight them, as he proves in this classic showdown with the count (Bela Lugosi) in the 1931 version of Dracula.

Ten Great *Dracula* Lines
Not in Stoker's Book

. . . .

Bram Stoker was no slouch at dialogue, and some of his best lines show up in the 1931 film version directed by Tod Browning. The screenplay was by Garrett Fort, working from Stoker's book and the stage play by Hamilton Deane and John L. Balderston. But a few of the most widely imitated phrases from that movie do not appear in the novel. They include:

Dracula never touches the stuff, but Vampire wine (the reds include Merlot and Cabernet Sauvignon) is a popular Romanian export.

"The spider spinning his web for the unwary fly. The blood is the life, Mr. Renfield."
—*Count Dracula (Bela Lugosi)*

"I never drink—wine."
—*Count Dracula*

"It reminds me of the broken battlements of my own castle in Transylvania."
—*Count Dracula*

"To die—to be really dead—that must be glorious."
—*Count Dracula*

"There are far worse things waiting man than death."
—*Count Dracula*

"The strength of the vampire is that people will not believe in him."
—*Professor Van Helsing (Edward Van Sloan)*

"I dislike mirrors. Van Helsing will explain. . . . For one who has not lived even a single lifetime, you are a wise man, Van Helsing."
—**Count Dracula**

"Be guided by what he says. It's your only hope. It's her only hope."
—**Renfield (Dwight Frye) pleading with Seward (Herbert Bunston) and Harker (David Manners) to follow Van Helsing**

"Isn't this a strange conversation for men who aren't crazy?"
—**Renfield**

"They're all crazy. They're all crazy, except you and me. Sometimes I have me doubts about you."
—**Martin the asylum guard (Charles Gerrard), to the maid (Moon Carroll)**

"The spider spinning his web for the unwary fly."

The Thrill of the Hunt:
Dracula as an Adventure Book

. . . .

"He think to escape, but no! We follow him. Tally Ho! As friend
Arthur would say when he put on his red frock! Our old fox is wily."
—*Professor Van Helsing,* Dracula, *chapter 23*

Bram Stoker's *Dracula* is a novel that has been endlessly and rightly stalked by literary detectives ferreting out clues that support psychological, philosophical, political, sexual, social, and religious interpretations. You'll find no shortage of compelling and provocative arguments out there, from Leonard Wolf's deeply meditative *A Dream of Dracula* (1972) to Nina Auerbach's challenging *Our Vampires, Ourselves* (1995). Dracula has been pursued with a vigilance and determination that would make Van Helsing and his band of vampire hunters look like Eagle Scouts going after the merit badge for emergency preparedness.

Freudians and feminists, socialists and scientists, historians and horror fans: they've all sifted through the text searching for subtext. Indeed, *Dracula* has undergone so much analysis, you'd be forgiven for thinking he's more at home reclining on a psychiatrist's couch than in a coffin.

But, as Stephen King has pointed out, horror works on many levels. It can be cerebral, emotional, and primal—blowing your mind, wrenching your heart, and turning your stomach. One of the amazing things about *Dracula* is that it works on all three of these levels. King, in his nonfiction book *Danse Macabre*, breaks down the three levels of scary fiction to "terror on top" ("the unpleasant speculation called to mind when the knocking on the door begins"), "horror below it" ("that emotion of fear that underlies terror"), and "lowest of all, the gag reflex of revulsion." Stoker would have understood King's stated philosophy, which is to aim high for terror. If you can't get terror, go for horror. "But if I find I cannot" terrify or horrify, King writes, "I'll go for the gross-out. I'm not proud."

You can just imagine Stoker aiming a knowing smile at King, nodding in agreement. That's because, at heart, both Stoker and King are storytellers. The risk in dwelling too long in the dense and tangled forest of analysis is that you'll miss out on the book's considerable power as an adventure story. In the splendidly crafted opening chapters of *Dracula*, Jonathan wonders what "sort of grim adventure" he will be facing in Transylvania. It is grim, and it is an adventure. Stoker, through Jonathan, is grasping your hand and inviting you to jump aboard for the ride.

In this way *Dracula* has much in common with the novels of English author H. Rider Haggard or the Sherlock Holmes stories of Stoker's friend Arthur Conan Doyle. The early Transylvania chapters are weird, exotic, erotic, and suspenseful. The final third of the book, the hunt for Dracula, bristles with the clue-chasing energy of a Holmes-and-Watson investigation. You certainly can imagine Van Helsing yelling to his comrades, "Come! The game is a-foot!" He all but does say this when comparing the search for Dracula to a fox hunt.

Like Holmes, Van Helsing can be insufferable at times. But also like Holmes, his iron will and sense of purpose are undeniably impressive. Like Dracula, Van Helsing is also a fascinating subject for analysis. That can wait, however. Your first duty on a roller coaster is to enjoy the roller coaster. There's plenty of time after the ride to ponder *why* you enjoy the roller coaster.

"I taught a course in which the students had to read *Frankenstein*, *Dracula*, and *1984*," comments English professor and *Dracula* expert Elizabeth Miller. "And, at the end, I always asked the students to rank the books. The favorite, as far as sheer reading enjoyment, always was *Dracula*."

This is not to sell the book short in the disquisition, exposition, and supposition departments. To be sure, if you pause to look down from the roller coaster ride, you might notice that the tracks span a psychological bottomless pit. Jolting over that pit for the first time can be just a stone cold gas. Later, you'll go back to explore the pit, and that, too, can be thrilling, but then it's an adventure of a different type.

Metaphors and Monsters:
What Does Dracula Represent?

· · · · · · · · · · ·

What does it all mean?
—Dr. *John Seward*, Dracula, *chapter 11*

Let us return for a moment to those three seminal horror classics—Mary Wollstonecraft Shelley's *Frankenstein* (1818), Robert Louis Stevenson's *The Strange Case of Dr. Jekyll and Mr. Hyde* (1886), and Bram Stoker's *Dracula* (1897). They are united in our consciousness by more than just genre. Yes, they were published in the same century. And, yes, each was the work of an author from the British Isles: the English Shelley, the Scottish Stevenson, and the Irish Stoker. But what truly creates the bond forever linking these three supernatural stories is their allegorical power.

Frankenstein isn't really about a scientist fashioning a creature in a laboratory. It's about a man taking the blasphemous step of playing God. Or it's about the individual cut loose in a lonely universe, feeling abandoned by God. Or it's a cautionary tale about the dangers of science running wild. Or it's a

morality tale about responsibility. Or . . . well, you get the idea. Go on. Pick one. Or another. There's plenty more where those came from.

Dr. Jekyll and Mr. Hyde isn't really about a doctor and his steaming green potion. It's about the struggle between good and evil within every individual. It's a psychological case study in duality. It's about a child (of man or of God) asking not to be judged for how he was made. It's a warning about the dangers of alcohol, or maybe drugs. It's a study of Victorian repression, which leads to a double life and a descent into decadence and addiction. We're just getting started.

And *Dracula* isn't really about a vampire. Deliberately or unconsciously, Stoker produced a volume open to a wide variety of allegorical interpretations. If all of the theories about this novel were laid end to end, they'd stretch from Jonathan Harker's home in Exeter to the front door of Castle Dracula. You could cover a vast amount of territory, with plenty of detours and side trips along the way.

The monster-as-metaphor tradition leads us back to Greek mythology, a landscape more overrun with paranormal parables than the pop-culture conceptualization of Transylvania. But our three nineteenth-century authors certainly refined the concept, using their monsters as remarkably versatile stand-ins for their era's fears, anxieties, doubts, and longings. Although their origins and personalities are radically different, Frankenstein's creature, Mr. Hyde, and Count Dracula pose the same troubling question: "What am I?" And by forcing us to confront this question, we are left with the bigger societal question: "What are we?"

What Shelley and Stevenson showed Stoker in the nineteenth century was similar to what Rod Serling and Gene Roddenberry showed a generation of television writers in the next century. Weary of battling network censors and worried sponsors, Serling realized that fantasy was the ideal vehicle for carrying profound stories to a mass audience. He examined the human condition and submitted it for our approval in *The Twilight Zone*, and Roddenberry followed his enterprising example with *Star Trek*. Roddenberry could present stories about racism and intolerance in outer space, and nobody objected, because, after all, these were merely stories about aliens and rocket ships.

Fantasy, from Homer to the recent TV series *Heroes*, has provided us the context for grappling with monstrously big ideas. That's true of the subset genre, science fiction. And it's true of that other subset genre, horror, which is at its best when allegorical storytelling is on the line. How frighteningly good can the horror novel get at this game?

Consider that the creatures Hyde and Dracula are not only astonishingly versatile, they are incredibly durable. They hop from generation to generation, taking on new meanings and possible meanings with each passing decade. Van Helsing calls *Dracula* immortal. Well, yeah.

There is no definitive answer, therefore. What does it all mean? There are, of course, many who will tell you that any discussion of *Dracula* must consider the sexual implications, but even here, there is no consensus on what those implications are.

"I think each generation fashions a vampire in its own image, or at least according to its own societal make-up and concerns," notes J. Gordon Melton, author of *The Vampire Book: The Encyclopedia of the Undead*. "The Dracula character is extraordinarily malleable. Stoker created a very, very powerful character that can keep coming back at us, like Sherlock Holmes. These may be the two characters most often portrayed on the screen, and you can understand why."

Drop-Dead Sexy: Sex, Sexuality, and Seduction in *Dracula*

· · · · · · · · · · ·

"Yes, I too can love. You yourselves can tell it
from the past. Is it not so?"
—*Count Dracula*, Dracula, *chapter 3*

Your mother and I have been putting off this talk for a while, but it's time we had that little discussion about (shhhh!) s–e–x. It's unavoidable, particularly when you're talking about Dracula.

Hollywood depictions of vampires have emphasized one of two approaches taken by Bram Stoker in his novel. Compare the first two screen versions of *Dracula* and you'll see what I mean. German director F. W. Murnau's silent classic *Nosferatu* (1922) gave us the plague-carrying, rodentlike Orlok, a repugnant yet fascinating vampire played by Max Schreck. Universal's 1931 film, taking its cue from the play, gave us the vampire as matinee idol—a mysterious Valentino-like foreigner played in evening clothes by Bela Lugosi. Sensuality won out, and, even though the Valentino look quickly went out of vogue, later Dracula interpretations became more overtly sexual and sexy. Christopher Lee

Hey, good lookin'! Despite his rodent-like appearance, Max Schreck's vampire had seduction on the mind in the 1922 silent classic, Nosferatu.

appropriately titled his autobiography *Tall, Dark and Gruesome*, splendidly allying both the terrifying and alluring aspects of his most famous screen character. And Frank Langella smoldered across the screen as the most sensual Dracula of them all.

"We cleaned him up and dressed him for the stage, so he could enter an English drawing room," said *Dracula* expert J. Gordon Melton. "He lost the fangs, the mustache, the bad breath. Lugosi was this handsome, urbane, intriguing

Dracula on the prowl: Michael Nouri and Carol Baxter in NBC's 1979 Cliffhangers series.

European nobleman. Lee much more consciously sexualized the role, and Langella completes that process. With Langella, he became a full-fledged sex symbol."

It's a view of the vampire that completely befuddles legendary fantasy writer Richard Matheson, who wrote the script for the 1974 *Dracula* TV movie starring Jack Palance. "I've never understood why anyone would find them attractive in any way," comments Matheson, whose other vampire credits include the novel *I Am Legend* (1954) and the script for the TV movie *The Night Stalker* (1972). "To me, when you think about it, vampires are pretty disgusting. They're dead people who smell bad and live by drinking people's blood. It's pretty ghastly. They try to romanticize it, but there's nothing romantic about it."

As Dracula said to the vampire hunter holding a sharpened stake, "You've made your point." Matheson, though, is in the minority. Sex has been associated with the *Dracula* story from the start, and the rise of Freudian analysis only widened and accelerated the speculation.

So most theories about *Dracula* can't get too far along without mentioning those repressed Victorians and sex. But where some see the novel as a study in repression, others see it as expression—an explosion of sexual wants and needs. The forthright Englishman Jonathan Harker is repelled by the three brides in Castle Dracula, but he sure seems to be enjoying the "languorous ecstasy" of being seduced by them. The fair one "went on her knees, and bent over me. . . . There was a deliberate voluptuousness which was both thrilling and repulsive." Deliberate, I'd say.

"In the England of 1897, a girl who 'went on her knees' was not the sort of girl you brought home to meet your mother," Stephen King writes in his nonfiction study *Danse Macabre*. "Harker is about to be orally raped, and he doesn't mind a bit."

If *Dracula* is about sex, it "sure isn't a book about 'normal' sex," King argues. "The sexual basis of *Dracula* is an infantile oralism coupled with a strong interest in necrophilia (and pedophilia, some would say, considering Lucy in her role as the 'bloofer lady')." More than twenty years before King penned that description, Maurice Richardson labeled *Dracula* "a quite blatant demonstration of the Oedipal complex." How complex can you get? To Richardson, Stoker's novel was nothing less than—ready?—"a kind of incestuous, necrophilous, oral-and-sadistic all-in wrestling match." Quoting Richardson, author Phyllis A. Roth endorses this view, writing that the "equation of vampirism with sexuality is well established." And then there's Stoker biographer Barbara Belford's contention that *Dracula* is riddled with fear of homosexuality and devouring women. There also was a wave of feminism in the 1890s, and the New Woman movement may have been perceived as an undermining of the traditional social, economic, political, and, yes, sexual roles of Victorian women. So it's all about sex? That's what it means? Well, maybe. Then again, maybe not.

Like Roth, Franco Moretti contributed a scholarly essay to the Norton Critical Edition of *Dracula*, but he argues that the novel isn't about sex—it's about money. He sees Count Dracula as capital setting out "on the conquest of the world." He quotes Karl Marx, who wrote, "'Capital is dead labour which, vampire-like, lives only by sucking living labour, and lives the more, the more labour it sucks.'" Others see the whole vampire thing as Stoker vamping on Darwinian theory concerning natural selection and evolution. Others see Dracula as the supernatural embodiment of the Nietzschean *Ubermensch* (superman). Still, even capital-minded Moretti can't avoid the whole sex and the single vampire thing, and he states that Dracula "liberates and exalts sexual desire."

Not surprisingly, the count's role in the *Dracula* sexcapades also is hotly debated by scholars and vampire enthusiasts. To some he is the seducer, sneaking into the bedroom with promises of forbidden lust. To others he crosses the line from seducer to sexual predator. "My interpretation of the book is that Dracula is a serial rapist, and that the bite is a metaphor for sexual intercourse," Melton contends. "So the forced bite becomes

rape. Lugosi's interpretation turned Dracula from a rapist into a seducer, and Langella's portrayal completed that process. I don't think Lee and Palance were the right actors to complete that process, but they certainly pushed it. The process, though, has taken us away from the book's depiction."

Must we accept this view of Count Dracula? Not at all, say some academics, who view Van Helsing and the vampire hunters as the agents of repression or ignorance. History, after all, is written by the winners, and Harker, Seward, and Van Helsing are among those writing the history. Maybe just as the name Dracula was misunderstood (the name was thought to mean "devil"), Dracula himself was misunderstood, thought to be a devil. Maybe Dracula is a romantic hero in the Byronic tradition.

Yeah, Sigmund, and sometimes a wooden stake is just a wooden stake. Hollywood, though, has been more responsible than Stoker's novel for our view of Dracula as a sensual being. As David J. Skal observes in his 1996 book *V is for Vampire*, "Stoker's ugly, animalistic conception of the count has been stubbornly resisted by filmmakers and dramatists."

Still another view of *Dracula* is that it's a book steeped in homoeroticism. This interpretation starts in the same scene that drew King's attention: the attempted seduction of Harker by the three wives. Some see great significance in Dracula's angry declaration, "This man belongs to me!" This phrase first appears in a March 1890 chapter outline made by Stoker. It survived every reworking, although it

originally continued with three more provocative words: "I want him."

There are those who argue that Dracula
merely wants Harker for planning purpos-
es, and for proof they cite Dracula's assur-
ance that the wives can have him "when
I am done with him." They also point out
that Dracula's primary victims are women,
although others see homoerotic aspects to
the count's dominance of Renfield and in
the male bonding that is so much a part of
the friendship shared by Arthur, Quincey,
and Seward.

*Count Dracula (Bela Lugosi) about to enjoy
a midnight snack provided by a sleeping Lucy
(Frances Dade) in the 1931 film version of
Dracula.*

In her essay, "'A Wilde Desire Took
Me': The Homoerotic History of *Dracula*,"
Talia Schaffer builds the case that Dracula
was inspired by the Stokers' friend Oscar
Wilde: "Stoker used the Wildean figure
of Dracula to define homosexuality as
simultaneously monstrous, dirty, threatening, alluring, buried, corrupting, conta-
gious, and indestructible." The 1895 tri-
als that resulted in Wilde's imprisonment
may well have sparked some deep psychological responses in Stoker (it would
be rather amazing if they didn't), but it's
difficult to see much of the witty, stylish
Wilde in the brutish Count Dracula of
the novel. Schaffer, however, sees parallels between Wilde's time in Reading
Prison and Harker's imprisonment in
Castle Dracula: "the first part of the
book swings wildly between utter hatred
of Wilde and utter sorrow for Wilde."
Whether you accept this interpretation
or not, a strong case can be made for
Stoker having produced a book steeped
in ambivalence.

Stoker left behind no comments on
Wilde's prosecution and prison sentence. Some see this as a case for
Victorian repression; others see it as
discretion. Still others see it as proof of
guilt and regret, and some see it as all of
the above. Without real proof, however,
the interpretive ruminations and speculation are destined to continue. Stoker,
after all, also didn't leave behind any
detailed or definitive thoughts on his
intentions for writing the novel. Even if
he had, the debate and deconstruction
probably would be no less intense.

No scene inspires more debate than
Dracula's attack on the Harkers in chapter 21. Stoker has Dracula invade the
couple's bedroom. Harker is rendered
unconscious, and Dracula not only drinks
Mina's blood but forces her to drink his
(an exchange of bodily fluids that eventually could propagate his kind). What kind
of ménage a trois is this?

The bedroom is the acceptable
domain for acceptable sex, but remember that the bedroom also was the
place of new life (childbirth) and death
to Victorians. Hmmm, sex, life, and
death—symbolically speaking, not much
going on in this scene.

Blood Will Out:
The "Fluid" Nature of the Novel

. . . .

"I saw it drip with the fresh blood!"
—*Mina Harker,* Dracula, *chapter 21*

Sex, sex, sex! Is that all these *Dracula* scholars think about? Must every interpretation of the book be about sex? Well, no, there's always violence. Even by modern horror standards, there are some disturbingly gory passages in Bram Stoker's novel, including the ghastly staking of Lucy and the brutal death of Renfield.

Dracula is a book that's drenched in blood. On one level, it's all about the blood. Care to guess how many times the word appears in the course of the book's twenty-seven chapters? The blood count is 110. That's just in its simplest five-letter form. Moving into the adjective realm, *bloody* shows up 5 times, *blood-stained* makes 3 appearances, and *bloodless, blood-curdling,* and *cold-bloodedness* are used once each. *Lifeblood* is also used once, pushing the final tally of blood words to 121.

But the blood in *Dracula* pulses with (you guessed it) metaphoric meanings. The Victorians were obsessed with blood, from bloodlines that defined class distinctions to blood as the carrier of diseases that terrified them. Dracula is a foreigner, representing one kind of menace to British blood. Yet he's also a plague carrier (thought by some to be

Christopher Lee, out for blood, plays the vampire king closer to how Stoker described, complete with mustache, in the 1970 film Count Dracula.

the literal meaning of the word *nosfer-atu*), draining away the fluid of life and, at the same time, contaminating it.

It is no wonder that Harker is so appalled by the thought of Dracula turned loose in London, where, among "its teeming millions" (a phrase used independently by both Jonathan and Mina), he can "satiate his lust for blood." Talk about a danger to the blood supply! Dracula's game plan is to invade and infiltrate, consume and corrupt, contaminate and propagate. You can bloody well see how he represents a whole range of condition-red threats to true-blue British blood. He is the foreigner hoping to establish a new bloodline on British soil—one that threatens the established order. He is syphilis or some other disease of the blood that threatens to reduce hale and hearty Englishmen to Renfield-like slaves of madness. He is the corrupter of women, turning them into carriers of contagion.

And, hey, don't look now, but we've just swerved back to sex. Well, metaphorically, it works that way, too.

Still, there's no getting around that Stoker meant all the blood references to have religious significance as well. Under the influence of his dark master, Renfield perversely quotes scripture ("The blood is the life!") to justify the consumption of bugs, birds, and, ultimately, Dr. Seward's blood. Catholic imagery looms significantly here, which is intriguing, since Stoker, like the heroic Harker, was not raised Catholic.

The young, vibrant blood of English manhood provides the muscle and brawn that battles Dracula. But it is the Catholic Van Helsing who provides the brains, the spiritual resolve, and the means with which to defeat this prince of darkness. If Count Dracula is a pestilence emerging from a Catholic region of continental Europe, so then Van Helsing is the force for good, racing to England from Catholic Europe. This juxtaposition symbolizes the central spiritual tussle of the book, framed in Catholicism yet played out in a Protestant culture.

If Van Helsing is right (and he is) and his methods are correct (and they are), *Dracula* almost reads like recruitment propaganda for the Vatican. And this is just one more aspect that, from what we know of Stoker, must have been unintended.

The drinking of Christ's saving blood is a central part of the Catholic Mass. The drinking of the satanic Dracula's blood is what corrupts Mina. The symbols of Catholicism, including the crucifix and the rosary, are what the Catholic landlady and Van Helsing hand out for protection against the agents of evil. Harker tell us that, as "an English Churchman, I have been taught to regard such things as in some measure idolatrous," but it becomes "a comfort and a strength to me whenever I touch it." The captain of the *Demeter* resolves to save his soul by lashing his hands to the wheel with the object the vampire "dare not touch," a crucifix. And it is the other element of transubstantiation, the sacred Host, that Van Helsing uses to repel Dracula. Van Helsing is so spot-on correct about confronting Dracula, you

Jack Palance does a little necking in the 1974 TV movie version of Dracula.

almost are left wondering why Harker, Seward, and Holmwood don't convert to Catholicism at the end of the story.

When Harker escapes the evil that is Castle Dracula, his place of refuge, survival, and salvation is a Catholic hospital in Buda-Pesth. Sister Agatha, "a sweet, good soul," is the nurse and protector. She reunites Jonathan and Mina. And although a chaplain from the English mission is summoned to marry them, the ceremony takes place in the safety of the Hospital of St. Joseph and Ste. Mary.

Blood is life to the undead Dracula. He needs it to survive. It will make his soulless body immortal. To Van Helsing, the doctrinal meaning of "the blood is the life" refers to salvation for the immortal soul. Mere matters of life and death no longer are high enough stakes for the book's conclusion. That battle,

as Van Helsing tells his comrades, is for Mina's soul. He understands this, and so does Dracula.

Her pure blood has been corrupted by the blood of Dracula. "Unclean!" she shouts, recalling the cry of the leper. Is this a spiritual contamination? Or is Stoker suggesting that exposure to dangerous sex corrupts the ideal Victorian woman who requires the protection of chivalrous Victorian men? Is this what's threatening the soul of good Christian women, and, as must naturally follow, good Christian men? Remember, Harker is nearly lost in ecstasy when being seduced by Dracula's three vampire brides. And if this is what Stoker had in mind, even unconsciously, has the flow of blood carried us back to sex? Maybe. This interpretation is far from conclusive, yet the discussion is inevitable.

Publishing History: London, America, Today

· · · · · · · · · · · ·

This was the being I was helping to transfer to London . . .
amongst its teeming millions.
—*Jonathan Harker*, Dracula, *chapter 4*

Bram Stoker's *Dracula* is second only to the Bible in terms of international sales. I know that's true; I read it in a magazine. I think it was *Famous Monsters of Filmland*, although it might have been *Castle of Frankenstein*. I think I was ten years old when I first stumbled on this astounding "fact," so, of course, either of these prestigious periodicals would have been treated as an unimpeachable source.

It sure sounded great back then, but over the decades I've also seen this astounding fact attributed to Margaret Mitchell's *Gone With the Wind*, Arthur Conan Doyle's *Sherlock Holmes* stories, John Bunyan's *Pilgrim's Progress*, J. R. R. Tolkien's *Lord of the Rings*, Dan Brown's *The Da Vinci Code*, Dr. Benjamin Spock's *Baby and Child Care*, Agatha Christie's mysteries, and the Boy Scouts of America's manual *Scouting for Boys*. And about the only thing *Dracula* and a Boy Scout handbook have in common is that they both offer instruction on pounding stakes.

It's similar to the oft-made claim about Count Dracula holding the record as the fictional character most often portrayed in movies and on television. Easy to say; hard to figure out all the tie breakers, particularly when you factor in television and non-English movies. Do you count the Count

on *Sesame Street*? How about Al Lewis as Grandpa on *The Munsters*? The battle seems to be between the count and Sherlock Holmes, and if you limit the discussion to English-speaking films, Holmes appears to have a slight edge. Television complicates matters, as it usually does, but these two cloaked figures from Victorian literature certainly lead the pack.

The "second only to the Bible" claim is even more difficult to verify. Still, the fact that *Dracula* is in the discussion demonstrates the strength of its enduring popularity. It was not a runaway bestseller when published in England by A. Constable and Company in May 1897, but it sold briskly and never has been out of print. Stage and screen versions insured that the book would be constantly reissued and reintroduced to new generations. The first American edition, with a cover showing Castle Dracula surrounded by bats, was published in 1899 by Doubleday, McClure and Company. The first paperback edition, featuring a black-and-white cover illustration of Harker observing Dracula crawling down the castle wall, was published by Constable in 1901. The same wall-crawling scene, more lavishly drawn, graced the cover of W. Rider and Company's 1912 London reissue. Constable reprinted the novel in 1920.

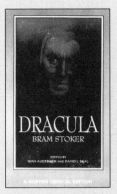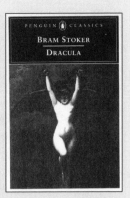

The dozens of paperback editions of Dracula *include those published by Norton, Oxford, and Penguin.*

Rider reprinted it in 1916, 1921, 1931, and 1947. Doubleday reprinted it in 1913, 1917, 1919, 1920, 1927, and 1928.

With Bela Lugosi having made a Broadway sensation as Count Dracula in 1927, rebinding specialists Grosset and Dunlap published a 1928 edition, reissuing it a few years later with pictures from the 1931 Universal film. Stoker's novel took a big step toward classic status with the Modern Library edition of 1932.

Only two translations appeared during Stoker's lifetime: one in German in 1908 and—don't even try to guess this one—one in Icelandic in 1901. French, Italian, and Spanish editions appeared in the 1920s. In Stoker's native country, Ireland, *Dracula* appeared, translated into Gaelic, in 1933. In Vlad the Impaler's native land, the book was translated into Romanian in the early 1990s. It has remained a genuine international bestseller, also translated into Chinese, Danish, Dutch, Finnish, Flemish, Greek, Hebrew, Hungarian, Indonesian, Japanese, Korean, Malaysian, Norwegian, Polish, Portuguese, Russian, Swedish, Thai, and Ukrainian.

There were more than twenty-five unabridged English versions available in 2007, including mass-market paperback editions from Bantam, Oxford, Penguin, and Signet. Since the 1972 appearance of Raymond T. McNally and Radu Florescu's *In Search of Dracula*, several illustrated and annotated editions have appeared. The most significant, useful, and engaging of these are:

The Annotated Dracula (1975), with an introduction, notes, and bibliography by Leonard Wolf; art by Sätty; and illustrated with maps, drawings, and photographs (and revised as *The Essential Dracula* in 1993).

Dracula: The Definitive Edition (1996), with introduction and appendixes by Marvin Kaye, and illustrations by Edward Gorey.

Dracula: A Norton Critical Edition (1997), edited by Nina Auerbach and David J. Skal, with the authoritative text, contexts, reviews and reactions, dramatic and film variations, and essays and criticism.

"Dracula's Guest": The Missing Chapter?

· · · · · · · · · · · ·

"Nay, sir, you are my guest. It is late, and my people are not available. Let me see to your comfort myself."
—**Count Dracula,** Dracula, *chapter 2*

Blame the widow. Florence Stoker contributed a brief preface to *Dracula's Guest, and Other Weird Stories*, published by George Routledge & Sons of London in 1914. Writing that *Dracula* "is considered my husband's most remarkable work" she explained that the story "Dracula's Guest" was the novel's original opening. "It was originally excised owing to the length of the book." Well, not quite.

Still, this misconception continued to hang around *Dracula* like a damp black cape. We did, after all, have it on the widow's authority. "Dracula's Guest" became the novel's missing first chapter, cut because of length.

It's yet another *Dracula* myth that needs a wooden stake hammered through it. Bram Stoker's original opening was an exchange of letters between Dracula and Peter Hawkins. The episode that became "Dracula's Guest" appears to have been intended, at some point, as a second chapter. But Stoker wisely jettisoned both ideas, greatly enhancing the mood and pace of the wonderfully evocative Transylvania chapters. In other words, "Dracula's Guest" is the abandoned second chapter, and was cut by Stoker long before the book was heading down the home stretch.

Stoker was planning three volumes of collected material near the end of his life. *Dracula's Guest, and Other Weird Stories*, containing nine supernatural tales, was the only one near completion at the time of his death in 1912. "Had my husband lived longer, he might have seen fit to revise this work, which is mainly from the earlier years of his strenuous life," Florence Stoker wrote. "But, as fate has entrusted to me the issuing of it, I consider it fitting and proper to let it go forth practically as it was left by him."

The title story begins with Jonathan Harker in Munich on April 30. He has engaged a carriage for an afternoon drive into the surrounding countryside, but his superstitious driver fears the coming of *Walpurgisnacht* (Walpurgis Night, or the Witches' Night). When the driver refuses to continue in the direction of a long-deserted village ("'It is unholy.'"), the curious Jonathan tells him, "'You are afraid, Johann—you are afraid. Go home, I shall return home alone; the walk will do me good. . . . Walpurgisnacht doesn't concern Englishmen.'"

A storm breaks, and Jonathan seeks shelter among some trees. When the tempest passes, moonlight reveals that he is in a cemetery. He sees the tomb of "Countess Dolingen of Gratz in Styria—Sought and Found Death—1801." This chapter would have given Stoker's novel a literal connection to Styria, the southeast Austrian state that was the setting for Joseph Sheridan Le Fanu's 1782 "Carmilla" (and the pre-Transylvania choice of homeland for Stoker's vampire).

Jonathan has a nightmarish encounter with Countess Dolingen and a guardian werewolf (who could be the count himself). He is rescued by a search party and carried back to Munich. There he learns that Count Dracula had sent a letter: "Be careful of my guest—his safety is most precious to me. Should aught happen to him, or if he be missed, spare nothing to find him and ensure his safety. . . . Lose not a moment if you suspect harm to him. I answer your zeal with my fortune."

When Jonathan believes he recognizes one of Dracula's wives in chapter 3, presumably it's because the fair one ("with great, wavy masses of golden hair and eyes like pale sapphires") is Countess Dolingen.

The posthumously published "Dracula's Guest" has enjoyed a long life, becoming (thanks to its title) Stoker's most widely anthologized terror tale. It easily has outdistanced the best of his supernatural short stories, which include "The Judge's House" (1891), "The Squaw" (1893), "The Secret of the Growing Gold" (1892), "The Red Stockade" (1894), "Death in the Wings" (1908), "The Dualitists" (1887), "The Spectre of Doom" (1881), and "The Burial of the Rats" (1914). "Dracula's Guest" also achieved notoriety as the loose—very loose— inspiration for *Dracula's Daughter*, the *Dracula* film sequel released by Universal Studios in 1936. It starred Gloria Holden as Countess Maria Zaleska, who, as the title suggests, is the count's undead offspring.

The Stoker family—young Noel, at left, Florence and Bram— sketched by Trilby *author George du Maurier for the British magazine* Punch.

Mark Twain Meets Dracula

· · · · · · · · · · · ·

"I heard once of an American who so defined faith, 'that faculty which enables us to believe things which we know to be untrue.' For one, I follow that man. He meant that we shall have an open mind. . . ."
—*Professor Van Helsing,* Dracula, *chapter 14*

Does Mark Twain make a cameo appearance in *Dracula*? Well, at the very least, the reports of his being mentioned in the novel are not greatly exaggerated. Mark Twain undoubtedly is the American Van Helsing is referring to in chapter 14.

Compare Van Helsing's paraphrase above with the actual Twain line in *Following the Equator* (1897): "Faith is believing what you know ain't so."

Mark Twain, born Samuel Langhorne Clemens in 1835, was just one of the many literary celebrities Bram Stoker counted among his friends. They may have met in England through Irving during the summer of 1879 (when Twain also met Charles Darwin, Henry James, and James Whistler). Or they may have met in New York during the Lyceum Theatre's 1883 tour of the United States. There would be many more meetings on both sides of the Atlantic. The two writers last saw each other in 1907, when Twain received his honorary degree from Oxford University. They corresponded until Twain's death in 1910.

Twain invited both Henry Irving and Stoker to invest in the Paige Compositor, an ill-fated typesetting machine that played a key part in Twain's financial ruin (he returned Stoker's money when it was obvious that the typesetter was too complicated and accident-prone to succeed). "I can't get up courage enough to talk about this misfortune myself, except to you," Twain wrote to Stoker.

To repay his debts dollar for dollar, Twain embarked on a world lecture tour in July 1895. The author of *The Adventures of Tom Sawyer* (1876) and *Adventures of Huckleberry Finn* (1885) reached London one year later, and, at this heroic moment of triumph, he learned that his favorite daughter, Susy, had died of spinal meningitis at the family's home in Hartford, Connecticut. She was twenty-four.

Devastated, the Clemens family went into seclusion at a rented house in the Surrey town of Guilford. In October, they moved to a rented house at 23 Tedworth Square in London's Chelsea district. Many of their closest English friends didn't even know they were in London. One of the few people they saw during this period was Stoker, whose friendship, loyalty, and discretion were great-

Bram Stoker's wide circle of friends included Mark Twain, who might have subtitled Dracula, *"The Reports of His Undeath Are Not Greatly Exaggerated." (Drawing by Mark Dawidziak)*

ly valued by Twain. During this period, Twain was working on *Following the Equator*, his travel book about the world tour. He drafted Stoker to act as his British agent for the book with the London publishing firm of Chatto and Windus. It was published in England as *More Tramps Abroad* in 1897, the same year as the first edition of *Dracula*.

It was not the first time Twain had sought such representation from Stoker. Always trying (and failing) to write a successful play, Twain once asked him to be his agent in Britain for dramatic works. This did not prove a demanding assignment. "Confidentially I have always had an idea that I was well equipped to write plays," Twain said in 1895, "but I have never encountered a manager who has agreed with me."

During one of their meetings, the two men exchanged tales of witchcraft before a literary crowd at Brown's Hotel on Dover Street in London. "Fine, tell us some more," Stoker said to Twain. "I have a short story on witchcraft in hand." Some Twain scholars have suggested this "short story" grew into *Dracula*, but this conversation, recorded by American journalist Eugene Field, was in 1907, ten years after the book was published. Still, during their first meetings, "they exchanged views on the conflicts of duality, on nightmares, and on the unconscious," as Barbara Belford points out in her biography of Stoker, and their "discussions of dreams and dual personalities continued." This was almost an obsession with Twain, who also carried on a warm correspondence with Robert Louis Stevenson, author of *The Strange Case of Dr. Jekyll and Mr. Hyde* (1886). Twain was more taken with this horror tale than Stoker's novel, and Stevenson's story was on his mind during his final days.

In late 1896, however, Twain certainly would have been well aware that his friend was about to publish a vampire novel. Stoker made sure to send Twain a presentation copy of *Dracula*.

Related by Daniel Farson in his biography of his great-uncle Bram Stoker, a family legend tells of Bram's wife, Florence, inviting the famous American author to tea. She gave the maid strict orders not to admit anyone but Mark Twain. When the time for Twain's arrival had slipped by, Florence sent for the maid. No word had been received of Mark Twain being delayed, the maid told her. "'I thought I heard the doorbell,'" Florence said. "'Yes,'" replied the maid, "'it was a Mr. Clemens, but I told him you weren't at home.'"

The Six Degrees of Stokeration

. . . .

"Oh, what have I done to be blessed with such friends?"
—Lucy Westenra, Dracula, *chapter 10*

Walking into the parlor of Thomas Donaldson's Philadelphia home, Bram Stoker spotted a burly, balding, and bearded old man seated on the opposite side of the room. He recognized him at once. It was March 20, 1884, and a dream was about to come true for Stoker. He was seconds away from being introduced to his literary hero, Walt Whitman. "I found him all that I had ever dreamed of, or wished for in him: large-minded, broad-viewed, tolerant to the last degree; incarnate sympathy; understanding with an insight that seemed more than human," Stoker recalled more than twenty years later. He promised to visit Whitman at his cottage in Camden, New Jersey, making good on that promise in November 1886.

Whitman's view of Stoker was recorded by Donaldson: "'My gracious, he knows enough for four or five ordinary men, and what tact . . . He's like a breath of good, healthy, breezy, sea air.'" The American poet's response to Stoker was hardly unique. Although not a literary lion like Whitman or Twain, Stoker was known, embraced, and trusted by a staggering number of American and British writers, politicians, and stage luminaries. He seemed to know everybody.

Friends with both Mark Twain and Walt Whitman? That would be enough, certainly, but you're just beginning to chart the circumference of the Stoker friendship circle. In England, he was friends with both Arthur Conan Doyle and Oscar Wilde (once a suitor to Stoker's wife, Florence). On May 25, 1895, the same day that Queen Victoria knighted both Henry Irving and Thornley Stoker, Wilde was convicted on charges of gross indecency. Sentenced to two years in prison, Wilde was abandoned by most acquaintances. There are accounts of Stoker taking money to Wilde, destitute in Paris, but Stoker's feelings about the trial and Wilde were never committed to paper.

Stoker, though, unquestionably remained close friends with W. S. Gilbert, the notoriously prickly playwright best known for his operetta collaborations with Arthur Sullivan. He also counted Henry Dickens (the novelist's son) and Baroness Angela Burdett-Coutts (a Dickens partner in philanthropic projects) among his acquaintances. And journalist-explorer Henry Morton Stanley, also friends with Twain, encouraged Stoker to pursue literature as a career.

Both painter James Whistler and aging poet Alfred, Lord Tennyson sought Stoker's advice. At the center of London's theatrical world with Henry Irving and Ellen Terry, he got to know Sarah Bernhardt, Edwin Booth, and George Bernard Shaw (an Irishman, like Stoker and Wilde). Among the leading political figures, he was admired by Winston Churchill, William Ewart Gladstone, and Theodore Roosevelt. If you're judged by the company you keep, Stoker's marks are off the chart.

Stoker was both great in number of friends and friends with the great of his era. While Irving and Whitman were the two who made the strongest impressions on him, one must be a little bit awed by the impression Stoker made on the likes of Roosevelt and Twain in America and Gilbert and Gladstone in England.

The Six Degrees of Stoker-ration
Bram Stoker's Wide Circle of Friends and Associates

Oscar Wilde   Mark Twain   George Bernard Shaw   Walt Whitman

Henry Irving   Arthur Conan Doyle

Ellen Terry   W.S. Gilbert

Theodore Roosevelt   William E. Gladstone   Winston Churchill   Lord Tennyson   James Whistler

Stoker collected an amazing array of friends and acquaintances from the worlds of literature, art, theater, and politics.

Vampirism: Psychology, Pathology, and Porphyria

· · · · · · · · · · ·

"Ah, it is the fault of our science that it wants to explain all,
and if it explain not, then it says there is nothing to explain."
—*Professor Van Helsing,* Dracula, *chapter 14*

Various branches of medicine and science have taken swings at providing a factual basis for the mythological and folkloric roots of vampirism. If the vampire legend has its origins in a medical or psychological condition, then perhaps so does Count Dracula. The botanist points to such parasitic plants as rafflesia, mistletoe (nicknamed the vampire plant), and witchweed. The zoologist can site examples of nature's bloodsuckers: mosquitoes, leeches, ticks, and, of course, vampire bats. Psychologists present cases of clinical vampirism, a condition that leads to an obsession with drinking blood, human or animal. And pathologists have linked several diseases with vampire beliefs, including tuberculosis and rabies.

The medical condition that has become most persistently associated with vampirism is porphyria, a general medical grouping for at least eight metabolic illnesses with widely differing symptoms. The common cause for each disease is a buildup of porphyrins, a natural body chemical. This buildup causes a hemoglobin deficiency in heme, a substance found in all body tissue, but the greatest concentration is found in red blood cells, bone marrow, and the liver. The lack of heme can cause physical, psychiatric, and neurological disturbances. A rare and inherited blood disorder, porphyria can attack the nervous system, leading, in extreme cases, to seizures and hallucinations. It can result in skin problems (itching, swelling, blisters) and abdominal pain, and can leave sufferers with an acute sensitivity to light.

Porphyria wrongly became "the vampire disease" when the media jumped on a 1985 paper presented by respected

Count Dracula (John Carradine) seeks a scientific reason for vampirism in this scene (with Onslow Stevens and Martha O'Driscoll) from House of Dracula.

Canadian scientist David H. Dolphin to the American Association for the Advancement of Science. A biochemist at the University of British Columbia, Dolphin put forth the theory that, historically, porphyria sufferers might have been driven to drinking blood to combat the disorder. After causing a sensation, the theory was widely challenged by skeptical vampire experts, distressed porphyria sufferers, and worried organizations like the American Porphyria Foundation.

Porphyria sufferers don't crave blood, and there's no known instance of them indulging in vampiric behavior. In short, they understandably resented being viewed as potential vampires. From the other direction, there's no evidence that suspected vampires of history suffered from porphyria. Indeed, reports of human blood drinkers clearly don't describe people afflicted with porphyria.

All right, couldn't porphyria explain the avoidance of sunlight? It could, if the avoidance of sunlight was part of

the vampire folklore. But it isn't, being instead a post-*Nosferatu* (1922) concept formalized by twentieth-century fiction writers for the printed page and the silver screen.

Dolphin's research credits are impressive, by the way. He is the lead creator of a medication used in connection with laser eye surgery, and, in 2005, he was awarded the prestigious Gerhard Herzberg Canada Gold Medal for Science and Engineering.

Still, as provocative as Dolphin's theory seemed in 1985, his hypothesis, according to vampire researcher J. Gordon Melton, "has no viable exponents at present." "The notion of vampire legends originating in porphyria is right up there with Vlad the Impaler being the inspiration for Stoker's Dracula," adds Elizabeth Miller, whose many scholarly books include *Dracula: Sense and Nonsense*. "It sounded like it could be right at the time, then it rapidly spread, turning into a misconception without any real foundation."

Nosferatu:
Taking *Dracula* to the Max

· · · · · · · · · · ·

. . . so for a while we were all silent.
—Dr. John Seward, Dracula, *chapter 10*

The vampire played by Max Schreck in the 1922 silent film *Nosferatu: Eine Symphonie des Garuens* is named Graf (German for Count) Orlok. But a count by any other name still would smell of Transylvanian soil. Call him what you will—and Florence Stoker called him an infringement of her copyright—he's still Count Dracula.

Filmed during the summer of 1921 by German director Freidrich Wilhelm Murnau, *Nosferatu* presented a vampire more in keeping with European folklore than Bram Stoker's conception. Schreck, whose name means terror in German (and it was his real name), made a terrifying bloodsucker, but he no more resembled the character in the book than such later screen Draculas as Frank Langella, Christopher Lee, and Bela Lugosi.

Still, although set in Germany in 1838, *Nosferatu* is a remarkably atmospheric adaptation of the *Dracula* story. It's also a silent-screen masterpiece. Full of metaphoric flourishes and deeply disturbing images, Murnau's film remains a haunting experience more than eighty-five years after its opening. Some of the "special" effects, like a stop-motion sequence meant to depict supernatural speed, routinely get laughs when the creepy classic is shown today. But many, not without reason, view *Nosferatu* as the greatest screen version of Stoker's novel.

The director and his screenwriter, Henrich Galeen, took great liberties with the story, changing far more than just the location and the names. The Jonathan Harker character, Waldemar Hutter (Gustave von Wangenheim) bids farewell to his wife, Ellen (Greta Schroeder-Matray), and heads for the castle of Graf Orlok. Hutter's employer, the eccentric Knock (Alexander Granach), eventually goes completely mad and is confined to an asylum. He, therefore, comes across as a combination of two characters from the novel, lawyer Peter Hawkins and R. M. Renfield.

Enchanted by a picture of Ellen, Orlok leaves Hutter a prisoner in the castle, departing for his captive's home, the port city of Bremen. Meanwhile, Professor Bulwar (the Van Helsing character, played by John Gattowt), is experimenting with vampiric plants. Orlok lands in Bremen, which soon finds itself in the grip of a deadly plague (an actual plague did ravage the city in 1838). Ellen reads that a vampire can be destroyed if a virtuous woman permits him to stay with her until dawn. Orlok does and is reduced to a puff of smoke by the rising sun. Ellen dies, but her sacrifice ends the plague ravaging Bremen (not only that but she sets in motion the notion that a vampire can be killed by sunlight).

This memorable and incredibly influential ending was, perhaps, the greatest departure from Stoker's book. Mina, after all, does not die, and Dracula, of course, dies on his home turf. In many regards, however, it is more faithful to Stoker's novel than the many film versions to follow.

Premiered at the Berlin Zoological Gardens in March 1922, *Nosferatu* was the first screen adaptation of Stoker's *Dracula*. It did not use the name Dracula, but a film released the year before did trade on the monstrous moniker. Director Karoly Lathjay's *Drakula, The Death of Drakula* (1921) starred Paul Askonas as an insane musician who believes he is Dracula. The Hungarian film, however, did not use Stoker's plot.

Nosferatu did use that plot, and Florence Stoker was not amused. She enlisted the aid of the British Incorporated Society of Authors, who didn't exactly go after Orlok

It was not authorized, but it was brilliant: Max Schreck as the Dracula character, Graf Orlok, in Nosferatu *(1922).*

with the same vigor as did Van Helsing and the boys when hunting down Count Dracula. Nonetheless, after several court skirmishes, a final settlement was reached in July 1925. Part of the agreement was that all known copies of Murnau's film would be destroyed. Finding all of Dracula's scattered earth boxes proved an easier task. Copies of *Nosferatu* kept turning up to taunt and infuriate the aging widow. When Florence Stoker died in 1937 (a year after Max Schreck), the threat of litigation disappeared like Orlok at the end of the film. By the 1960s, the movie's reputation was growing among film scholars and the general public.

The film Florence Stoker tried to destroy had come roaring back, now recognized as a silent-screen horror classic worthy of mention in the same sentence as Robert Wiene's *The Cabinet of Dr. Caligari* (1920), John Barrymore's *Dr. Jekyll and Mr. Hyde* (1920), and Rupert Julian's *The Phantom of the Opera* (1920). For a movie quickly withdrawn from widespread circulation, *Nosferatu* certainly has exerted a profound impact on vampire lore and literature. Its depiction of the vampire king, though, quickly would be supplanted by another interpretation for another medium. Dracula was about to take to the boards—and I don't mean the ones used to construct his earth boxes.

Dracula Takes to the Stage

· · · · · · · · · · ·

. . . as far as the imagination could grasp it
through the gloom of the night.
—Jonathan Harker, Dracula, *chapter 1*

As a man of the theater, Bram Stoker undoubtedly realized that *Dracula* could do boffo business as a stage play and that his boss Henry Irving could make a sensation as the title character. This was more than just the instincts of a capable theater manager. Stoker had good reasons for believing in *Dracula* as a play and in Irving as Dracula.

Dating back to the 1820s, vampire plays had been hits in England, France, and Germany. And Irving had demonstrated an ability to sink his teeth into dark characters in such roles as Richard III, Macbeth, Iago in *Othello*, Iachimo in *Cymbeline, Peter the Great*, Louis XI, Mephistopheles in *Faust*, and Mathias in *The Bells*.

It may have been partly to convince Irving that Stoker arranged for a staged reading of *Dracula* at the Lyceum Theatre on the morning of May 18, 1897. This was about a week before the official publication of the novel, so the reading almost certainly was also designed to protect the story's theatrical copyright on the author's behalf. Believed to be a safeguard against piracy, this was a common step taken by authors and playwrights, even though its legal force was questionable. Fifteen actors took part in the reading, which ran over five hours. A player listed as Mr. Jones became the first actor to portray Count Dracula. No one has done more solid research on the count's journey from novel to stage and screen than *Dracula* scholar David J. Skal, and he believes that Mr. Jones is Lyceum company member T. Arthur Jones.

When asked what he thought, Irving reportedly gave a resounding and devastating one-word response: "Dreadful!" This may be a myth. Or it may have been merely a judgment on the quality of the reading, rather than the story and the characters. The marathon, after all, spanned five acts and forty-five scenes. But those looking for evidence of a Dracula-like Irving manipulating and dominating a Harker-like Stoker have made much of this monstrous moment.

Stoker was his constant friend, his loyal employee, his staunch defender. Could Irving have been this cruel? This callous? This unfeeling? If so, perhaps it is a great shame that he never played Dracula.

As devoted as she was to Irving, Ellen Terry left behind memories that suggest there was a distance and coldness to the Lyceum's "governor." But whether or not Irving actually dissed and dismissed *Dracula* as a theatrical property, the actor was destined never to play the vampire king whose fame would outlive and outshine his own. And Stoker was destined to see no other stage version of his novel.

An actual and authorized *Dracula* play wouldn't materialize until after Stoker's widow had gone to war against the unauthorized silent-film version, *Nosferatu*. While successfully driving a legal stake through German director F. W. Murnau's brilliant 1922 movie, Florence Stoker gave her permission for an English stage production. The task of turning the novel into a play fell to actor-director-playwright Hamilton Deane, who wrote a first draft while confined to bed with a severe cold. The Hamilton Deane Company was a touring troupe that specialized in crowd-pleasing melodramas: Deane courted box-office receipts, not glowing reviews.

He adapted *Dracula* in a way that would significantly alter the public's perception of the story and several of its characters. Following the conventions of the English drawing-room play, Deane threw out the Transylvania chapters. He put a cape and evening clothes on Count Dracula, creating a vampire uniform that has become the Halloween and pop-culture standard. He also turned Quincey Morris into a woman and filled his three-act play with astonishingly clunky dialogue.

Deane took on what he considered the more substantial role of vampire hunter Abraham Van Helsing. Thus, in 1924, Edmund Blake became the first actor to play Dracula in a fully staged, authorized dramatic version of the novel.

Rather than take the production to London, where it was unlikely to get a warm reception from the major theater critics, Deane kept *Dracula* in the repertoire of his company's touring shows. Raymond Huntley replaced Blake in the title role, wearing a wig with gray streaks that resembled satanic horns. Huntley was still playing Dracula when the Deane version finally opened in London at the Little Theatre on February 14, 1927. Although it was Valentine's Day, the critics threw no roses—as Deane had feared might be the case. Despite the largely negative reviews, the play soon was selling out the 300-seat venue, and, by the end of the summer, was moved to a larger theater.

Deane, by all accounts, was not a great playwright. But he was the road-company visionary who put Count Dracula on the path to true immortality. He convinced Florence Stoker to sanction a stage version. He fashioned the theatrical property that, despite its structural weaknesses, was sturdy enough to provide a foundation on which the character would grow to iconic stature. And he demonstrated that there was gold in them thar chills. Now, the count would be the first to tell you that there's always a price to be paid for immortality. The ruthless vampire king had become, in the words of Dracula historian Skal, "almost perversely sanitized." Deane had fashioned "the 'new' image of the master vampire in evening dress and opera cloak, one polite enough to be invited into a proper Knightsbridge living room," Skal writes in *Hollywood Gothic*, the authoritative source for the count's journey from book to stage to screen.

Still, without Deane, Stoker's book might have been no more than a literary footnote—an obscure Victorian novel by an even more obscure Victorian author.

This pivotal figure in *Dracula* history also possessed the heart of a barnstorming showman. When a newspaper reporter joked that there be a uniformed nurse in attendance at every performance of the play, Deane seized on the wisecrack and turned it into one of the theater's legendary publicity stunts. He called Queen Alexandra Hospital, engaging the services of an experienced nurse armed with smelling salts and brandy. Advertising warned Londoners that *Dracula* was so frightening that "a nurse will be in attendance at all performances." The stunt would be later be used by the copycat masters of Hollywood.

Behind the scenes, though, the lucrative *Dracula* was a troubled production. Deane fought with Florence Stoker, who commissioned a second stage version (this one by Charles Morrell, and not successful). Deane broke with Huntley. Still, *Dracula* rolled on, raking in the profits in London and the provinces. Huntley stayed

in the London production with bug-eyed Bernard Jukes as the bug-eating Renfield. Deane returned to his beloved road.

Huntley eventually would set the still-unbroken record for most stage appearances as Dracula. Blake and Huntley were followed in the London and touring productions of Deane's play by such cape wearers as W. E. Holloway, Frederick Keen, John Laurie, Keith Pyott, and, eventually, Deane himself. Deane played the role for the first time in a 1939 London production directed by none other than Jukes (back as Renfield, of course).

The drawing power of this drawing-room version of *Dracula* was not lost on hard-drinking, hard-partying publisher and producer Horace Liveright. While recognizing the many problems with Deane's script, the enterprising American saw visions of bats over Broadway, dropping doubloons in his pocket as they swooped over New York's theater district. Florence Stoker didn't like Liveright any more than she liked Deane, but American playwright and journalist John L. Balderston proved a charming and effective go-between.

A deal was struck. Balderston got the assignment of putting the Deane play through a thorough rewrite for Broadway, and a New York opening was set for October 1927. Liveright asked Huntley and Jukes to make the move across the Atlantic. Jukes jumped at the chance. Huntley got left out when he held out for more money. So now Liveright and his team had to find just the right actor to play Dracula on the Great White Way.

Bela to Broadway to
Hollywood to Immortality

· · · · · · · · · · · ·

. . . he suddenly made a grab at my throat.
—*Jonathan Harker,* Dracula, *chapter 2*

Those hands . . . those eyes . . . that accent . . . the commanding gestures! It would seem that Bela Lugosi was born to play Dracula. But, um, he wasn't born Bela Lugosi—unless, of course, you look at his name from a symbolic point of view, which is precisely what we're going to do in a few paragraphs.

Bela Ferenc Dezsö Blasko was born near the western border of Transylvania on October 20, 1882, in Lugos, Hungary. Located on the River Timis, the city was then part of the Austro-Hungarian empire. Now in western Romania, with a population more than eighty percent Romanian, the city is known as Lugoj.

The youngest child of a banker, Bela was bit not by a vampire bat but by the acting bug when a touring theater troupe stopped in Lugos. He ran away from home at twelve, hoping to find work as an actor. Lacking education, training, and experience, he was des-

The most popular image of Dracula: Bela Lugosi in 1931.

tined for early disappointment. He found work in mines and on railroad lines, but not on a stage. An older sister managed to find him a spot with a provincial theater, yet even in small roles the adolescent Bela was awkward and inept. Far from being discouraged, however, the determined young man set out on an extensive self-education program, reading widely and voraciously. His studies included strict attention to volumes on acting theory and method.

After a few false starts, he made what's considered his actual stage debut in 1902, portraying, of all things, a count—Count Konigsegg in the play *Brigadier General Ocskay*. Also perhaps foreshadowing the career turns ahead, he appeared in a 1903 Transylvania production of *The Bat*. That same year, he played Gecko, Svengali's servant, in *Trilby*. It was about this time that he adopted the stage surname of Lugosi (meaning "one from Lugos" or "of Lugos"). He became, therefore, "Bela, One from Lugos," a name that was both symbolically ideal and technically accurate.

It was a busy time for the young actor. In 1910 alone, he had roles in more than twenty-five plays. During the second decade of the century, he was a featured player with both the Hungarian Royal Theater and the National Theater of Budapest, appearing in everything from melodramas and operettas to religious dramas and Shakespearian productions. With the outbreak of World War I, he joined the Austro-Hungarian army, serving as an infantry lieutenant.

Returning to the stage, Lugosi decided to take a chance on the movies. Adopting yet another stage name, Arisztid Olt, he made his film debut in 1917. He appeared in eleven more movies before the end of 1918, then rolled the career dice yet again. He moved to Germany, rapidly becoming a leading center for film production. He was forced to remain in Germany when a change in government put labor activists at risk. Lugosi had helped organize an actors' union in Budapest, so he

now found himself an exile. Knowing little English, he arrived in the United States in March 1921. The big break was being cast as Fernando, an Apache dancer, in the 1922 Broadway production of *The Red Poppy*. Still unable to speak English, Lugosi learned his role phonetically, impressing the critics. The reviews were not as enthusiastic about the overall play, and *The Red Poppy* closed after a six-week run. Lugosi's performance, though, earned him the role of a German spy in J. Gordon Edwards's 1923 action film *The Silent Command*. It was his American screen debut, and again his reviews were good.

Still, major roles eluded him. He appeared with Leslie Howard in the 1924 Chicago run of *The Werewolf*, an adaptation of a German play. He returned to Broadway the following year for another brief run, playing the Valentino-like Sheik of Hamman in *Arabesque*. Then Horace Liveright came calling, apparently at the suggestion of Jean D. Williams, a director who knew Lugosi. The producer was looking for the perfect actor to star in his Broadway production of the spooky London hit *Dracula*. Lugosi was the perfect actor for the role.

Following brief September runs in Hartford and New Haven, Connecticut, *Dracula* opened on October 5, 1927, at New York's Fulton Theatre. John L. Balderston had greatly improved Hamilton Deane's clunky adaptation of Bram Stoker's novel. The American had polished the dialogue, tightened the three-act structure, and reduced the number of roles from eleven to eight. Gone from the Deane original were one of the two maids, the female Quincey P. Morris, and Arthur Holmwood. Balderston also gave Mina the name of her doomed friend, Lucy.

Directed by Ira Hards, this production cemented the public perception of Dracula and of Stoker's story. Van Helsing, played by Edward Van Sloan, was the bespectacled, whitehaired symbol of wisdom. The significantly aged Dr. Seward, played by Herbert Bunston, was no longer Lucy's suitor but her father (or the Mina character's father, if you will, since Lucy was now called Mina and Mina was now called Lucy). Jonathan Harker, played by Terence Neill, was the well-groomed image of a proper leading man. Renfield, with Bernard Jukes on his way to setting the record for appearances in the role, was a raving, spider-swallowing lunatic wildly swerving from ranting to pleading. And Dracula . . . well, Dracula was Bela Lugosi.

The six-foot-one, forty-five-year-old actor was truly making the part his own. And the part was making him a matinee idol. Despite mixed reviews, the New York production of *Dracula* duplicated the London success. It ran for 261 performances on Broadway, closing in May 1928. At that point, the gross receipts for the production were more than $350,800. Lugosi and Jukes were dispatched to California, where they repeated their Dracula-Renfield act for eight weeks in Los Angeles and four weeks in San Francisco. That added more than $108,000 to the kitty.

Liveright moved quickly to put together a tour of the Midwest and the eastern states, and, this time, Huntley agreed to terms and sailed for America.

Huntley played the role in Atlantic City, Boston, the Bronx, Cleveland, Detroit, Philadelphia, and Washington, D.C. By May 1929, the play's gross receipts had topped a million dollars. Several tours would follow over the next quarter of a century in both North America and Great Britain. Deane continued to tour his version. American audiences saw the Balderston rewrite. More than thirty years after the publication of Stoker's novel, Dracula had successfully invaded England . . . and the United States.

Yet the number of people introduced to the count in all these theaters was miniscule compared to the mass audience reached by movies. Since the day of the Hungarian *Drakula, The Death of Drakula* and the German *Nosferatu*, movies had learned to talk. And the Deane-Balderston play was, if nothing else, talky.

Hollywood lore has it that Universal Pictures purchased the film rights to *Dracula* in 1928, with director Tod Browning thinking it an ideal vehicle for the planet's reigning horror star, Lon Chaney. Then Chaney died in 1930, clearing the way for Bela Lugosi to repeat his stage triumph on the silver screen. It sounds right. Chaney had created two of his most elaborate and grotesque make-up designs for Universal films based on French novels set in Paris: Wallace Worsley's *The Hunchback of Notre Dame*

(1923) and Rupert Julian's *The Phantom of the Opera* (1925). And Browning had been Chaney's director on *The Unholy Three* (1925), *The Road to Mandalay* (1926) and, most significantly, *London after Midnight*, a 1927 spooker with Chaney playing both a cagey investigator and a suspected vampire. Chaney also made an impressive transition to talkies with the 1930 remake of *The Unholy Three*, so it seems perfectly logical that *Dracula*, Universal, Chaney, and Browning were on a straight road leading to the 1931 film.

It's logical—and it's also wrong, at least as far as the straight road goes. Universal did try to nail down the complicated rights to *Dracula* in 1928, but, at that point, Chaney was under contract to MGM. And Universal was seeking the property not for Chaney but for the silent screen's other leading horror actor, Conrad Veidt. The sharp-featured German actor had delivered memorable performances as the murderous somnambulist in Robert Wiene's *The Cabinet of Dr. Caligari* (1920), the title character in Wiene's *The Hands of Orlac* (1925), and the disfigured carnival performer in Paul Leni's *The Man Who Laughs* (1928). Like Chaney's *The Hunchback of Notre Dame*, *The Man Who Laughs* was based on a Victor Hugo novel. Like *The Phantom of the Opera*, it was a Universal film co-starring Mary Philbin.

So Veidt, not Chaney, was Universal's first choice to play Count Dracula. Negotiations for the film rights dragged on, however, as Universal went several extra miles to ensure clear title to the Transylvania property. The legal waters were greatly muddied by nagging appearances of *Nosferatu*, as well as financial concerns raised by Deane, Balderston, Liveright, and Florence Stoker. Delay cost Universal both their leading man and its seeming lock on the property. By late 1929, Veidt had returned to Germany, possibly believing that his thick accent would sabotage any chance of making it in American talking pictures. He would flee Germany when the Nazis took full power, returning to America and playing Nazis in such Warner Brothers films as Michael Curtiz's *Casablanca* (1942) and Vincent Sherman's *All Through the Night*. Into the breach jumped several interested studios, including Columbia, Metro, and Paramount.

It's entirely probable that at this point Universal did set its sites on a *Dracula* starring Chaney. Browning was the Universal director who most coveted the story, and he reportedly discussed concepts for an adaptation with Chaney. Film historian and *Dracula* expert David J. Skal theorizes that Universal might have gone so far as to sign Browning to a multifilm deal in hopes of getting Chaney to play the count. But Hollywood's "Man of a Thousand Faces" was diagnosed with bronchial lung cancer. He died at the age of forty-seven on August 26, 1930. So then the field surely was open for Lugosi, right?

Not even close, although both Lugosi and Jukes tried to negotiate film deals with themselves attached as stars. Jukes peppered the studios with startling stills of himself as the wide-eyed, maniacally laughing Renfield. These photographs later were widely believed to be of the actor who did play Renfield in the 1931 film, Dwight Frye. It was a picture of Jukes, not Frye, for instance, that inspired the cover painting used for the eighteenth issue of *Famous Monsters of Filmland*.

In August 1930, the same month Chaney died, Universal finally was in position to tie up film rights to *Dracula*. The studio ended up holding four properties titled *Dracula*: Stoker's novel, the Deane play, the Balderston rewrite of the Deane play, and yet another play (this one written at Florence Stoker's behest by Charles Morrell). This proved unfortunate, because cost-conscious studio executives felt that if they owned the play they should use the play. Browning's reliance on this stage-bound concept would haunt the second half of his film.

At this time Universal was riding the wave of rave reviews for its acclaimed film version of Erich Maria Remarque's World War I novel *All Quiet on the Western Front* (1930; directed by Lewis Milestone). Horror films made studio founder Carl Laemmle Sr. uneasy. His son, known as Junior, loved them, and *Dracula*, over Dad's objections, became his pet project.

Nervous about the morbidity of the subject and eager to promote *Dracula* as a prestigious literary project, Universal announced that Pulitzer Prize–winning novelist Louis Bromfield would author the script. Browning was officially named the film's director, but his screenwriter was frustrated by budgetary concerns and the studio's demands that he use the book and the play.

Dudley Murphy was brought in to collaborate with the struggling Bromfield. Their efforts were turned over to another writer, Garrett Fort, who received final credit for the screenplay (with Murphy receiving a continuity credit). This screenplay, filmgoers were told, was based on the novel by Stoker and the stage play by Deane and Balderston. It was, although the second half of the movie was based far more on the play than the novel.

The Deane-Balderston play was set in Purley, England. The film moved the action and the location of Dr. Seward's sanitarium to Whitby. The play had Dracula reach England by plane. The movie restored Stoker's grim sea voyage, using some stock footage from a Universal silent film. Carfax, an estate near London in the novel, becomes an abbey in the film, perhaps a nod to the ruined abbey in Whitby.

On the road to this final screenplay, the unfortunate Renfield replaced Jonathan Harker as the young English agent traveling to Count Dracula's Transylvania castle. A final chase back to the castle was cut to keep expenses down. And then the die was cast, as far as the plot was concerned. But Dracula himself wasn't cast.

Even with Veidt's return to Europe and Chaney's passing, Lugosi was not the front-runner. John Wray, who had played the drill sergeant Himmelstoss in *All Quiet on the Western Front*, was announced for the role, yet nothing came of this. Ian Keith was said to be the leading candidate for the role, although New York stage actor William Courtenay, as well as Chester Morris, Paul Muni, and Joseph Schildkraut, were among those considered. It has been reported that young John Peter Richmond was considered, although there is no hard evidence that the actor later known as John Carradine ever came to Universal's attention in 1930.

Lugosi continued to lobby, and Universal executives, realizing that the actor's desperation meant they could get him cheap, offered the insulting salary of five hundred dollars a week. Fearful of the part going to someone else, Lugosi swallowed the deal and, on September 11, 1930, signed to star in Browning's film.

Two other veterans of the Broadway production were asked to re-create their roles: Van Sloan as Van Helsing and Bunston as Dr. Seward. Lew Ayres, the star of *All Quiet on the Western Front*, was the first choice for Harker. He wanted to play Renfield, though, and David Manners was cast as Harker. Helen Chandler, not yet twenty-one, was cast as Mina. Frances Dade, just twenty-one, was cast as Lucy. And Frye, a versatile Broadway player, landed the part Ayres had wanted and that Jukes would play thousands of time on stage.

The cameras started rolling on September 29. It was a seven-week shoot, so Lugosi was paid just $3,500 for playing the movie's lead role. The shooting script described scenes with Dracula bearing his fangs, but Universal, already

queasy, ruled that the vampire must go fangless. The official New York premiere of Universal's *Dracula* was on Thursday, February 12, 1931. The opening weekend, therefore, gave birth to the legends that the studio's first talking horror movie debuted on Friday the 13th and Valentine's Day (when Deane's play had opened in London four years earlier).

The seventy-five-minute film that opened at the Roxy Theatre was indeed a strange one, and not just because it was a vampire story. There are those armadillos, native to the southwestern United States and South America, crawling around Castle Dracula. There is poor Lucy turned into a vampire, then dropped from the story without another mention (and since she is left unstaked, undead, and unresolved, Lucy presumably still is out there, stalking the streets of London). There are the stilted performances of Chandler and Manners, almost as stilted as the camerawork in the second half of the film.

Even without these odd elements, however, *Dracula* still would be one strange vampire movie. It suffers from a Jekyll-and-Hyde quality, to borrow a split-personality from another classic horror novel. The first half of the film, from the wonderfully atmospheric Transylvania scenes to Dracula's appearance at the London opera house, is a fabulous showcase for Lugosi's widely impersonated portrayal of Count Dracula. The actor's stage-honed delivery and unease with English only seem to feed the creepiness of his characterization: "I . . . am . . . Dracula." Why, yes . . . yes, he is.

When the lights go down at the conclusion of the opera scene, Browning's *Dracula* starts to go downhill—fast. It becomes a static and stagy film, relying on the Deane-Balderston play and taking little advantage of the material's jump to a new medium. That's not to say this part of the movie is without its stellar moments. There is the count's smashing of the mirror box: "I dislike mirrors." There is the classic battle of wills between Lugosi's count and Van Sloan's Van Helsing: "Your will is strong, Van Helsing." There is the pathetic Renfield's death on that magnificent stone staircase in Carfax Abbey: "I am loyal to you, master!" But after such a bloody terrific opening, this half of the film does seem terribly anemic.

In his book *V is for Vampire: The A–Z Guide to Everything Undead*, Skal goes so far as to call *Dracula* "Perhaps the most influential bad movie ever made." Eeeouch! It is a disappointing film, and parts of it unquestionably have dated badly.

While readily conceding the film's many faults, vampire expert J. Gordon Melton just settles for calling Browning's *Dracula* "the most influential vampire film of all time." Why, yes . . . yes, it is. *Dracula* not only had a profound impact on vampire movies and books to follow, it established Lugosi's count as an iconic figure. We recognize his voice, his face, his mannerisms, his outfit. He . . . is . . . Dracula.

"I think the reason that we continue to read Stoker and look at *Dracula* today is as much a product of Bela Lugosi's performance as it is the novel," Melton

comments. "The performance pushed it into popular culture in a way the book never did. It really established the character in the public mindset."

His performance has been much maligned by some film historians and horror enthusiasts, but ask someone to do an impression of Count Dracula, and, folks, you're going to get Bela Lugosi.

"He is my favorite Dracula by far," comments Jeanne Keyes Youngson, who founded the Count Dracula Fan Club more than forty years ago. "Bela is my Dracula. Because of his accent and his appearance, I just believe in him more. Christopher Lee always seems like Christopher Lee. Bela always seems like the genuine article to me. You wonder what would have happened if Paul Muni or Ian Keith got the role. I don't think we'd be having this conversation right now."

Dracula also set off the talking-pictures horror boom of the 1930s. That's because, at the box office, Lugosi had scared up long lines of Depression-rocked filmgoers eager for some chilling diversions. It was Universal's top-grossing film of the year, saving the strapped studio from bankruptcy.

Universal, the studio so squeamish about a vampire movie, opened the graveyard gates with a vengeance. *Dracula* was followed by James Whale's *Frankenstein* (1931; with Boris Karloff in the role Lugosi turned down), Karl Freund's *The Mummy* (1932; Karloff again, with a screenplay by Balderston), Whale's *The Invisible Man* (1933), Edgar G. Ulmer's *The Black Cat* (1934; teaming Karloff and Lugosi), Whale's *Bride* of *Frankenstein* (1935), Stuart Walker's *Werewolf of London* (1935), and Lew Landers's *The Raven* (1935; with Lugosi and Karloff again). Paramount got into the horror racket with its own versions of classic novels: Rouben Mamoulian's version of Robert Louis Stevenson's *Dr. Jekyll and Mr. Hyde* (1932), which claimed prestige points by winning Fredric March an Oscar, and Erle C. Kenton's *The Island of Lost Souls* (1933; based on the H. G. Wells novel *The Island of Dr. Moreau*). Warner Brothers responded with two films that teamed future Universal player Lionel Atwill and Fay Wray: Curtiz's *Doctor X* (1932) and *The Mystery of the Wax Museum* (1933). And RKO stomped into the genre in 1933 with Wray and her outrageously tall leading man in *King Kong* (directed by Merian C. Cooper and Ernest B. Schoedsack).

Horror films were big business, thanks to *Dracula* and Lugosi, who would continue to be haunted by his most famous role and by the bad contract he had signed with Universal. Hollywood, time, and medical misfortune would not be kind to Lugosi, of whom Karloff rightly observed, "'Poor Bela, he was worth a lot more than he got.'"

There were bright spots, including Lugosi's portrayal of the broken-necked Ygor in Rowland V. Lee's *Son of Frankenstein* (1939) and his splendid return to the Dracula role in *Abbott and Costello Meet Frankenstein* (1948; directed by Charles Barton). But Tinseltown had typecast him as the man in the cape, and Lugosi returned to Dracula-like roles in Browning's *Mark of the Vampire* (a 1935 remake of Browning's own *London after Midnight*, starring Chaney) and Landers's *The Return of the Vampire* (1943). He also traded on the Dracula image by appearing in such low-budget efforts as Jean Yarbrough's *The Devil Bat* (1940), Phil Rosen's *Spooks Run Wild* (1941), and John Gilling's *Old Mother Riley Meets the Vampire* (a 1952 British film also known as *My Son, The Vampire*). And there were the predictable mad-scientists roles in the lamentable likes of William Beaudine's *Bela Lugosi Meets a Brooklyn Gorilla* (1952) and the notorious Ed Wood's *Bride of the Monster* (1955). He returned to the stage for *Dracula* tours, and when he died in Los Angeles of a heart attack at age seventy-three on August 16, 1956, it was in a town that had turned its back on him.

Deane, who continued to play Dracula on stage until 1941, died two years later. Jukes, Lugosi's Renfield on Broadway, had died in 1939. Frye, his Renfield on film, had died in 1944. Liveright had died in 1933, Florence Stoker in 1937, Fort in 1945, and Balderston in 1954.

"'Dracula never ends,'" Lugosi told an interviewer after returning from an ill-fated 1951 British revival of the play. "'I don't know whether I should call it a fortune or a curse, but it never ends.'"

Lugosi was buried in Holy Cross Cemetery in full Dracula costume, including the cape. Perhaps he always knew that donning the cape was what would make him immortal.

CAPSULE

The Count Goes Spanish

· · · · · · · · · · ·

I think had there been any alternative I should have taken it. . . .
—*Jonathan Harker,* Dracula, *chapter 1*

There is no question that Tod Browning's *Dracula* (1931) is a film overloaded with missed opportunities. Even those who dote on Bela Lugosi's performance and the eerie opening scenes fess up to a hankering for a more fully realized interpretation of Stoker's novel. This point was underscored by film historian David J. Skal's rediscovery of Universal's Spanish version of *Drácula* (1931). Filmed at night on the same sets being used by Browning's crew during the day, the Spanish-language *Dracula* follows the American blueprint almost scene by scene. Yet, working within this struc-

ture (and on a tighter budget), director George Melford and Universal's head of foreign productions, Paul Kohner, were able to outpace their A-team counterparts both technically and visually.

Melford's cast included Carlos Villarias as El Conde Drácula, Lupita Tovar as Eva (the renamed Mina character), Barry Norton as Juan Harker, Pablo Álvarez Rubio as Renfield, Eduardo Arozamena as Van Helsing, José Soriano Viosca as Dr. Seward, and Carmen Guerrero as Lucia.

While admitting that the Spanish version "does suffer from the same stage-bound sluggishness as the

Filmed on the same sets as the American version, Universal's Spanish-language Drácula *starred José Soriano Viosca as Dr. Seward, Carlos Villarias as El Conde Dracula, Lupita Tovar as Eva, Barry Norton as Juan Harker, and Eduardo Arozamena as Van Helsing.*

American film," Skal praises Melford's *Drácula* for being "consistently resourceful in enhancing the mood and action." The lighting is more effective. The women's costumes are more revealing and more sensual (one not always following the other). The camera angles are more intriguing. The camera movement is more . . . well, there is some actual camera movement. And the trick shots are . . . well, there are some actual trick shots, including a double exposure that allows Dracula to rise from his coffin, emerging from a shroud of mist.

The Spanish *Drácula* is so imaginative in its use of the same source material, Skal observes in *Hollywood Gothic*, that it "today can be read as an almost shot-by-shot scathing critique of the Browning version."

That's true, as far as the direction and cinematography go. And Tovar's Eva certainly displays more life and luster than Helen Chandler's frail and vapid Mina in the Browning version. Frequently overlooked is the splendid work of Soriano Viosca as Seward. His scenes with Tovar glow with the warmth and devotion of a loving father-daughter relationship—an emotional note hardly even struck by Herbert Bunston and Chandler in Browning's film. Scoriano Viosca and Tovar make you feel how much these characters care. Bunston and Chandler ask you to take their word for it.

But these are the only performances that register as major advantages for the Kohner-Melford version. Where the American film has it all over the Spanish *Drácula* is in the starring cast—particularly Lugosi's Count, Dwight Frye's Renfield, and Edward Van Sloan's Van Helsing.

Villarias gives it his best, but his portrayal simply lacks the elegance and bearing of Lugosi's interpretation. Lugosi's overwhelming identification with the role is no way dented by watching Villarias don the cape and slink through a technically superior film. Arozamena is a gifted character actor who has his moments as Van Helsing, but he lacks the steely authority of Van Sloan. And Álvarez Rubio throws everything into his performance, but his manic, often hysterical portrayal lacks the levels Frye brings when he shows Renfield heartbreakingly lurching back to momentary sanity and the burden of his crimes.

Still, a screening of the Kohner-Melford film does make you yearn for an American version produced, directed, and filmed with the vitality, ingenuity, and imagination of the Spanish *Drácula*. It's Browning's direction that rightly gets called into question when you compare his *Dracula* either with Melford's movie or with James Whale's *Frankenstein*, which was also released in December 1931. As directorial efforts, both of these films have a spark that's sadly missing from Browning's effort.

CAPSULE

Universal Horror

· · · · · · · · · · ·

. . . as if it were the centre of some sort of imaginative whirlpool. . . .
—Jonathan Harker, Dracula, *chapter 1*

Having been the home of Lon Chaney's silent classics *The Hunchback of Notre Dame* (1923; directed by Wallace Worsley) and *The Phantom of the Opera* (1925; directed by Rupert Julian), Universal Pictures ushered in a new era of horror with the 1931 releases of Tod Browning's *Dracula* and James Whale's *Frankenstein*. Although not to the tastes of most studio executives, these terror tales kept Universal solvent in the early 1930s, much as the comedies of Abbott and Costello would save it from bankruptcy in the early 1940s. Perhaps it was fitting, therefore, that some of Universal's leading monster stars, including Dracula, would meet Bud and Lou in a 1948 film that both revitalized the comedy team's career and put an affectionate exclamation point on the studio's golden age of horror.

For the seventeen years between the releases of *Dracula* and *Abbott and Costello Meet Frankenstein* (1948; directed by Charles Barton), Universal's back lot was a landscape where torch-bearing mobs went in search of werewolves, invisible men, and man-made monsters. Ernest Thesiger's Dr. Pretorius might have been overlooking this terror territory when he offered his infamous toast in

Bud Abbott and Lou Costello meet Frankenstein (Glenn Strange). . . and Dracula (Bela Lugosi). . . and the Wolf Man (Lon Chaney Jr.). . . and the Invisible Man (Vincent Price, not pictured, of course).

Bride of Frankenstein: "To a new world of gods and monsters!"

There were two cycles within this golden age that begins and ends with Bela Lugosi playing Count Dracula (significantly, the only two times he would play the role on the screen). The first and far more noteworthy cycle ended in 1939 with Rowland V. Lee's *Son of Frankenstein*, Boris Karloff's third and final appearance as the Frankenstein monster. This period gave us Lugosi in Robert Florey's *Murders in the Rue Morgue* (1932), Karloff as ancient Imhotep in Karl Freund's *The Mummy* (1932) and back as the monster in Whale's *Bride of Frankenstein* (1935), Lugosi and Karloff in Edgar G. Ulmer's *The Black Cat* (1934) and Lew Landers's *The Raven* (1935), Claude Rains in Whale's *The Invisible Man* (1933), and Henry Hull in Stuart Walker's *Werewolf of London* (1935).

The second cycle was dominated by a new horror star, Lon Chaney Jr., who contributed a classic character to the paranormal pantheon with his tortured portrayal of lycanthropic Larry Talbot in George Waggner's *The Wolf Man* (1941). The year before, Vincent Price had starred in Joe May's *The Invisible Man Returns*, and cowboy specialist Tom Tyler had become the first Universal actor to play shuffling Kharis in Christy Cabanne's *The Mummy's Hand*. After the success of *The Wolf Man*, though, Chaney was suited up to play the monster in Erle C. Kenton's *The Ghost of Frankenstein* (1942; with Lugosi back as Ygor) and bandaged up to play Kharis in Harold Young's *The Mummy's Tomb* (1942; wrapped up in a hated role for the first of three times). But Universal didn't use Chaney in Arthur Lubin's 1943 remake of *The Phantom of the Opera*, which had starred Lon Chaney Sr. That role went to his costar in *The Wolf Man*, Claude Rains.

Starting in 1943, Universal tried to keep its horror franchise going by teaming up its monsters. The film that got this rolling was Roy William Neill's *Frankenstein Meets the Wolf Man*, which teamed Chaney as Talbot with Lugosi as the monster (the role he had turned down twelve years earlier

because it had no dialogue).

Dracula's presence can be felt throughout this golden age, and reissues of the Lugosi film helped keep Bram Stoker's novel a steady seller. Lambert Hiller's *Dracula's Daughter*, a sequel to the 1931 movie, was released in 1936. The screenplay by Garrett Fort was supposedly based on the "Dracula's Guest" chapter cut from Stoker's novel, but it bears little resemblance to Harker's account of an encounter with a female vampire.

Although Lugosi was supposed to return as Dracula for the sequel, a reworked concept reduced the count's presence to that of a wax dummy burned by his undead daughter, Countess Marya Zaleska (a.k.a. Countess Dracula, played by Gloria Holden). With Edward Van Sloan back as Van Helsing (this time inexplicably named *Von* Helsing), *Dracula's Daughter* is a moody and stylish horror film that holds up quite well today. One of the movie's most discussed scenes has become the title character's pick up and seduction of the starving Lili (Nan Grey). The lesbian subtext doesn't seem all that subtle as the countess leers longingly at the disrobing Lili. Holden's countess is also the first vampire seeking a cure for her undead state (a notion that would be taken up three decades later in the supernatural soap opera *Dark Shadows*).

Robert Siodmak's *Son of Dracula* (1943) is also an intriguing vampire film, despite the horrible miscasting of the beefy Lon Chaney Jr. With its Southern Gothic touches and John P. Fulton's special effects, it plays like a collaboration between Stoker and William Faulkner. All of the splendid touches almost (but not quite) make up for Chaney's stiff and awkward performance as Count Alucard (I know—but the backward pseudonym was a fresh idea at that point).

By this time, thanks to producer Val Lewton (*Cat People*, 1942; *I Walked with a Zombie*, 1943), RKO had taken over the lead in Hollywood's horror field. Universal's response was to pack as many monsters as possible into one film.

When Chaney returned to his cherished Wolf Man for the monster-rally films, John Carradine, not Lugosi, put on Dracula's cape and ring. He was a lean, mustached, sonorous count for Kenton's *House of Frankenstein* (1944) and *House of Dracula* (1945), both of which featured Western heavy Glenn Strange as the fourth actor to play the monster for Universal. All three actors to follow Karloff as the monster—Chaney, Lugosi, and Strange—were back for the swan song, *Abbott and Costello Meet Frankenstein* (with Vincent Price making a closing-scene "appearance" as the Invisible Man).

There were notable non-Universal vampire films released during the studio's golden horror age, including *Vampyr* (producer-director Carl Theodor Dreyer's 1931 movie wrongly said to be based on Joseph Sheridan Le Fanu's story "Carmilla"), Browning's *Mark of the Vampire* (1935, with Lugosi as the Dracula-like Count Mora), Landers's *The Return of the Vampire* (1943, with Lugosi as the Dracula-like Armand Tesla), and Sam Newfield's *Dead Men Walk* (1943, starring George Zucco). Universal, though, became as much a home for Dracula as was Transylvania. Stoker created him. Deane gave him the cape and evening clothes. Lugosi gave him a face and voice. And Universal gave him international icon status.

Carradine's count is destroyed by sunlight in *House of Dracula*, but not before infecting well-meaning doctor Franz Edelmann (Onslow Stevens) with his blood, bringing him under the vampiric influence. Making like the crafty count, Universal had infected 1930s and '40s moviegoers with regular doses of vampire drama, bringing them under the vampiric influence. Dracula himself couldn't have mapped out a better plan for extending his reach to the planet's teeming millions.

Dracula or Not?

Ten Films in Which the Central Character Isn't Dracula—Or, Is He?

. . . .

"I only used that name because I was in doubt."
—Professor Van Helsing, Dracula, *chapter 13*

Dracula-like, Dracula-inspired, Dracula-influenced, and Dracula-based characters can be found in dozens of films released over the last eighty-five years. Almost none of the following are called *Dracula*, so what's in a name? Are any of them meant to be the count himself? Dig deep into each for the bottom line:

Graf Orlok (Max Schreck) in F. W. Murnau's *Nosferatu* (1922): Who were they trying to kid? The names were changed to protect the filmmakers from litigation (it didn't work). German director Werner Herzog's 1979 remake with Klaus Kinski made no such effort to distance itself from the count. The bottom line: Unquestionably Dracula.

He's the son of the great Lon Chaney, but is his Count Alucard the son of Dracula or the vampire king himself?

Count Mora (Bela Lugosi) in Tod Browning's *Mark of the Vampire* (1935): Sure looks and sounds like Dracula. But that's the trick. Mora is revealed to be an actor hired to play a vampire. The bottom line: Not Dracula.

Armand Tesla (Bela Lugosi) in Lew Landers's *The Return of the Vampire* (1943): Universal wouldn't permit Columbia Pictures to use the Dracula name, but the audience was asked to draw its own conclusions about a vampire wearing a cape and played by Lugosi. The bottom line: Close, but not really Dracula.

Count Alucard (Lon Chaney Jr.) in Robert Siodmak's *Son of Dracula* (1943): Most film buffs take it for granted that Chaney is playing the original Count Dracula. There is some confusion here, though, thanks to the title. Are we meant to take it literally, as we take the title of Universal's first sequel, Lambert Hillyer's *Dracula's Daughter* (1936)? Is Chaney intended to be a Dracula descendant, making him *a* Count Dracula, but not *the* Count Dracula? While the majority opinion sides with him portraying *the* Count

Dracula, there's evidence that Universal itself didn't hold with this interpretation. Both Dracula and his son, Alucard, were intended to appear in Charles Barton's 1948 monster rally *Abbott and Costello Meet Frankenstein*. How, then, could Alucard be the original Count Dracula? Cut from the Bud-and-Lou film were Alucard and Kharis the Mummy. And there is no finer, more authoritative source on Universal horror than film historian Gregory William Mank. In his marvelously detailed book *It's Alive!* (1981), Mank, fully aware of *Son of Dracula*, states in his entry on 1944's *House of Frankenstein* that Dracula "had not stirred at Universal since the original 1931 film." The bottom line: Maybe Dracula, maybe not.

Von Housen (Bela Lugosi) in John Gilling's *Old Mother Riley Meets the Vampire* (a.k.a. *Vampire over London* and *My Son, The Vampire*; 1952): Sad appearance for Lugosi in British comedy starring English drag performer Arthur Lucan as his popular washerwoman character, Old Mother Riley. Lugosi was hoping to make money by taking the *Dracula* play on tour in Britain, but the enterprise was shut down due to mismanagement. Without funds to get home, he agreed to appear in this low-budget movie about an evil scientist planning to use uranium deposits to build an army of robots. The bottom line: Not Dracula, not even a vampire.

Baron Roderico da Frankurten (Christopher Lee) in Steno's *Tempi duri per i vampiri* (Hard Times for Vampires, 1959; retitled *Uncle Was a Vampire* in the United States: The comedy definitely trades on Lee's portrayal of the count a year earlier in Terence Fisher's *Dracula* (a.k.a. *Horror of Dracula*). Bottom line: The association is strong, but this is not Dracula.

Baron Meinster (David Peel) in Terence Fisher's *The Brides of Dracula* (1960): This was the Hammer Studios sequel to Fisher's *The Horror of Dracula*, and Peter Cushing was back as Van Helsing. The bottom line: Meinster is a vampire and a Dracula disciple, but not Dracula.

Count Yorga (Robert Quarry) in Bob Kelljan's *Count Yorga, Vampire* (1970) and *The Return of Count Yorga* (1971): He has the title, the outfit, the cape, and the widow's peak. The bottom line: The influence is undeniable, but Yorga is not Dracula.

"Blacula" Prince Mamuwalde (William Marshall) in William Crain's *Blacula* (1972) and Bob Kelljan's *Scream, Blacula, Scream* (1973): Dracula (Charles MacCauley) turns the African prince into a vampire. The bottom line: Dracula is responsible, but Blacula is not Dracula.

Kurt Barlow (Reggie Nadler) in Tobe Hooper's *'Salem's Lot* (1979): Nadler's makeup for this miniseries version of Stephen King's novel is meant to resemble Max Schreck as Orlok, who was supposed to be Dracula. So is this another Dracula? The bottom line: Not really; in King's book, Barlow is disarmingly human in appearance.

John Carradine: A New Kind of Dracula

· · · · · · · · · · ·

*. . . a tall old man, clean shaven save for a long white
moustache, and clad in black from head to foot. . . .*
—*Jonathan Harker,* Dracula, *chapter 2*

Many reasons have been given for Bela Lugosi not getting the role of Dracula in Erle C. Kenton's *House of Frankenstein* (1944). In *It's Alive!*—his definitive history of the studio's eight *Frankenstein* films—Gregory William Mank notes that those reasons ranged "from the actor's poverty row commitments and his poor health to the studio's lingering displeasure over his *Frankenstein Meets the Wolf Man* performance" (in which he had been badly miscast as the monster). It has also been suggested that Universal Studios executives were peeved at Lugosi for appearing as vampire Armand Tesla in what amounted to an unauthorized *Dracula* sequel for Columbia, Lew Landers's *The Return of the Vampire* (1943).

Lugosi was sixty-one. He needed the money. He was the actor most associated with the role, and he very much wanted the part. Had the stars aligned,

Universal could have billed all three of their golden-age horror stars in one film: Lugosi, Boris Karloff, and Lon Chaney Jr. It was not to be.

Universal awarded the role to thirty-eight-year-old John Carradine, who had played small roles in several of the studio's horror films: James Whale's *The Invisible Man* (1933), Edgar G. Ulmer's *The Black Cat* (1934), and Whale's *Bride of Frankenstein* (1935). He had also made a memorable villain in such movies as John Ford's *The Prisoner of Shark Island* (1936) and Henry King's *Jesse James* (1939). He was a versatile actor, though, playing the tough sailor Long Jack in Victor Fleming's *Captains Courageous* (1937), courtly Southern gambler Hatfield in Ford's *Stagecoach* (1939), and the spiritual Casy in Ford's *The Grapes of Wrath* (1940). He knew (and liked) Lugosi, having just worked with him and George Zucco in one

John Carradine's suave Count Dracula uses the famous ring to cast a spell on the lovely Rita (Anne Gwynne) in House of Frankenstein.

of those poverty-row movies, William Beaudine's *Voodoo Man* (1944). Both Carradine and Zucco were hired for *House of Frankenstein;* not so Bela Lugosi.

Whatever the reason for Lugosi not getting the call, the casting of Carradine opened up new possibilities for vampire characters in general and Dracula in particular. First, the cadaverous Carradine's interpretation was, in many ways, closer to Stoker's conception of the vampire king in the novel: tall, gaunt, mustached, with streaks of white in his hair. Universal agreed when Carradine asked if his count could be more faithful to Stoker's description, although studio executives did make him trim back the mustache and retain the evening clothes first ordered off the rack by Hamilton Deane.

And the voice choice? Dwell on that for a moment. From his first appearance in the 1931 film, Lugosi's Dracula clearly is nowhere close to mastering English inflections. But Stoker has Harker remark on the count's excellent command of English (although Dracula himself realizes that, to better fit in, he "must learn the English intonation"). Carradine gives us a Dracula who has followed through on this resolve, so that his English grammar and intonation will not mark him a stranger. Lugosi's Dracula oozed Old World charm, but Carradine's Dracula has a suavity and easy manner that allows him to move without notice through the concert halls of Paris or the casinos of Monte Carlo. While he lacks the sheer physical strength of such later

Draculas as Christopher Lee and Jack Palance, Carradine makes up for this with that resonant voice, that penetrating gaze, and that arch of the eyebrow that conveys incredible cunning.

It would be a mistake to place a claim on Carradine rekindling Stoker's concept, which was more cold-blooded predator than sensual seducer. Indeed, building on the Lugosi characterization, Carradine's Dracula is even smoother and more stylish as the courtly count. Lugosi's Dracula never drinks wine, but Carradine's Dracula sips merrily away in *House of Frankenstein*. "It is the bond that links us together," Carradine's Dracula tells the mesmerized Rita (Anne Gwynne). "I will come for you before the dawn." Woohoo!

What makes Carradine's portrayal so pivotal in the Dracula lexicon is yet another departure from Stoker. Carradine introduces a world-weariness that seems somewhat logical in an immortal being living through the centuries under a terrible curse. This actually is expressed in the opening sequence of the 1945 sequel to *House of Frankenstein*, Kenton's *House of Dracula*. Dracula has presented himself to brilliant scientist Franz Edelmann (Onslow Stevens): "Yes, doctor, I am Count Dracula. You see before you a man who has lived for centuries, kept alive by the blood of innocent people. That's why I've come to you; to seek release from a curse of misery and horror, against which I'm powerless to fight alone." Picking up on an idea that surfaced in *Dracula's Daughter* (1936; directed by

Lambert Hillyer), Carradine's Dracula is searching for a cure. There is weariness. There is regret. There is the hope for change. This desire goes out the castle window, of course, when he spots the doctor's lovely assistant, Miliza (Martha O'Driscoll). "You left Schoenheim just as we were becoming acquainted," this truly continental Dracula says in the guise of Baron Latos. "Now that chance has brought us together again, I hope to see you quite often."

The scripts for *House of Frankenstein* and *House of Dracula* hardly allowed Carradine to fully explore the hints of regret and the longing for release, but many vampires to follow him— from Jonathan Frid's Barnabas Collins in the TV series *Dark Shadows* to David Boreanaz's Angel in the eponymous TV series—would become victims of conscience and battle against their monstrous nature. While this advance on the vampire character did not reach fruition until Barnabas in *Dark Shadows* (1966–71), the tortured path to undead introspection is indicated in Carradine's performance.

Carradine was by no means as overwhelmingly identified with Dracula as Lugosi, but his association with the character was strong. He played the count on stage in the 1950s, then packed up his cape and jumped into yet a third medium, starring in a live television production of *Dracula* that was aired on January 6, 1956, by NBC's Emmy Award–winning daily afternoon series, *Matinee Theatre* (1955–59). Carradine almost certainly was television's first Dracula.

Created and produced by Albert McLeery, *Matinee Theatre* presented a mix of classics (*Wuthering Heights, Much Ado About Nothing, The Tell-Tale Heart*) and original stories, each introduced by host John Conte. The target audience for this golden-age anthology was women at home. Although not as well-remembered as such acclaimed primetime cousins as *The U.S. Steel Hour, Goodyear TV Playhouse,* and *Playhouse 90,* McLeery's program did manage to attract teleplays by Nathaniel Benchley, Frank Gilroy, Helene Hanff, Ira Levin, Abby Mann, Rod Serling, John Van Druten, and Gore Vidal. The stars for these one-hour productions included such dependable players as Jim Backus, Fay Bainter, Billie Burke, Hermione Gingold, Edmund Gwenn, Cedric Hardwicke, Oskar Homolka, Edward Everett Horton, Victory Jory, Kevin McCarthy, Roddy McDowall, Agnes Moorehead, Arthur O'Connell, Geraldine Page, and Vincent Price. Seven months after playing Dracula on *Matinee Theatre* Carradine appeared as Jeffrey Pyncheon in the program's adaptation of Nathaniel Hawthorne's *The House of Seven Gables.* On February 12, 1957, *Matinee Theatre* aired a live version of *Frankenstein* featuring former heavyweight boxing champion Primo Carnera as the monster. Little of substance is known about Carradine's TV Dracula, however, because no copies have surfaced, not even a grainy kinescope (a filmed version of a TV program, a method used before the advent of videotape).

A third film appearance as the count, in Beaudine's *Billy the Kid versus Dracula* (1966), was every bit as awful as it sounds. Carradine's Dracula this time sported a beard, which was about the only hair-raising thing about this goofy bargain-basement movie. Sad to say, there were two even more forgettable films with Carradine as Dracula: Federico Curiel's *Las Vampiras* (a 1968 Mexican production) and Adrià García and Victor Maldonado's *Nocturna* (a 1979 release also known as *Granddaughter of Dracula*). Somewhat better was his portrayal of aging horror actor Loren Belasco (who may or may not be you-know-who) in "McCloud Meets Dracula," a 1977 episode of NBC's *McCloud* TV series. Although crippled by arthritis, Carradine has some stirring moments, booming in grand style, "How many policemen, how many torchbearers in the night, seeking out the soul of Dracula? They're the bloodsuckers, not I!" He also appeared in two low-budget films, Al Adamson and Jean Hewitt's *Blood of Dracula's Castle* (1967; as a butler named George, not the count) and Paul Aratow and Adamson's *Doctor Dracula* (1977; as a cult leader named Radcliff). Fans of *The Munsters* TV series fondly remember his appearances as Herman's boss, Mr. Gateman.

The reports of Carradine's death had a theatrical flair and were not greatly exaggerated. He died on November 27, 1988, in Milan, where he was the guest of honor at a showing of *Stagecoach.* He suffered a heart attack after climbing the 328 cathedral steps of the city's Duomo. He was eighty-three.

Making the Most of Life:
Abbott and Costello Meet Frankenstein

. . . .

They whispered together, and then they all three laughed. . . .
—Jonathan Harker, Dracula, *chapter 3*

Lon Chaney Jr. bitterly blamed the comedy team of Abbott and Costello for turning the classic Universal monsters, including Count Dracula, into clownish figures. "Abbott and Costello ruined the horror films: they made buffoons out of the monsters," Chaney griped.

The complaint is by no means legitimate, and it only proves how little the disillusioned Chaney appreciated the magical appeal of Charles Barton's *Abbott and Costello Meet Frankenstein*. Unlike TV's *The Munsters* (1964–66) or such all-out horror spoofs as Mel Brooks's *Young Frankenstein* (1974) and Stan Dragoti's *Love at First Bite* (1979), this 1948 Universal release did not play the monsters for laughs. Indeed, no small part of the film's magic is that it works equally

well as a Universal horror film and as an Abbott and Costello comedy. The monsters get to play their roles reasonably straight, and that genuine sense of menace makes the Bud-and-Lou hijinks all the more hilarious. The reverse is also true. The monsters, "contrasted to the madcap antics around them," notes film historian Leonard Maltin, "were that much more terrifying."

The proof is in the sheer number of horror fans—me included—who became horror fans because of this film. Maltin rightly calls *Abbott and Costello Meet Frankenstein* "the best horror-comedy ever made, and, in many ways, one of the best horror films ever produced at Universal."

Abbott and Costello had reigned as Top 10 box office stars for most of the 1940s. Their films were incredibly popular during

Dracula (Bela Lugosi) puts the whammy on Wilbur (Lou Costello) in Abbott & Costello Meet Frankenstein.

the war years, and the duo kept America laughing with such routine-packed efforts as Arthur Lubin's *Buck Privates* (1941), *In the Navy* (1941), *Hold That Ghost* (1941), *Keep 'em Flying* (1941), and *Ride 'em Cowboy* (1942); Erle C. Kenton's *Pardon My Sarong* (1942) and *Who Done It?* (1942); Charles Lamont's *Hit the Ice* (1942); and Jean Yarbrough's *The Naughty Nineties* (1945). They also kept Universal solvent. By 1948, however, the Universal horror cycle had run its creepy course, and the studio's top comedy team seemed to be slipping.

Abbott and Costello Meet Frankenstein both rejuvenated Bud and Lou's career and provided a fitting film farewell to Universal's terror triumvirate: Dracula, the Frankenstein monster, and the Wolf Man. In later films the comedians would go on to meet, among others, the Invisible Man, Dr. Jekyll and Mr. Hyde, and the Mummy, but none of these meetings were as inspired as the comedy-horror collision of 1948.

"Most happily, the film returned Bela Lugosi to the screen as Dracula," Universal authority Gregory William Mank wrote in *It's Alive!* "The Hungarian actor had not worked in a Hollywood studio since the spring of 1946." It has been reported that Universal, as it had in 1931, considered casting Ian Keith as Dracula, but this time Lugosi always seemed to be the first and only choice.

Although sixty-five and too old for the role, Lugosi is magnificent in *Abbott and Costello Meet Frankenstein*. Bud and Lou are in top comic form throughout the beautifully paced film, but Lugosi's Dracula is *the* performance. There are moments when he is both wonderfully menacing and funny. "Ah, you young people, making the most out of life," he tells Lou, taking just the right pause before ominously adding, "while it lasts!"

This would be only the second time Lugosi officially played Dracula on screen, and he makes the most of it. If anything, he seems more cunning, more comfortable, and more in command than he did in the 1931 film.

Lugosi's decline, physically and professionally, was swift after this meeting with Abbott and Costello. He lived only eight more years, battling health problems and appearing in increasingly low-budget movies. Hollywood was pretty much done with him, so, from a major-studio standpoint, it ended where it began for the actor—at Universal, in the role of Count Dracula.

Riding the Crest:
The Dracula Ring

· · · · · · · · · · ·

. . . the living ring of terror. . . .
—*Jonathan Harker,* Dracula, *chapter 1*

Bela Lugosi wears a marvelously distinctive ring in *Abbott and Costello Meet Frankenstein*. It carries the same symbol found on Dracula's coffin in that film. It was known at Universal as the Dracula Crest: a shield emblazoned with a *D* that is topped by a bat and surrounded by four crowns. Over the bat is a fifth and larger crown.

This was not the crest of Vlad the Impaler. It was not the ring Lugosi wore on Broadway or in the 1931 film version of *Dracula*. It's not based on anything described in Bram Stoker's book (Stoker doesn't even mention Dracula wearing a ring).

Yet this ring has become an integral part of Dracula folklore. Where did it come from? Try the Universal prop department. An early version of the Dracula ring and crest were designed for Robert Siodmak's *Son of Dracula* (1943). But the Dracula Crest ring makes its first starring appearance, so to speak, on John Carradine's hand in Erle C. Kenton's *House of Frankenstein* (1944). The ring reappears in Kenton's *House of Dracula* (1945), and Doctor Edelmann recognizes the symbol on his night visitor's coffin, exclaiming, "The Dracula Crest!"

The ring went back into storage until Lugosi was brought back to Universal in February 1948 to start work on *Abbott and Costello Meet Frankenstein*. He liked the ring so much that he took it away and had several copies made. Christopher Lee wore one of these copies in his third Hammer Studios film as the count, Freddie Francis's *Dracula Has Risen from the Grave* (1968). *Famous Monsters of Filmland* magazine creator Forrest J Ackerman has one of the Lugosi rings. Cortlandt Hull, great nephew of Henry Hull, the star of *Werewolf of London* (1935; directed by Stuart Walker), has another. Even some high-priced limited-edition replicas of the ring have become collector's items. They are popular with illusionists, who, after all, know magic when they see it.

The Return of Dracula: A Cold-Blooded Vampire for the Cold War

. . . .

It is cold, cold.
—*Professor Van Helsing,* Dracula, *chapter 27*

A decade after the count met Abbott and Costello, two *Dracula* films hit the movie screens in the same year. Dracula hadn't made an appearance in an English-speaking movie since 1948. He'd gone underground for most of the 1950s, a period dominated by such city-shattering monsters as Godzilla, Tarantula, Rodan, and the giant ants of Gordon Douglas's *Them!* (1954). Audiences seemed to crave horror tinged with science fiction, so this was the decade in which moviegoers were, in 1951, paid a visit by *The Thing from Another World* (dir. Christian Nyby), paused that same year to see *The Day the Earth Stood Still* (dir. Robert Wise), tested the water in 1954 with *The Creature from the Black Lagoon* (dir. Jack Arnold), and witnessed an *Invasion of the Body Snatchers* in 1956 (dir. Don Siegel). It was also the happy-days era that gave us the teen monster movie, so in 1957, American International released Herbert L. Strock's *Blood of Dracula* (followed that same year by Strock's *I Was a Teenage Frankenstein* and Gene Fowler Jr.'s *I Was a Teenage Werewolf*). But this bloodless spooker set at a private girls' academy merely traded on the infamous name. Dracula never

showed up as a character in the low-budget film about a troubled teen (Sandra Harrison) turned into a vampirish killer by a mad science teacher (Louise Lewis).

Then, after a ten-year absence, Drac was back on the big screen. Why were producers suddenly so interested in digging him up?

One reason, certainly, was Universal's 1957 release of its vintage horror films as the *Shock* package sold to television stations across the country. Syndicated by Screen Gems, this creepy cinematic collection created a rabid new generation of fans for Dracula, the Frankenstein monster, the Wolf Man, the Mummy, the Invisible Man, and the rest of Universal's ghoulish gang. The revival also fueled the late-night careers of such local horror hosts as New York's Zacherley (John Zacherle), Vampira (Maila Nurmi, already a Los Angeles phenomenon before the advent of *Shock* therapy), mad scientist Morgus the Magnificent (Sid Noel) in New Orleans, and Gorgon the Gruesome (Bill Camfield), whose eerie laugh echoed throughout the Dallas–Fort Worth area. Bela Lugosi died one year and one month before the *Shock* troops sparked new interest in his career and in *Dracula*.

So two new Draculas emerged from their coffins in 1958. The far more important of these was, of course, Christopher Lee. He first put on the vampire cape for Terence Fisher's *Dracula* (a.k.a. *Horror of Dracula*). But the other 1958 release, *The Return of Dracula* (a.k.a. *The Curse of Dracula*), is not without its intriguing elements. Francis Lederer plays the count in this moody updating of the Dracula story. (Lederer himself seemed bound for eternal life before he died in 2000 at the age of 100.) Directed by Paul Landres, the film opens in the Balkans with a Van Helsing-like vampire hunter (John Wengraf) leading a group of men toward a tomb. Stake and mallet ready, they open Dracula's coffin to find . . . it's empty. He's gone. "But where?" asks one of the vampire hunters. "Where?"

The scene shifts to a railroad station, where artist Bellac Gordal (Norbert Schiller) is bidding his parents an emotional farewell. "At least in America I will be welcome," Bellac says. "I can paint life as I see it. An artist must have some kind of expression." Yes, his father agrees, "You are lucky to

Dracula (Francis Lederer), right, closes in on Rachel (Norma Eberhardt) and her boyfriend, Tim (Ray Stricklyn), in the climactic show-down in The Return of Dracula.

be free." But his luck is about to run out. Encountering Bellac on the train, Dracula kills the artist and assumes his identity. Escaping from behind the Iron Curtain, he travels to the small California town of Carleton, into the loving arms of Bellac's widowed cousin, Cora Mayberry (Greta Granstedt). Cora hasn't seen Cousin Bellac since they were children, so she accepts the courtly European as the genuine article.

Bellac/Dracula soon sets his sight on the neck of lovely cousin Rachel (Norma Eberhardt), but not before turning the blind Jenny Blake (Virginia Vincent) into a vampire. Dracula eventually is done in by the all-American goodness of Rachel and her boyfriend, Tim (Ray Stricklyn).

Wearing a long overcoat like a cape, Lederer's Dracula is a cold-blooded Eastern European agent infiltrating a cozy American town during the Cold War. He is the ultimate Red Scare nightmare, the danger from behind the Iron Curtain that threatens to contaminate and undermine the Eisenhower Era normalcy of life in these here United States. The symbol of anticommunist goodness, European secret agent Meyerman (Wengraf) recognizes this threat. So does the symbol of religious goodness, the Reverend Doctor Whitfield (Gage Clark).

The Return of Dracula, therefore, plays like a Cold War horror parable, much in the same way that Siegel's *Invasion of the Body Snatchers* and Nyby's *The Thing from Another World* used science fiction to metaphorically probe the fears, insecurities, and anxieties of the era that gave us the very real terrors of the Red Scare and the anticommunist blacklisting. Dracula isn't just invading a small American community. He's being welcomed into the American home by God-fearing, patriotic citizens who embrace him as a loving relation seeking refuge. Don't trust him! He's not who he says he is!

Communists hiding under the bed? *The Return of Dracula* can do better than that. This soulless being is hiding in a coffin. He carries out his evil plot in the shadows of night. Of course he does. Dragged into the daylight, this evil will shrivel and die.

The Return of Dracula is Cold War–era proof of Dracula's metaphoric flexibility. Fear of foreigners is part of Stoker's book, after all, and here is that xenophobia updated and filtered through the Iron Curtain. Each generation creates its own Dracula? Here's a Dracula made in the 1950s, set in the 1950s, and symbolic of the 1950s. Lugosi gave us a Dracula that suited his time. Frank Langella would later do the same in the 1970s. And so we shouldn't dismiss Lederer in the 1950s.

Like almost every other *Dracula* film, this one has its champions and its detractors. But even if the Cold War allegory doesn't work for you, *Return of Dracula* can be enjoyed as a nifty and unnerving horror film. There are a few made-you-jump scares. There are several deeply disturbing images that linger long after Dracula's ghastly death throes (impaled on a jagged wooden stake). And there's the staking of poor Jenny (depicted in this black-and-white movie with a few feet of color film showing the gushing blood).

Lederer would later distance himself from horror films, expressing astonishment that so many fans expressed an interest in Dracula. But only Lugosi brought more of an Eastern European, Old World quality to his portrayal of the count. There's also an underplayed sincerity to his performance, and this allows him to be chillingly and seductively effective when intoning such lines as, "There's only one reality, Rachel, and that is death. I bring you death—a living death. I bring you the darkness of centuries past and centuries to come. Eternal life, and eternal death. Now do you fear?"

Although the association with Count Dracula never would be as strong for Lederer as it would be for John Carradine, Lee, and Lugosi, he did return to the role on one more memorable occasion. On October 27, 1971, NBC aired an episode of *Rod Serling's Night Gallery* titled "The Devil is Not Mocked." Based on a short story by Manly Wade Wellman, this installment of the horror anthology series tells of Nazi troops storming into an Eastern European castle. General Von Grunn (Helmut Dantine), accuses the master of the castle (Lederer) of leading underground resistance forces. How right he is. At midnight, Von Grunn's soldiers are torn to shreds by the castle inhabitants. Their bullets are useless. "You must forgive my servants and our primitive Transylvania customs," the master of the castle says. "If it's any consolation, General, this is the headquarters of the secret resistance . . . and I am its proud commander—Count Dracula."

Radio-Free Dracula

. . . .

. . . and in the air the heavy, oppressive sense of thunder.
—*Jonathan Harker,* Dracula, *chapter 1*

Yes, 1958 was a big year for Dracula, thanks to Christopher Lee and Francis Lederer. A little more than sixty years after the publication of Bram Stoker's novel, the count had exerted his considerable powers in the realms of literature, theater, film, and even television. Did you notice that there's a major medium missing from the cultural spectrum? What happened to radio, which, for most of the 1930s and '40s, had a cherished place in almost every American home?

Well, twenty years before the Lee-led 1958 revival, there was a notable radio adaptation of *Dracula*. One of the reasons for its notability was that this *Dracula* was the very first offering of *First Person Singular*. Oh, sorry, you probably know the CBS series by the more imposing moniker soon formalized as its official title: *The Mercury Theatre on the Air*. And this, of course, was the radio extension of the acclaimed theater company founded by Orson Welles and John Houseman. The one-hour program premiered July 11, 1938. Welles, just twenty-three at the time, had already established himself as a Broadway prodigy with the Mercury Theatre's modern-dress staging of William Shakespeare's *Julius Caesar*. Welles made the jump to radio with the network hyping him as the show's creator, director, producer, writer, and star. He took the Mercury players along for the ride, planning to start a nine-week summer run with an adaptation of Robert Louis Stevenson's *Treasure Island*. That became the second *Mercury Theatre on the Air* broadcast after Welles decided to lead with one of his favorite books, *Dracula*.

The resonant Welles voice rolled out of radio speakers that July evening, mellifluously welcoming listeners across America:

Orson Welles provided the voices for Count Dracula and Dr. Seward for his 1938 Mercury Theatre on the Air *radio adaptation of* Dracula.

Good evening. The Mercury Theatre faces tonight a challenge and opportunity for which we are grateful. We will present during the next nine weeks, many different kinds of stories—stories of romance and adventure, biography, mystery and human emotion. Stories by authors like Robert Louis Stevenson, Emile Zola, Dostoyevsky. Edgar Allan Poe, and P. G. Wodehouse. . . . We are starting off tonight with the best story of its kind ever written. You will find it in every representative library of graphic English narrative. It's Bram Stoker's *Dracula* . . . and so, for the moment, goodbye, ladies and gentlemen. I'll see you in Transylvania.

Welles truly did love Stoker's novel. And he was keenly aware of how unfaithful the stage versions and the Lugosi film had been. "*Dracula* would make a marvelous movie," Welles would later tell fellow director Peter Bogdanovich. "In fact, nobody has ever made it; they've

never paid any attention to the book, which is the most hair-raising, marvelous book in the world."

Believing Stoker an underrated writer, Welles went back to the book for the *Dracula* radio adaptation he wrote with Houseman. The script wasn't exactly written in blood, but gallons of beverages were involved. Working on a crushing deadline, the dynamic duo worked, according to Welles biographer Simon Callow, over "several meals and without benefit of sleep, awash with bottles of wine, balloons of brandy and great pots of coffee."

Long stretches of their adaptation were, indeed, drawn directly from the novel. They reinstated Dracula's drooping white mustache, hairy palms, and "peculiarly sharp white teeth." They used Bistritz, Romania, and Purfleet, England, as well as other locations ignored by stage and film versions. In major and subtle ways, Welles and Houseman seemed intent on distancing themselves from the 1931 Universal movie.

Still, they only had an hour in which to tell the entire story, and an incredible amount of streamlining was necessary. Needing to tighten the action as much as possible, they jammed together the characters of Arthur Holmwood and John Seward, calling the composite Dr. Arthur Seward.

Welles couldn't resist playing both Seward and Dracula (and several small roles). His vampire voice—serviceable, if not mesmerizing—was enhanced by engineers with an echo effect.

Most of his cast was drawn from the

ranks of the Mercury Theatre company: George Coulouris as Jonathan Harker, the always-dependable Martin Gabel as Van Helsing, Agnes Moorehead as Mina, Elizabeth Farrell as Lucy, Ray Collins as the captain of the *Demeter*, and Karl Swenson as the ship's mate.

Still available on cassette and compact disc, the *Mercury Theatre on the Air* production of *Dracula* is a vintage radio delight. It has been wildly overpraised by some, and there are a few undeniably hokey moments, but the major performances are rock solid and great fun in a grand theatrical manner. The countless sound effects (what Callow rightly calls the "continuous wall of sound"), are impressive, even by today's technological standards. And many of the musical choices are downright stirring. That's hardly shocking since Bernard Herrmann, the composer for Hitchcock's *Psycho*, was the musical director. On the other side of the ledger, many of the scene-ending music cues are melodramatically overwrought and overdone, while the constant fascination with sound effects actually gets distracting.

Still, the Welles biographers have valued this *Dracula* highly. Charles Highman, author of *Orson Welles: The Rise and Fall of an American Genius*, regards it as a triumph: "The results were extraordinarily powerful: 'Dracula' became a masterpiece in its own right, faithful to the spirit and letter of the book. . . . To this day, Welles's 'Dracula' is the best performing version."

Callow, in *Orson Welles: The Road to Xanadu*, cheers the broadcast's "old-fashioned barnstorming" feel—the "excitement and intensity of the transmission." With *Dracula*, Callow observes, Welles "launched a passionate assault on radio, thrilled by its techniques."

Throughout the summer of 1938, Welles and his team followed *Dracula* with such classics as *Treasure Island* and *A Tale of Two Cities*, concluding their nine-week run with an adaptation of G. K. Chesterton's *The Man Who Was Thursday*. The critical success of these broadcasts led CBS to renew *The Mercury Theatre on the Air* for the fall. In December, the series picked up a sponsor and became *The Campbell Playhouse*, continuing under this title until the spring of 1940.

Although it all started with *Dracula*, the program's most famous (and infamous) production was the "panic broadcast" of October 30, 1938. Aired the night before Halloween and taken by many listeners as the real thing, this Martian invasion was the Orson Welles take on H. G. Wells's 1898 novel, *The War of the Worlds*.

CAPSULE

Christopher Lee: The Hammer Horror

. . . .

*But the Count! Never did I imagine such wrath and fury,
even to the demons of the pit.*
—*Jonathan Harker,* Dracula, *chapter 3*

Terence Fisher's *Horror of Dracula*
(1958) introduced Christopher Lee as
Count Dracula, and Lee introduced an
aspect to the character never before
captured on screen: that chilling combination of animal cunning and brute
strength. As fresh as Lee's portrayal
seemed in 1958, however, he was
merely reclaiming the power given the
vampire king by Bram Stoker.

Stoker's novel tells us that Dracula
has the strength of twenty men. You
don't quite buy that in the earlier
performances of John Carradine, Bela
Lugosi, and Max Schreck. Schreck
seems plenty animalistic, all right, but
his Orlok-Dracula suggests rodent-car-
ried pestilence, not muscle. Carradine
and Lugosi have cunning and Old
World charm, but you can't imagine
either of their Draculas mopping the
floor with the offensive line of the
Chicago Bears. Only Lon Chaney Jr.
as Count Alucard has the sheer brute
strength described by Stoker—and
that's about all he has.

From our first glimpse of Lee in
Horror of Dracula, however, we have
no trouble believing that he possesses
the strength of twenty men. Lugosi's
Dracula can be cruel. Lee's Dracula is

*No actor stood taller as Count Dracula
than Christopher Lee, seen here in* The
Horror of Dracula.

not only cruel but can erupt in a snarl-
ing fit of awesome savagery and feroc-
ity. Nobody goes for the jugular like
Christopher Lee.

We also have no doubt that Lee's
Dracula is smart—terribly smart, and
that it would be a fatal mistake to
underestimate him. You can see him
at the head of an army in the fifteenth

century, crossing the River Danube to match wits with the Turks. He must be, as Van Helsing says in the book, that very same "Voivode Dracula . . . no common man; for in that time, and for centuries after, he was spoken of as the cleverest and the most cunning, as well as the bravest of the sons of the 'land beyond the forest.'" In Lee's portrayal, we find the realization of both that "mighty brain and that iron resolution."

There's more. Lee's Dracula is also a being of raw sensuality, great nobility, and tragic isolation. Don't skip over that last element: Lee was intent on making that part of his portrayal, and that became a key element in all of the Dracula interpretations and most of the vampire portrayals to follow.

"Vampires are the monsters that people relate to," comments writer-producer Joss Whedon, the creator of TV's *Buffy the Vampire Slayer* and *Angel*. "They look like everybody else, but they're not like everybody else. The vampire is the most beautiful, exalted, superior version of something that is not human and is all alone. And they represent that kind of aloneness, but they represent that in a very romantic fashion. And people relate to that because everybody ultimately feels alone. And everybody is alone and different. There always is that sense of isolation."

It is indeed a shame that Lee never got the chance to play the role in a faithful adaptation of Stoker's novel. As effective as it is, after all, *Horror of Dracula* is hardly a model of fidelity to its source.

Hammer Studios got rolling in the horror field with the 1957 release of *The Curse of Frankenstein*. Terence

Fisher directed, Jimmy Sangster wrote the script, Peter Cushing played Victor Frankenstein, and Lee portrayed the monster. The four Hammer horror pioneers reunited for the following year's *Horror of Dracula*. Although Sangster's screenplay successfully shattered the hold of the 1920s play by Hamilton Deane and John L. Balderston, it, too, took great liberties with Stoker's story.

The film opens with Jonathan Harker (John Van Eyssen) traveling to Transylvania to become the new librarian at Castle Dracula. He is not there to tell the count of an estate secured for him near London. This Jonathan Harker is on quite a different mission: he is there to kill Count Dracula. The librarian gig is just a ruse to get close to the vampire, who admires a picture of Harker's fiancée, Lucy (Carol Marsh). In case things go wrong, Harker is keeping a secret journal for his associate, Van Helsing (Cushing).

Things do go wrong. Instead of destroying Dracula, Harker is transformed into a vampire. Van Helsing arrives to find Dracula gone and his friend now one of the undead. He stakes Jonathan, little knowing that Dracula is on his way to England and Lucy. We've strayed a good distance from the Lugosi film, but we're plenty far removed from Stoker's book as well.

Sangster has made Lucy and Mina (Melissa Stribling) sisters, and Mina isn't Jonathan's intended; she's the wife of Arthur (Michael Gough). Dropped completely are John Seward, Quincey P. Morris, and Renfield.

Lucy, too, is turned into a bloodlust creature of the night granted release by a well-pounded wooden stake (folks, these Hammer films just sizzle with sexuality). Dracula takes aim on Mina, escaping back to his castle. Van Helsing confronts him there, and, after a terrific tussle, fashions a cross from two candlesticks and forces the count into the morning sunlight. The dawn's rays reduce Dracula to dust, making a sequel tough (but not impossible, as *Dracula, Prince of Darkness* would prove in 1966).

Any claims of faithfulness to the book disintegrated long before the count. Sunlight, of course, was not fatal to Stoker's Dracula. Harker, instead of being killed, is in on the kill at the end of the novel. Van Helsing is an observer to Dracula's demise, not the direct combatant. And, well, as Lee himself pointed out many times, this really wasn't the book.

Yet it was an energetic and energizing effort. It reestablished Dracula as the king of the monsters, and it established a Hammer horror formula that kept moviegoers entranced into the early 1970s: Lee and/or Cushing in starring roles, plenty of blood, plenty of young women in revealing outfits. And it established Cushing and Lee as the Boris Karloff and Bela Lugosi of their generation. What Karloff and Lugosi had been to Universal Studios, Cushing and Lee were to Hammer.

Lee was thirty-five when this film was made; Cushing was forty-four. Thanks greatly to their robust performances, *Horror of Dracula* positively crackles with intensity and vitality. Fresh blood, I'd say. Compare the Bela Lugosi–Edward Van Sloan face-off

with the Lee-Cushing showdown—the first being a drawing-room stare-down, the second being an all-out brawl. Try to picture Lugosi and Van Sloan in the fierce finale of *Horror of Dracula*: it doesn't work.

What does work is Lee's portrayal, which kicks open exciting possibilities previously closed off by the Deane-Balderston concept. That takes strength, and Lee, standing tall—really tall—in the title role, has strength to spare. And that's saying a mouthful.

Speaking of a mouthful, Lee earned the distinction of becoming the first actor to sport fangs while playing Dracula in an English-speaking film. The screenplay for the 1931 called for fangs, but Universal yanked them. Lee was not, however, the first screen Dracula to wear fangs. An interesting footnote (or headnote, as the case may be) to *Dracula* history is the discovery of the 1953 Turkish film *Drakula Istanbul'da* (Dracula in Istanbul). It starred a fang-bearing Atif Kaptan, who donned evening clothes like Lugosi and sported the bald look like Schreck. Even though this movie was the first to use many scenes from Stoker's novel, it also made wholesale changes. More intriguingly, almost twenty years before the publication of Raymond T. McNally and Radu Florescu's *In Search of Dracula*, director Mehmet Muhtar's film made a link between Stoker's vampire and the historical figure of Vlad the Impaler. Stoker's book is listed as a source, as is Ali Riga Seifi's *Kastgli Voyvoda* (The Impaling Voivode).

Interview with the Vampire (Actor)

· · · · · · · · · · · ·

". . . he saw a tall, thin man, who was not like any of the crew."
—*Captain's log of the* Demeter, Dracula, *chapter 7*

No actor has made more screen appearances as Count Dracula than Christopher Lee. He first donned the vampire cape for Terence Fisher's *Horror of Dracula* (released in England as *Dracula*) in 1958, returning to the role for six sequels: *Dracula, Prince of Darkness* (1966; dir. Terence Fisher), *Dracula Has Risen from the Grave* (1968; dir. Freddie Francis), *Taste the Blood of Dracula* (1969; dir. Peter Sasdy), *Scars of Dracula* (1970; dir. Roy Ward Baker), *Dracula A.D. 1972* (1972; dir. Alan Gibson), and *The Satanic Rites of Dracula* (1973; dir. Alan Gibson; a.k.a. *Count Dracula and His Vampire Brides*). In 1970, he starred in director Jess Franco's *El Conde Dracula* (Count Dracula), which Lee hoped would be a faithful adaptation of Stoker's novel. He also narrated and appeared as Vlad the Impaler in the 1974 documentary *In Search of Dracula*, based on the Raymond T. McNally and Radu Florescu book. And he appeared as the Dracula-like Baron Roderico da Frankurten in the 1959 Italian comedy *Tempi duri per I Vampiri* (Hard Times for Vampires, a.k.a. *My Uncle the Vampire* and *Uncle was a Vampire*; dir. Steno) and as the count again for the 1976 French comedy *Dracula pere et fils* (Dracula and Son; dir. Édouard Molinaro). For those keeping count at home, that's nine films as Dracula and two more with Dracula connections.

Born May 27, 1922, Lee's range as an actor extends well beyond horror roles. But the six-foot-five actor stands tall as a screen villain in fantasy films in general and supernatural stories in particular. In the midst of playing Saruman in Peter Jackson's *Lord of the Rings* movies, Count Dooku in the *Star Wars* films, and Flay in Andy Wilson's BBC miniseries of Mervyn Peake's *Gormenghast* novels (2000), Lee talked about horror roles, fantasy projects, villains, and Dracula.

What follows are some pertinent quotes from Christopher Lee.

On being linked to some of literature's great fantasy titles:

I seem to be associated with these authors who, like Jonathan Swift, swept readers to these wonderfully imaginative worlds with bizarre characters: J. R .R. Tolkien and *The Lord of the Rings*, Mervyn Peake and *Gormenghast*, Bram Stoker and *Dracula*. The difference, of course, is that *The Lord of the Rings* and *Gormenghast* are extraordinary realizations of books people said could never be brought to the screen. They're stunning and they're faithful, whereas *Dracula* never has been brought to the screen in a manner that's either stunning or faithful.

On the appeal of fantasy stories:

We are fascinated with what's outside our knowledge, outside our experience. Fantasy takes us away from the drab realities of everyday life into an enchanted world. That's fascinating, whether the fantasy is exciting, funny, inspiring, sad, horrifying. You find contemporary parallels in all of these books, and that's because human nature doesn't change. Horror stories always are about what people are capable of doing.

On how to play a monster:

I go back to how John Barrymore played Mr. Hyde in the silent version of Stevenson's story. Barrymore still managed to maintain the human appearance, although it was evil. It's a remarkable performance. Fredric March's interpretation was more simian, and the Spencer Tracy portrayal was almost non-human. I think that's wrong, because he is human,

although the personification of the essence of evil. I always kept that in mind when playing Dracula. If you don't let people see the human part, no matter how evil, you miss the bigger meaning of the character.

On how to play Dracula:

Anthony Hopkins said, and I'll borrow it, "I don't play villains, I play people." That was my approach to Dracula. He had this great nobility and this great dignity, which you get from Stoker's book. And I played this great strength, power, and cunning, which you also find in the book. But I also tried to invest him with a sense of sadness. He is cursed, after all, and he is isolated, and he is evil. All of that makes a very lonely man, and I certainly tried to get that into the performance. He's inhuman, but you can't make him non-human.

On leaving behind the role in 1976:

I never said I wouldn't play Dracula again. Indeed, if someone had stepped forward with a superior script that was faithful to Stoker's novel, I would have loved to play it. That never happened.

On his huge fan following from fantasy projects:

I am aware of it. I've always had a vast amount of mail from the United States, and it's always so positive and so refreshing and so encouraging. And I'm very grateful.

On being known for horror roles:

Once in a while, people do mistake the image on the screen with the actor. They might say, "I saw you as

Dracula and it scared the hell out of me." But most people are very savvy about that. I knew Boris Karloff very well. I was in three films with him. And he was the most wonderful man. You look at people known for horror roles: Lon Chaney, Boris Karloff, Bela Lugosi, Claude Rains, Basil Rathbone. These were splendid actors. These weren't splendid horror actors. They were splendid actors.

SIDEBAR

Model Behavior

· · · · · · · · · · ·

He made no motion of stepping to meet me, but stood like a statue. . . .
—*Jonathan Harker,* Dracula, *chapter 2*

The 1957 Universal Studios release of the *Shock* films series to television created a monster merchandising boom. Publisher James Warren and editor Forrest J Ackerman helped fuel the explosion by unleashing the first issue of their *Famous Monsters of Filmland* magazine in February 1958. It stuck around for twenty-five years (190 issues) in its original run, inspiring such other monster-minded magazines as *Castle of Frankenstein, Cinefantastique,* and *The Monster Times.* Dracula

made his first appearance on a *Famous Monsters* cover with issue number 22 in 1963 (Bela Lugosi's count putting the death squeeze on Dwight Frye's Renfield). In all, the count would appear on the magazine's cover fifteen times (six with the face of Lugosi, five with Christopher Lee).

Aurora, a Long Island company specializing in "all plastic assembly kits," took the next major merchandising step in 1961. They issued the first in what ultimately would be a series of thirteen monster model kits. It was not a step taken lightly. The plastic-model industry had long been dominated by cars and airplanes, although some companies, like Aurora, also offered historical figures, presidents, knights, soldiers, cowboys, horses, birds, battleships, tanks, submarines, sailing ships, ocean liners, and helicopters. Aurora executives weren't at all sure that it was appropriate to market monsters to kids. Would monster models cause nightmares? Would they lead to aberrant behavior in youngsters? Would they damage frail psyches?

Dracula was a frequent cover boy for Famous Monsters of Filmland *magazine and its many successors, including* Cinefantastique (*this December 1992 issue shows Gary Oldman as the Count*).

Aurora Plastics Corp., headquartered in West Hempstead, New York, went so far as to consult child psychologists, who gave the company the okay to ink a deal with Universal. Aurora was told that the monster models might actually be beneficial in helping children cope with fears. So the first kit, Frankenstein, appeared in 1961 with an eye-catching color drawing by James Bama on its thirteen-inch "long box" format cover. It was a monster hit.

The second Aurora monster model, sculpted by Bill Lemon and issued in 1962, was Dracula. The cover, another Bama stunner, showed Dracula on the stairs of his castle, surrounded by bats, ready to lure his victim (or the buyer) into a hypnotic trance. The drawing was based on a publicity picture taken of Lugosi for Charles Barton's *Abbott and Costello Meet Frankenstein* (1948).

Aurora's 1962 Dracula model.

Inside the box were the kit's forty-two black pieces, along with instructions on how to paint and assemble them: "Do not hurry. Work carefully and patiently." The joy of this process is unimaginable to those who have never spread newspaper across the dining room table, carefully lined up the necessary bottles of enamel paint, and thrilled to the odor wafting from an opened tube of plastic cement (glue, to you civilians; and the odor typically was followed by a mother's warning not to "smell that stuff").

The instructions told you to paint the inside of the cape red, the shirt front white, weed patches green, the rocks gray. When you were done, you had an eight-and-a-half-inch model of the count standing next to a tree in which hung two bats. For Dracula fans, it just didn't get any better than this. For the first time, budding horror enthusiasts could display a Lugosi-like Dracula on shelves in their rooms, drifting off to sleep with visions of vampire bats dancing in their heads.

The same year that Aurora's Dracula model became a best-seller, Bobby "Boris" Pickett had a smash hit with the novelty song "Monster Mash." Pickett talked his way through the number, imitating Boris Karloff and tossing in a quick impression of Lugosi: "Whatever happened to my Transylvania Twist?"

The first seven Aurora monster models were based on Universal Studios classics. Frankenstein and Dracula were followed by the Wolf Man, the Mummy, the Phantom of the Opera, the Creature from the Black Lagoon, and the Hunchback of Notre Dame. Dr. Jekyll as Mr. Hyde, King Kong, and Godzilla joined the lineup in 1964. The Bride of Frankenstein and the Witch hit stores in 1965. And the thirteenth Aurora monster model, the Forgotten Prisoner of Castle-Mare (a skeleton chained in a dungeon), put in his appearance in 1966.

Cars helped drive the model industry after World War II, so perhaps it was inevitable that Aurora would find a way to give the monsters wheels. In 1964, the company unveiled Dracula's Dragster, a plastic model of Dracula driving a coffin-style hot rod complete with spiderweb wheels, bat hubcaps, and candlestick headlights. Holding a martini glass filled with blood, the count sported a driving cap, his cape trailing behind him like a scarf. Following him down this Aurora road were four other monster cars: Frankenstein's Flivver, the Wolf Man's Wagon, the Mummy's Chariot, and King Kong's Thronester. The following year, AMT issued the Dragula, a plastic model kit based on Grandpa's coffin hot rod designed by car customizer George Barris for the *The Munsters* TV series. Barris used an actual coffin for the working car, introduced in "Hot Rod Herman," the episode that aired May 27, 1965.

AMT released a plastic model version of the Dragula, Grandpa's coffin hot rod on The Munsters.

Other merchandisers took notice when Aurora scared up big business with its monster models. There were soon Universal-sanctioned toys, puzzles, Pez candy dispensers, drinking glasses, and masks. Dracula was noticeably absent from the set of six plastic Universal monster figures—Frankenstein, the Wolf Man, the Mummy, the Phantom, the Creature, and the Hunchback—marketed by Louis Marx and Co. in 1968. But he was back in glow-in-the-dark versions of the Aurora models and later reissues by other companies. More than forty-five years after the Aurora Dracula model made its debut, the Internet or horror convention shopper can find Dracula models, busts, figurines, and action figures representing almost every incarnation of the character, from Lee and Lugosi to *Nosferatu* and Vlad the Impaler. They are made of plastic, plaster, resin, vinyl, fiberglass, paper, polystone, and many other substances. Standing still as statues, they speak volumes about the continuing fascination with the character that became the very model of how a vampire looks and acts.

Video Vampire: Dracula on TV

. . . .

"It's in the air."
—Mr. Swales, Dracula, *chapter 6*

The television history of Count Dracula is believed to start with John Carradine's portrayal in the title role of the live *Matinee Theatre* production of *Dracula* in 1956. It includes several documentaries and specials, and, on Halloween night 2000, the USA network premiered *Dark Prince: The True Story of Dracula* starring Rudolf Matin as Vlad Tepes. "My sacred mission is to bring order to Romania," decreed this Dracula. "If someone lies or commits any injustice, he is not likely to stay alive, whether nobleman, priest, or common man. . . . If they say I'm a vindictive man, they fear me. And that is well."

Here are ten landmark TV moments that followed this January 1956 presentation.

The Munsters (CBS, 1964–66): Universal turned its classic monsters into a suburban sitcom family, much to the delight of young horror fans watching *Shock Theatre*, buying Aurora model kits, and reading *Famous Monsters of Filmland* magazine. Al Lewis, cast as Grandpa, gave us Dracula as a Borscht Belt comic. He had a marble slab in the attic, a mad scientist's laboratory in the basement, a pet bat named Ygor, a cigar in his jacket's inside pocket, and an accent that was more Ebbets Field than Borgo Pass.

Mystery and Imagination (BBC, November 1968): Denholm Elliot, perhaps best known to movie audiences later as Coleman in *Trading Places* and Marcus Brody in the three *Indiana Jones* films, was an unlikely choice to play Dracula in this fourth-season episode of the British anthology series. The supporting cast included Corin Redgrave as Jonathan Harker, Susan George as Lucy Weston (changed from Westenra), Suzanne Neve as Mina, James Maxwell as Dr. Seward, Bernard Archard as Van Helsing, and Joan Hickson (who would later play Miss Marple) as Mrs. Weston. During its 1966–70 run, the program also presented adaptations of Joseph Thomas Sheridan Le Fanu's "Carmilla," Edgar Allan Poe's "The Fall of the House of Usher" and "The Tell-Tale Heart," Robert Louis Stevenson's "The Body Snatcher" and "The Suicide Club," Mary Wolstonecraft Shelley's

Frankenstein, and Oscar Wilde's "The Canterville Ghost."

Rod Serling's Night Gallery (NBC, October 27, 1971): Francis Lederer, star of Paul Landres's *The Return of Dracula* (1958) returned to the role for "The Devil is Not Mocked," a dandy episode in Serling's horror anthology series.

Sesame Street (PBS, 1972): The educational children's series introduced Count von Count, a Lugosi-like vampire Muppet who helped youngsters learn to count.

Bram Stoker's Dracula (CBS, February 8, 1974): *Dark Shadows* creator Dan Curtis was the producer and director behind this TV movie starring Jack Palance as the vampire king. Palance was terrific, and Curtis had the ideal writer adapting Stoker's novel: Richard Matheson had written the landmark vampire novel *I Am Legend* (1954) and the teleplay version of Jeff Rice's *The Night Stalker* for the 1972 Curtis-produced TV movie. Matheson had planned a largely faithful three-hour adaptation, but wholesale changes were required when CBS gave Curtis only two hours for the story. "I think it came as close as you could with just two hours, but there was quite a bit missing," Matheson has said. "I would have loved to see it at three hours. . . . That would have been dandy. Then we could have done it to a fare-thee-well. But even at the shorter time, it still came off very well." Matheson, unlike most previous screenwriters, actually used Stoker's book, and he incorporated scholars Raymond T. McNally and Radu Florescu's recently published research

on Vlad the Impaler. He also borrowed the *Dark Shadows* TV series' idea of the vampire being drawn to the reincarnation of his lost love (an idea later used in director Francis Ford Coppola's 1992 film *Bram Stoker's Dracula*). The TV movie is something of a missed opportunity, but it is very effective, with strong performances by Simon Ward as Arthur, Nigel Davenport as Van Helsing, Penelope Horner as Mina, Fiona Lewis as Lucy, Murray Brown as Harker, and, of course, Palance as Dracula. "Jack suggested unbelievable power by his very presence," Curtis comments. "You believed that Jack could pick you up by the throat and lift you off the ground. That's because he really could do that."

Count Dracula (BBC, 1977): Aired as a three-part miniseries, this lavish British production remains the most faithful adaptation of Stoker's novel. Many passages from the book are dramatized here for the first—and thus far the only—time. The strong cast includes Frank Finlay as Van Helsing, Judy Bowker as Mina, Bosco Hogan as Harker, Susan Penhaligon as Lucy, Mark Burns as Seward, Richard Barnes as Quincey (yes, Quincey finally made it—sort of), and Jack Shepherd as Renfield. Some baffling choices were made: the BBC team decided to make Mina and Lucy sisters; they combined Quincey Morris and Lord Godalming into the composite character of American diplomat Quincey P. Holmwood; and Dracula, played by Louis Jourdan, was portrayed as a suave seducer in the Lugosi mold (no mustache, no white hair). Jourdan's performance is the main drawback to this handsome miniseries; there are scenes where he's downright creepy, but the French actor lacks the raw power and towering presence of Christopher Lee or Jack Palance. Take Palance from the 1974 TV movie, put him in this often-daring production, and you're awfully close to having the definitive screen *Dracula*.

Cliffhangers (NBC, 1979): Michael Nouri, one of several actors later considered for the lead role in Coppola's film, played the count in the "Curse of Dracula" segment of this series that presented three continuing stories in an hour of prime-time television. His Dracula is a history professor teaching (night classes, of course) at a California university.

Dracula: The Series (syndicated, 1990–91): In this American TV series, Geordie Johnson played Dracula posing as Alexander Lucard, a blonde millionaire businessman who was more investor than impaler. The hip, modern Dracula routinely tangled with two boys living with their Uncle Gustav (Bernard Behrens), the great-grandson of Professor Van Helsing. Gustav's son was played by Geraint Wyn Davies, who would later star as vampire police detective Nick Knight on TV's *Forever Knight* (1989–96).

Buffy the Vampire Slayer (WB, February 26, 2000): German actor Rudolf Martin, who that same year played Vlad Tepes in the TV movie *Dark Prince: The True Story of Dracula*, made a memorable guest star as the vampiric count in the episode "Buffy versus Dracula."

Dracula (BBC, 2006): American fans of Stoker's novel bared their fangs

when this plodding and listless version showed up on the American PBS series *Masterpiece Theatre* in 2007. Worse than undead, it was deadly dull. Writer Stewart Harcourt took an anti-Stoker approach, sapping all the sense of excitement, suspense, and eerie fun from the mighty terror tale. His ill-advised revisionist script was so stridently intent on delivering a treatise about Victorian hangups that it ultimately owed far more to Henry James than Bram Stoker. The ninety-minute adaptation cavalierly tossed away the best elements of the book. More a radical reinvention than a reworking of the novel, it has the noble Arthur (Dan Stevens) suffering from syphilis and, believing that Count Dracula (Marc Warren) can cure him, actually sending Jonathan Harker (Rafe Spall) to Transylvania to arrange the vampire king's trip to London. Right about here, any devotee of the book is approximating Dracula's snarl when confronted by a fresh box of garlic. But wait, it gets worse: David Suchet's Van Helsing enters the story acting more like the deranged Renfield (who isn't in this adaptation). I'm not sure what this was, but it wasn't Bram Stoker's *Dracula*. It wasn't even a close blood relation.

Buffy Summers (Sarah Michelle Gellar), pictured here with vampire Spike (James Marsters), met Dracula (played by German actor Rudolf Martin) in a 2000 episode of Buffy the Vampire Slayer.

145

The Bloodlines: Dracula's Descendants

. . . .

"The vampire live on, and cannot die by mere passing of the time. . . ."
—*Professor Van Helsing,* Dracula, *chapter 18*

There were romanticized vampires before Bram Stoker's creation of Count Dracula, but the vampire king was, for the most part, pure predator. He was a thing of evil, driven by his lust for blood. And thus the vampire remained for about seventy years.

Sure, there were hints of regret and weariness in John Carradine's portrayal of Dracula, and there was the longing to be free of the vampire curse in Lambert Hillyer's *Dracula's Daughter* (1936). But the predatory nature of the vampire remained the driving force from 1897 until 1967. Richard Matheson significantly advanced the vampire novel in 1954 with *I Am Legend*. The future screenwriter of Dan Curtis's 1974 TV movie *Bram Stoker's Dracula* explored logical reasons behind aspects of vampire lore: the aversion to garlic, the avoidance of sunlight, the need for blood. "I think it was unusual in the fact that I considered it to be science fiction, not a horror story," Matheson comments. "I thought I was pretty clever in how I examined the vampire legend and explained it with scientific means. I

tried to take each of the vampire legends and find a scientific reason behind it. I did research with a doctor, for instance. I did a lot of research for that book."

But as important a book as *I Am Legend* was, it did not significantly advance the vampire character. That job fell to Barnabas Collins, the vampire played by Shakespearean actor Jonathan Frid on the ABC afternoon soap opera *Dark Shadows* (1966–71). Frid gave us the vampire as Hamlet—a brooding figure tortured by a conscience and self-doubt. Barnabas, unlike Dracula, was a vampire fighting against his own nature: "Must I be this way? Is it possible to change?"

Dan Curtis, the producer behind the supernatural soap opera, introduced Barnabas as a 175-year-old vampire let out of his chained coffin in April 1967. Barnabas was first intended to be a New England version of Dracula—a monster that, at the end of three months, would have a stake driven through his heart. "I brought the vampire in, and it suddenly became this gigantic hit," Curtis recalls. "Then I thought, 'Now what am I going to do?' I couldn't kill him off, so

146

that's when I turned him into the reluctant vampire. It really caught the imagination of the audience."

Barnabas blasted the way for Anne Rice's endlessly introspective vampires, most notably Louis and Lestat. He also paved the way for new, increasingly sympathetic interpretations of Dracula. This was evident in the portrayals by Jack Palance (in the 1974 TV movie written by Matheson and directed by Curtis), Frank Langella (on stage and screen), and Gary Oldman (in Francis Ford Coppola's 1992 *Bram Stoker's Dracula*). Pastiche novels built on this, giving us Dracula as a crime fighter, dashing hero, and romantic figure. This, in turn, created the path for *Angel*, the *Buffy the Vampire Slayer* TV spinoff that premiered in 1999. David Boreanaz played the brooding title character, a vampire with a soul/conscience.

"The longer the vampire character has been around, the more he has evolved from predator to wanting to be more human," Boreanaz comments. "There's the battle between the desire for blood and the desire to be more human—the inner battles, the exorcising of demons. But the basic allure has remained the same, and that's the combination of immortality, power, and sensuality. And it's wrapped up with a worldly charming appeal. There are so many spices and ingredients in the appeal."

Novels and movies have gone back and forth, fielding both predatory and romanticized vampires. On the predatory side of the street, you would find Kurt Barlow in Stephen King's, *Salem's Lot* (1975), Janos Skorzeny in Jeff Rice's *The Night Stalker* (1973), and Prince Vulkan

Gloria Holden had the title role in the 1936 film Dracula's Daughter.

David Boreanaz's Angel was one of the most notable post-Dracula vampires.

in Robert R. McCammon's *They Thirst* (1981). The movies gave us Robert Quarry in the starring role in Bob Kelljan's *Count Yorga, Vampire* (1970), Chris Sarandon as Jerry Dandridge in Tom Holland's *Fright Night* (1985), Edward Herrmann as Max in Joel Schumacher's *The Lost Boys* (1987), Rutger Hauer as Lothos in Fran Rubel Kuzui's *Buffy the Vampire Slayer* (1992), Thomas Ian Griffith as Valek in John Carpenter's *Vampires* (1998), and the vampire hordes in Robert Rodriguez's *From Dusk till Dawn* (1996).

On the heroic side of the street, television series gave us Geraint Wyn Davies as vampire police detective Nick Knight in *Forever Knight*, Boreanaz as Angel, Kyle Schmid as Henry Fitzroy in *Blood Ties,* and Alex O'Laughlin as vampire private detective Mick St. John in *Moonlight.*

Caught somewhere between were William Marshall as Prince Mamuwalde in the early 1970s *Blacula* films and James Marsters as the ever-changing Spike on the *Buffy* TV series. These are just a few of the Dracula descendants. Whether sinister or sympathetic, they all qualify as his "children of the night."

The Changing Face of Van Helsing

· · · · · · · · · · ·

*"No trifling with me! I never jest! There is grim purpose in what
I do, and I warn you that you do not thwart me."*
—*Professor Van Helsing,* Dracula, *chapter 10*

The 1931 film version of *Dracula* gave us an image of the count that remains prevalent more than seventy-five years later. It did the same for stalwart vampire hunter Abraham Van Helsing. Edward Van Sloan seemed everything one would want in a Van Helsing—wise yet wily, professorial yet personable, soft-spoken yet iron-willed, religious yet rational.

Like Bela Lugosi (and *with* Lugosi), Van Sloan perfected his paternal portrayal on the Broadway stage. Night after night, Van Sloan delivered the play's closing curtain speech: "Just a moment, ladies and gentlemen! Just a word before you go. We hope the memories of Dracula and Renfield won't give you bad dreams, so just a word of reassurance. When you get home tonight and the lights have been turned out and you are afraid to look behind the curtains and you dread to see a face appear at the window . . . why, just pull yourself together and remember that, after all, *there are such things.*"

There are such things. It was Van Helsing's basic message in Stoker's book. Van Sloan filmed the famous speech, which was included in the original release of Tod Browning's 1931 *Dracula*. It was cut from the 1938 rerelease, and the footage lost. We have only stills and a few seconds of Van Sloan standing on a stage, in front of a movie screen.

Yet the impact of Van Sloan's performance wasn't lost on audiences. His Van Helsing, embracing both science and superstition, became the model for the fearless vampire hunter. But as our image of Dracula changed through the decades, so did that of his equally cagey adversary: each generation fashioned a Dracula in its own image, and each generation tended to do the same with Van Helsing.

After Van Sloan, the actor most associated with Van Helsing is Peter Cushing, who played Van Helsing or Van Helsing descendants in five horror films, starting with Terence Fisher's *Horror of Dracula* in 1958. He reprised the role for the

Dracula-less sequel, Fisher's *The Brides of Dracula* (1960), then played characters named Van Helsing in *Dracula A.D. 1972* (1972; dir. Alan Gibson), *The Satanic Rites of Dracula* (1973; dir. Alan Gibson; a.k.a. *Count Dracula and His Vampire Brides*), and *The Legend of the 7 Golden Vampires* (1974; dir. Roy Don Baker). The tall, lean, athletic, and very British Van Helsing of *Horror of Dracula* was a marked departure from Van Sloan's portrayal. This Van Helsing could leap across tables and believably engage in hand-to-hand combat with the count.

If you fast-forward to 2004 and Hugh Jackman's star turn in Stephen Sommers's *Van Helsing*, there might be a tendency to assume that the good professor became younger, hunkier, and more vital with each new interpretation. Pitting the vampire hunter against Count Vladislaus Dracula (Richard Roxburgh), *Van Helsing* gave us the title character as dashing comic-book action hero.

But between Cushing and Jackman were many types of Van Helsings. Recalling both Van Sloan and Cushing, for instance, was Nigel Davenport in Dan Curtis's 1974 TV movie *Bram Stoker's Dracula*. Frank Finlay made the professor humorous and eccentric in the 1977 BBC miniseries. The stage was set, so to speak, for two Van Helsings who had won Academy Awards for best actor.

The most accomplished and acclaimed star to tackle the role was Laurence Olivier, who played Van Helsing in John Badham's 1979 film version of *Dracula*. Anthony Hopkins was not only eccentric, but at times manic, as Van Helsing in

Van Helsing goes Van Hunky, with Hugh Jackman as the monster-battling hero of Van Helsing.

Francis Ford Coppola's *Bram Stoker's Dracula* (1992). This was more in keeping with Stoker's novel than one might suspect. In the book, Van Helsing is by turns kind, cruel, subtle, blunt, chivalrous, and callous. At one point in the novel, he gives way to hysterics, laughing until he cries, then crying until he laughs. Later, Seward fears he is on the verge of a similar collapse.

The many shadings Stoker gave Van Helsing left him open to interpretation. Fred Saberhagen's 1975 novel *The Dracula Tape* had the count depict his adversary as a dangerous meddler. Patrick Lussier's *Dracula 2000* (2000) presented Van Helsing (Christopher Plummer) as a wealthy London antiques dealer keeping Dracula (Gerard Butler) prisoner and himself alive with injections of the vampire's filtered blood.

Dracula was played for laughs by Mel Brooks in his own *Dracula: Dead and Loving It* (1995), and as a shambling wreck by David Suchet in the BBC's 2006 TV adaptation. Bela Lugosi's Dracula calls Van Helsing a wise man for someone who has not lived even a single lifetime. Thanks to the movies and television, however, Van Helsing, like the count, has already been allowed several lifetimes—with the promise of more to come.

The Night Stalkers: Van Helsing's Descendants

. . . .

"You are hunters of the wild beast. . . ."
—*Professor Van Helsing,* Dracula, *chapter 23*

Bram Stoker's Van Helsing not only set the model for stalwart vampire hunters, he set in motion a battalion of supernatural sleuths plying their trade in books, movies, radio programs, comic books, and television shows. On the heels of *Dracula*, horror specialist Algernon Blackwood published stories featuring paranormal investigator John Silence that appeared in the first decade of the twentieth century.

Silence, the "physician extraordinary," was more of a general practitioner, however, and it was up to fantasy legend Richard Matheson to introduce a new kind of vampire-hunting specialist in *I Am Legend* (1954). Matheson's Robert Neville is the ultimate loner—a survivor isolated in a world overrun by vampires. He ventures out by day to stake as many of the undead as possible, even though the odds are overwhelming.

Matheson had a connection to the next significant vampire slayer, Carl Kolchak, the hard-nosed reporter played by Darren McGavin in the 1972 TV movie *The Night Stalker*. Kolchak had elements of Van Helsing and Neville, but, charging after a vampire in Las Vegas, he seemed more like a refugee from a 1930s Hollywood newspaper comedy.

There were several significant vampire hunters to follow Van Helsing, Neville, and Kolchak, including Blade the vampire slayer (an African American warrior created for Marvel Comics and played on screen by Wesley Snipes in Stephen Norrington's 1998 film *Blade*), Captain Kronos (played by Horst Janson in Brian Clemens's 1974 *Captain Kronos—Vampire Hunter*), and Peter Vincent (Roddy McDowall), the horror host who reluctantly battles the undead in Tom Holland's *Fright Night* (1985).

But none made a bigger impact than Buffy Summers, first played primarily for laughs by Kristy Swanson in Fran Rubel Kuzui's 1992 film *Buffy the Vampire Slayer*. Writer-producer Joss Whedon dug deeper into vampire lore, supernatural storytelling, and character development for the 1997–2003 TV version of *Buffy the Vampire Slayer*, which starred Sarah Michelle Gellar as the stake-wielding teen heroine.

The formula has remained constant since *Dracula*: if you play the vampire as stalker, you also get slayers. And you know Van Helsing would welcome Neville, Kolchak, Blade, Kronos, Vincent, and Buffy on his team.

Counting Up, Part One:
Nosferatu Revisited

. . . .

*". . . you would in time, when you had died, have become nosferatu,
as they call it. . . ."*
—*Professor Van Helsing,* Dracula, *chapter 16*

German writer-director Werner Herzog paid tribute to F. W. Murnau's *Nosferatu* with a very strange homage-remake of the 1922 silent classic. Released in 1979, it was known in America and the United Kingdom as *Nosferatu the Vampyre* (German title: *Nosferatu: Phantom der Nacht*). The film received mixed reviews, and it continues to be a topic of debate among Draculphiles.

It remains a great favorite with Herzog enthusiasts and many vampire fans, but what's stylish to some is stilted to others. So the full-color *Nosferatu* has its champions and its detractors. Leading *Dracula* authority David J. Skal certainly is no great admirer of the film starring Klaus Kinski as the count, Isabelle Adjani as Lucy, Bruno Ganz as Jonathan, and the French artist-writer Roland Topor as Renfield. Although Skal praises Kinski (made up to resemble Max Schreck in Murnau's original), he has little good to say about Herzog's direction or the other performances: "The film consists largely of preciously attenuated impressions of the Murnau

Klaus Kinski already had played Renfield when he was tapped to play Dracula in director Werner Herzog's remake of Nosferatu.

film," Skal writes in *Hollywood Gothic: The Tangled Web of Dracula from Novel to Stage to Screen,* adding that the "cast, director, and editor all appear to be stoned."

He'd get a lively argument from critics who find the film sensationally surrealistic. They see a mesmerizing visual masterpiece that's as moody as it is disturbing. Film historian Leonard Maltin calls the movie a "spooky, funny, reverent remake."

Well, the remake is not as faithful to the 1922 film as sometimes claimed. Major deviations include: Van Helsing driving a stake into the sun-exposed Dracula; Harker being turned into a vampire; Van Helsing arrested for "murdering" Dracula (as he is in the beginning of Lambert Hillyer's *Dracula's Daughter*, 1936).

Although dispatched by sunlight and a stake at the end of Herzog's film, Kinski returns (sort of) as an un-undead for Augusto Caminato and Mario Cainano's *Nosferatu a Venezia* (Nosferatu in Venice, 1988). This time the actor refused to shave his head, so his vampire, called Nosferatu for the Italian release, stalked the night with scraggly blond hair. Disappointing as it was, *Nosferatu a Venezia* featured one actor with a past *Dracula* connection and one with a future connection: Donald Pleasance had already played Dr. Seward (in John Badham's 1979 version of *Dracula*), and Christopher Plummer would go on to play Van Helsing in Patrick Lussier's *Dracula 2000* (2000).

Yet it is Kinski's performance in Herzog's film that provides the best trivia item. Having played Renfield to Christopher Lee's vampire king in Jess Franco's *Nachts, wenn Dracula erwacht* (1970; a.k.a. *Count Dracula*), he became the only actor to play both Renfield and Dracula in major screen adaptations of Bram Stoker's novel.

Gothic artist Joseph Vargo's Nosferatu *was inspired by the vampire look of Max Schreck in the 1922 silent film of the same name and Klaus Kinski in the 1979 remake. (Artwork © Joseph Vargo)*

Counting Up, Part Two: Hello, Sexy!

. . . .

By her side stood a tall, thin man, clad in black. His face was turned from us, but the instant we saw we all recognized the Count. . . .
—Dr. *John Seward,* Dracula, *chapter 21*

Three very different Draculas were on movie screens in 1979. Klaus Kinski was downright icky as the vile vampire in Werner Herzog's remake *Nosferatu the Vampyre*; George Hamilton was screamingly funny taking off on Bela Lugosi in Stan Dragoti's spoof *Love at First Bite*; and, grabbing most of the attention, Frank Langella sent hearts aflutter as the screen's sexiest count in John Badham's steamy updating of *Dracula*.

Dracula had been portrayed as a romantic and romanticized figure since the 1920s, and Hamilton Deane's drawing-room play. Langella, who had played the count in a 1967 production at the Berkshire Theatre Festival, became a Broadway matinee idol in the 1977 revival of the Deane-John L. Balderston work. Directed by Dennis Rosa, with sets and costumes designed by Edward Gorey, this *Dracula* ran at the Martin Beck Theatre for more than two years and nine hundred performances.

The play won Tony Awards for best revival and best costume design. Langella was followed in the production by David

Dukes, Raul Julia, and Jean LeClerc. Jeremy Brett, later Sherlock Holmes on television, and Martin Landau, later Bela Lugosi in director Tim Burton's *Ed Wood* (1994), played the title role in touring productions.

Like Lugosi, Langella flew with Dracula to the big screen, repeating his stage interpretation for the Universal Studios film. This *Dracula* featured Laurence Olivier as Van Helsing, Kate Nelligan as Lucy, Donald Pleasance as Dr. Seward, and Trevor Eve as Jonathan. Set in the 1920s and to the music of John Williams, this version felt no obligation to stick to the play, which had felt no obligation to stick to the book: the doomed Mina becomes Van Helsing's daughter; Van Helsing is killed in the final showdown with Dracula; Dracula is killed when snared by a hook and forced into the sunlight (although the knowing look on Lucy's face suggests the possibility of escape for her vampire love).

"I think there's an aspect of the Count that's never been explored before—his vulnerability, his sensitivity, his fear," Langella was quoted as saying in the Universal press kit for *Dracula*. He continued,

> We don't go into it heavily but we do go into it in the film. I've always felt that he's the kind of man if he has lived for 500 years and experienced different times and different cultures and different peoples, he's bound to have gained a certain amount of philosophy about life. . . . What I had to find was the key to what would make him work today. I decided he was a highly vulnerable and erotic man—not cool and detached with no sense of humor or humanity. I didn't want him to appear stilted, stentorian or authoritarian as he was so often presented. I wanted to show a man who was evil, but lonely, and who could fall in love.

With his blow-dried hairdo, a cape draped over his shoulders, and a billowy white shirt open to the waist, Langella's Dracula cut a dashing figure that wouldn't have been out of place on the cover of a romance novel. The movie posters for *Dracula* emphasized this aspect of his performance, proclaiming, "Throughout history, he has filled the hearts of men with *terror*, and the hearts of women with *desire*."

Some have criticized Badham's *Dracula* for going too far in romanticizing the count. Langella's portrayal, though, found a champion in vampire expert J. Gordon Melton, who credited the actor

Frank Langella steams up the screen in the 1979 version of Dracula.

with bringing "a new depth and dimension to a part that had become rather narrowly stereotyped. . . . Langella created the most appealing and human Dracula since Lugosi. He played the character not as a traditional monster, but a creature of a different species."

Langella followed Lugosi's stage-to-screen Dracula path, but that's where it stopped. Refusing to be stereotyped, he put the cape away for good, eventually adding a third Tony Award to his shelf for his portrayal of Richard Nixon in the 2007 production of *Frost/Nixon*. He also played two other iconic figures from nineteenth-century literature for high-profile New York stage productions: Sherlock Holmes in *Sherlock's Last Case* (1987) and Ebenezer Scrooge in the musical version of *A Christmas Carol* (2000).

Counting Up, Part Three: Bram Stoker's Dracula?

· · · · · · · · · · ·

As we travel on the rough road, for a road of an
ancient and imperfect kind there was. . . .
—Professor Van Helsing, Dracula, *chapter 15*

Unless you count Orson Welles and the 1938 *Mercury Theatre* radio production of *Dracula*, Francis Ford Coppola remains the biggest-name director to tackle an adaptation of Bram Stoker's novel. Here was an offer vampire fans couldn't refuse. The Academy Award–winning filmmaker behind the *Godfather* epics was setting out to deliver the definitive screen version of *Dracula*. He released this effort as *Bram Stoker's Dracula* in November 1992.

Lucy and Mina were called by their correct names. All of the major characters, including Arthur Holmwood and Quincey Morris, were used. The climactic race back to Transylvania was depicted. Surely, this at last was a completely faithful big-screen adaptation, right?

Don't count on it. This wasn't Bram Stoker's *Dracula*. This was Francis Ford Coppola's *Dracula*.

Straying from Stoker, Coppola and his team embraced innovations and deviations used in previous adaptations. From the 1974 TV movie starring Jack Palance, they borrowed the link to Vlad the Impaler and the notion of Mina being the reincarnation of the count's lost true love. From the 1979 film starring Frank Langella,

Oscar-winning director Francis Ford Coppola was at the helm of the 1992 version of Dracula.

they took the highly romanticized and sympathetic depiction of Dracula.

The result was a mixed bag of delights and drawbacks. Among the major drawbacks were two miscast American actors playing British characters: Keanu Reeves as a stiff and listless Jonathan Harker and Winona Ryder as a melodramatic Mina. Far better were Gary Oldman in the title role, Anthony Hopkins as an eccentric Van Helsing, Richard E. Grant as Seward, Cary Elwes as Arthur, Sadie Frost as Lucy, Bill Campbell as Quincey Morris, and Tom Waits as Renfield. Oldman lacks the physical stature of Christopher Lee and Jack Palance, but he brings a lot to the castle table—intensity, cunning, nobility, loneliness, longing, and creepiness.

While often splendidly eerie and at times great fun, Coppola's *Dracula* can also be self-consciously bizarre and unintentionally funny. Loaded with bloody and erotic images, it repeatedly goes way over the top, forgetting that Stoker's novel works on so many subtle levels. When restraint and stealth are called for, the movie becomes too wildly overt for its own good. Coppola has a firm grasp on the story's themes, yet he doesn't seem to understand that much of the book pounds along because it captures the thrill of the chase. For all of the sexy scenes and humorous touches, there are stretches when it drags like a vampire cape with an overlong hemline.

Ultimately, it goes down as another missed opportunity. Compared to previous Hollywood versions of the novel, it's not bad. Compared to the novel? Well, it's not exactly Bram Stoker's *Dracula,* now, is it?

Counting Up, Part Four: Batty *Draculas*

· · · · · · · · · · ·

They are very picturesque, but do not look prepossessing.
—*Jonathan Harker,* Dracula, *chapter 1*

Bela Lugosi, Christopher Lee, Frank Langella, Gary Oldman, and a clawful of others are the screen's major Draculas. But the count has been portrayed so often in movies, you've got to expect some odd Transylvania twists. Here are five—to put it charitably—lesser Draculas:

Blood of Dracula's Castle (1969): Alexander D'Arcy is Dracula in this film from low-budget specialist Al Adamson. John Carradine appears as a butler.

Dracula versus Frankenstein (1971): "The kings of horror battle to the death," promised the posters for another epic from director-producer Adamson. They should have battled for a better script. Zandor Vorkov plays Dracula with side-burns, a goatee, an Afro hairdo, an echo-chamber voice, and a ray-gun ring. This was the last film for two stars of Erle C. Kenton's *House of Frankenstein* (1944): Lon Chaney Jr. and J. Carroll Naish.

Some of the original laboratory equipment from James Whale's *Frankenstein* (1931) was used, Russ Tamblyn is in the cast, and there's a cameo by *Famous Monsters* editor Forrest J Ackerman. None of that helps.

Dracula Sucks (1979): James Gillis portrays the count in what has become the most famous of the countless adult films featuring the character. Directed by Philip Marshak.

Waxwork (1988): Former Tarzan Miles O'Keefe plays Dracula as a *waxwork* come to life in this teen horror film directed by Anthony Hickox.

To Die For (1989): Set in modern Los Angeles, director Deran Serafian's blend of romance and action gave us a Dracula (Brendan Hughes) who was a blend of Vlad the Impaler and Stoker's vampire. Michael Praed took over the role for a 1991 sequel.

Dracula on the Record

· · · · · · · · · · ·

How I miss my phonograph!
—*Dr. Seward,* Dracula, *chapter 25*

Dracula became a recording star in 1958 when Philadelphia horror host John Zacherle, with Dave Appell and the Applejacks backing him, scored a hit with the rock novelty number "Dinner with Drac." It flew to number six on the *Billboard* charts, earning the Cool Ghoul an appearance on Dick Clark's *American Bandstand*. Zacherle rode the wave of this success to WABC Channel 7 in New York, adding a *-y* to his onscreen credit, reportedly to make his name easier to pronounce (Zak-er-lee).

"Dinner With Drac" set the horror host's beloved limericks to a mellow rock beat:

> A dinner was served for three
> At Dracula's house by the sea.
> The hors d'oeuvres were fine,
> But I choked on my wine,
> When I learned that the main course was me!"

This hardly would be Dracula's only appearance on vinyl. Four years after this memorable dinner, Drac made his one-line cameo in Bobby "Boris" Pickett's hit novelty song, "Monster Mash."

Dracula had a good deal more to say with the 1963 release of the AA Records album *Famous Monsters Speak*. A tie-in with *Famous Monsters of Filmland* magazine, the LP featured a fiery full-color cover painting similar to the art being used for the boxes of Aurora's monster models. A Glenn Strange–ish Frankenstein and a Bela Lugosi–like Dracula were the dominant figures. The Wolf Man, the Creature from the Black Lagoon, and the Mummy lurked in the background, even though they were not featured on this album.

The back cover displayed eight black-and-white photographs: four of Boris Karloff as the Frankenstein monster, four of Lugosi from Tod Browning's 1931

Former Dead End Kid Gabriel Dell was the voice of Dracula for this 1963 album regularly featured in the ad pages of Famous Monsters of Filmland *magazine.*

film *Dracula*. The easiest way to purchase this record was, of course, though *Famous Monsters of Filmland* ($1.98, plus 25¢ for postage and handling). Side 2 was called "Dracula's Return," but it just as easily could have been titled, "The Original Interview with the Vampire." Starting with the clack-clacking sound of a typewriter, "Dracula's Return" was a reporter's account of a visit to the count's crypt. Side 1, also written by Cherney Berg, gave the Frankenstein monster the chance to tell his story. Who's doing the Lugosi/Dracula voice on *Famous Monsters Speak?* That's none other than Gabriel Dell, a founding member of the East Side Kids (later the Dead End Kids and the Bowery Boys). Dell, a gifted comedian, had perfected his Lugosi impression as a regular on TV's *The Steve Allen Show.*

A year after Dracula had his say on this album, the novelty of vampire songs in a funny vein hadn't worn off. With the American reissue of John Gilling's *Old Mother Riley Meets the Vampire* (1952; starring Bela Lugosi) as *My Son, the Vampire*, Warner Brothers Records released a 45-rpm single of song parodist Allan Sherman's title track. It contained the memorable passage

> My son, the vampire, he's a total loss,
> And if you should meet with him,
> Do not eat or drink with him.
> Run if he takes out his dental floss,
> 'Cause my son, the vampire, ain't collecting it for the Red Cross.

In 1974, Capitol Records released *Hammer Presents Dracula with Christopher Lee*, with Lee providing narration on a collection of music from several of Hammer Studios' Dracula films. That same year, Rapple (a division of Apple) released Ringo Starr and Harry Nilsson's *Son of Dracula* soundtrack. In 1975, Murray Hill Records released *The Great Radio Horror Shows*, a three-record set that included the 1938 Orson Welles *Mercury Theatre on the Air* broadcast of *Dracula*. That same year, Power Records courted young horror fans with *A Story of Dracula, the Wolfman and Frankenstein.*

Dracula continued his audio presence as first cassette tapes and then compact discs replaced LP records. Some of the finer adaptations of the novel include: the three-hour Penguin Audiobooks version by Richard E. Grant (who played Seward in director Francis Ford Coppola's 1992 *Bram Stoker's Dracula*); the full-cast Naxos Audiobooks abridgment starring Brian Cox and Heathcote Williams; Robert Whitfield's unabridged Blackstone Audiobooks release; and Brilliance Audio's unabridged multivoice presentation. Soundtrack albums have also been released in various formats for the *Dracula* film adaptations directed by John Badham (music by John Williams, available on CD since 1990) and Francis Ford Coppola (music by Wojciech Kilar, available on CD since 1992). Performed by the Kronos Quartet, the Philip Glass score composed for a special edition of Tod Browning's 1931 *Dracula* was released in 1999. And since vampires keep coming back at you, all those novelty songs, as well as the 1938 Welles radio show, are now available on CD.

You Could Die Laughing:
The Dracula Spoofs

· · · · · · · · · · ·

It was all very ridiculous. . . .
—*Jonathan Harker,* Dracula, *chapter 1*

Early on, Hollywood saw the comic possibilities in playing the Dracula character for laughs. A year after being rescued from economic horrors by director Tod Browning's *Dracula* (1931), Universal released a comedy short incorporating scenes from F. W. Murnau's *Nosferatu* (1922). It was appropriately titled *Boo!*

In 1933, Bela Lugosi himself did the spoofing in a short subject, Lewis Lewyn's *Hollywood on Parade*. This Dracula was a wax figure that comes to life and terrorizes Betty Boop (Mae Questel). And Lugosi was again having fun with the Dracula persona in Browning's 1935 film *Mark of the Vampire*.

The mixing of humor and horror was expertly handled with Lugosi as the count in Charles Barton's *Abbott and Costello Meet Frankenstein* (1948). So by the time John Zacherle served up his novelty radio hit "Dinner With Drac" in 1958, getting a laugh or two at

Dracula's expense was no longer a novelty. In 1957, a year after Lugosi's death, Gabriel Dell introduced his Dracula character on TV's *The Steve Allen Show*. On the stand-up comedy front, Lenny Bruce was making a Lugosi-Dracula impression a regular part of his infamous act in the 1950s and '60s. In 1971, another stand-up veteran, Woody Allen, published a humorous take on "Count Dracula" in his short story collection, *Getting Even*. Allen's Dracula mistakenly makes a house call during a total eclipse of the sun. "It's so rare to see him around this early," comments the Transylvania town's mayor. "In fact I can't ever remember seeing him around in the daytime."

But it was television that really opened up the bloodgates, giving us a steady flow of daffy Draculas and Dracula knockoffs played by the likes of Durwood Kirby (in a sketch on *The Garry Moore Show*), Bob Denver (on

Gillligan's Island), Vincent Price (in an episode of *F Troop*), Raymond Burr on (*The Sonny and Cher Comedy Hour*), Paul Lynde (in the TV movie *Gidget Gets Married*), Benny Hill (in a sketch for his British series), Joe Flaherty (as "oooo-scary!" horror host Count Floyd on *SCTV*), and, of course, Al Lewis as the cigar-smoking Sam Dracula (better known as Grandpa) on *The Munsters*.

Movies soon caught up in the Dracu-laugh department. *Mad Monster Party*, directed by Jules Bass and released in 1967, gave us Count Dracula as a stop-motion animation puppet. The film features music, a script by *Mad* magazine writers, and the voices of Boris Karloff and Phyllis Diller. Bass and producer Arthur Rankin Jr. were responsible for several stop-motion holiday specials, starting in 1964 with *Rudolph the Red-Nosed Reindeer*.

For whatever reason, 1974 was a big year for *Dracula* spoofs. *Andy Warhol's Dracula* was a loopy lampoon written and directed by Paul Morrissey; also known as *Young Dracula* and *Blood for Dracula*, it starred Udo Kier as a virgin-seeking vampire. That same year, in the wake of Mel Brooks's *Young Frankenstein*, David Niven starred in *Old Dracula*, a goofy horror spoof about the aging count reviving his wife; it was directed by Clive Donner, who would later helm George C. Scott's TV movie version of *A Christmas Carol*. Also in 1974, former Beatle Ringo Starr and Harry Nilsson (as the title character, Count Downe) collaborated on the comic rock opera *Son of Dracula*, directed by Freddie Francis

(another uninspired effort, it also was retitled *Young Dracula*). "It is not the best film ever made," was Ringo's less-than ringing verdict, "but I've seen worse." And, in 1976, Christopher Lee fared no better in the French comedy *Dracula père et fils* (Dracula and Son), directed by Édouard Molinaro.

The two highest-profile Dracula satires were:

Love at First Bite (1979; directed by Stan Dragoti): "Children of the night . . . shut up!" Count Vlad Dracula (George Hamilton) is kicked out of his castle, being served eviction papers by Romania's Communist government. It seems that Castle Dracula is needed as a training ground for Nadia Comaneci and the Olympic squad. He is given the choice of leaving the country or moving into "an efficiency with seven dissidents and one toilet." Not knowing what a dissident or a toilet is, he heads for New York and finds love in the arms of Cindy Sondheim (Susan Saint James).

It wasn't exactly Bela Lugosi and Edward Van Sloan when Leslie Nielsen and director Mel Brooks played Dracula and Van Helsing in the spoof Dracula: Dead and Loving It.

Arte Johnson plays the loyal Renfield (channeling his inner Dwight Frye), and Richard Benjamin is a crack-up as psychiatrist Jeffrey Rosenberg, a distant and bumbling descendant of Professor Van Helsing. Although no masterpiece, it is consistently funny—which is more than you can say for . . .

Dracula: Dead and Loving It (1995): *Young Frankenstein* director and comedian Mel Brooks (also playing Van Helsing) and a post—*Police Squad* Leslie Nielsen (playing the title role) teamed up for this wildly uneven parody of the *Dracula* films (the Lugosi version in particular). "This Dracula is constantly being tripped up by his own evil schemes and misfiring magic," Brooks was quoted saying in the Castle Rock press kit for the movie. "Every time he's ready to strike, something goes embarrassingly wrong." The same could be said of the script. The able cast also included Harvey Korman as Dr. Seward, Peter MacNicol as Renfield, Steven Weber as Jonathan, Amy Yasbeck as Mina, and Lysette Anthony as Lucy. Brooks and his team did do their homework, however, and that allowed them to score a few comedic bull's-eyes.

George Hamilton spoofs Lugosi's Dracula (with Arte Johnson spoofing Dwight Frye's Renfield) in Love at First Bite.

The Wit and Wisdom of Sam Dracula

. . . .

He is a funny old man. He must be awfully old. . . .
—Mina Murray, Dracula, *chapter 6*

Television's *The Munsters* gave us Dracula as a vaudeville vampire. Playing off the paranormal persona, Al Lewis got some of the series' best lines as Grandpa (a.k.a. Sam Dracula). Ten Grandpa gems:

"Will you stop arguing? There is enough noise in here to wake the living."

"Any place I hang myself is home."

"Why, I've never been so insulted since the day I died."

"Let's not bring up the past. For once in this family, let's let the dead stay buried."

"Don't try to hide anything. You know, in this family, nothing ever stays buried."

"I'm taking a plane home. I'd fly there myself, but I've had a very trying day."

"I wish she'd get married. We could use some fresh blood in this family."

"Why, in the old country, whenever we needed a man, didn't I always manage to dig somebody up?"

"Problems! Problems! Sometimes I wish I were back in the old country, where my biggest worry was who to put the bite on for three square meals a day."

And my personal favorite, Grandpa's reason for not joining a country club:

"I don't want to join the club because there's no one there of my class. After all, Herman, you know I'm a full-blooded count. And the closest thing they have to royalty there is the bartender—Duke Feinberg."

The Munsters, *here adorning a lunch box, gave us Dracula as a Borscht Belt comic (Al Lewis, at right, as Grandpa).*

Interviews with Other Vampires

· · · · · · · · · · · ·

"We are in Transylvania; and Transylvania is not England.
Our ways are not your ways. . . ."
—**Count Dracula,** Dracula, *chapter 2*

Here are some views of Dracula from three American actors who played him in the 1970s.

Frank Langella, star of the 1977 Broadway revival at the Martin Beck Theatre and director John Badham's 1979 film:

> As an actor, you can't start out to play your character as a monster. He doesn't see himself that way. He may be a vampire, but you still need to find those things that make him human. So I played him as an isolated and lonely nobleman with a terrible problem. And because of this problem, he's forced to live a life of great secrecy and compelled to satisfy a terrible thirst. I suppose you could read the book and see him as one who stalks and attacks innocent victims. I chose to play him, not as a stalker, but as a seducer. This made him romantic instead of repulsive.

This seemed to work for him. By the way, Langella's portrayal not only made women swoon, it earned him a Tony Award nomination.

Jack Palance, star of the 1974 TV movie directed by Dan Curtis and adapted by Richard Matheson:

> I think it was the only character I've ever played that frightened me. Even in the doing of it, I had a feeling of, perhaps on occasion, becoming too near to Dracula—too much the character. I used to walk away from the set hoping that the entire production would end as soon as possible. I didn't really want to become Dracula . . . it's kind of a spellbinding character, always was to that time and still remains so . . . I never thought of the character as being evil. Somebody else has said that "this is possibly the most evil character you've ever

played." I think I would accept their judgment, but certainly I would not give myself that same judgment. Dracula was no more evil than any other man. He was someone trapped in a situation. Evil is a term that is given him by others. . . . Since then, I've been offered Dracula several more times, and I didn't want to do it anymore. Once is enough.

Here is your real Vlad connection. Palance, who previously had starred in the Curtis-produced version of The *Strange Case of Dr. Jekyll and Mr. Hyde* (1968), was born Vladimir "Walter Jack" Palahnuik.

Michael Nouri, star of the *Curse of Dracula* segment of NBC's serialized *Cliffhangers* series, a short-lived three-in-one package that premiered in February 1979:

You know, early in my career, I played two characters on NBC shows that didn't last long, but people still seem to remember and ask me about: Dracula and Lucky Luciano on *The Gangster Chronicles*. They follow me around to this day. And they were both figures that represent dark power and danger. We continue to be fascinated by the vampire and the gangster, and I think that combination has a great deal to do with it. Dracula, though, adds the promise of immortality, and, with that, is a seductive quality that makes him incredibly alluring. Power, immortality, danger—that's an alluring formula. He's not only seductive, he's intriguing. You can't help thinking about what it would be like to exist as he does.

Some actors have found that vampire cape a heavy burden, but not Nouri. He remembers the old boy fondly, saying, "I had a great deal of fun playing him, even with all of the night hours."

And if you're in the neighborhood, drop on in for a drink: Jack Palance in front of his castle digs in the 1974 TV movie version of Dracula.

Landau as Lugosi

· · · · · · · · · · ·

. . . we should stand or fall by our act, and perhaps
some day this very script may be evidence. . . .
—*Jonathan Harker,* Dracula, *chapter 25*

Aging Bela Lugosi (Oscar winner Martin Landau) teaches
Ed Wood (Johnny Depp) how to make like a horror star in
this scene from director Tim Burton's Ed Wood.

Bela Lugosi never came close to winning an Oscar. But in 1995, Martin Landau won an Oscar for playing Lugosi in director Tim Burton's acclaimed biopic *Ed Wood* (1994). The heart of the film was the odd-couple friendship of an aging Lugosi with the ever-optimistic Edward D. Wood Jr., a director with high hopes but little talent.

Wood, played in the film with manic energy by Burton favorite Johnny Depp, cast the down-on-his-luck Lugosi in such low-budget movies as *Glen or Glenda* (1953) and *Bride of the Monster* (1955). He also edited silent test footage of the actor into the often-ridiculed

Plan 9 from Outer Space (1959), an unintentionally hilarious horror-science-fiction mishmash released three years after Lugosi's death (his character was played in several scenes by chiropractor Tom Mason, creeping into scenes with a Dracula-esque cape hiding his face).

Burton's movie offered sympathetic depictions of both Wood and Lugosi. Wood was the dreamer refusing to give into disillusionment. Lugosi was the disillusioned star who refuses to let dreams die. "I was struck by the great nobility of those last years," comments Landau, who had studied Lugosi's films and interviews. "Here he was, trapped in these awful films—really, really horrible films, like *Bela Lugosi Meets a Brooklyn Gorilla*. And yet he was giving it his all. He was summoning all the dignity and talent and commitment he could muster. I never wanted to do a caricature or impression of him, because I truly grew to admire him so much. He really was a remarkable actor—a consummate actor, and an underrated one."

There were deviations from fact. The film gets plenty of comic mileage out of Landau's Lugosi letting loose with angry outbursts of profanity. By most accounts, Lugosi was not a swearing man. Also, during this period, Lugosi was married to his fifth wife, Hope Lininger. Neither his wife nor son Bela Lugosi Jr. is depicted in the film.

Lugosi fans were upset with the many inaccuracies. Landau fans were upset when the actor, accepting his Academy Award for best supporting actor, had his thank-you speech cut short by the blaring orchestra. A visibly upset Landau pounded the podium and yelled, "No!" But he didn't get the chance to finish his comments—at least, not on the Oscar stage. "The reason I was so upset was that I was about to dedicate that win to Bela Lugosi," says Landau, who played Dracula in a 1980s touring production of the play. "It was my chance to express my admiration and my thanks. I very much wanted to do that. I wanted to honor him."

He also wanted to honor him with a nuanced performance in the Burton film. Although at first miffed by reports of how *Ed Wood* portrayed his father, Bela Lugosi Jr. saw the film with Landau and endorsed the performance.

Why No Definitive Dracula Film Exists

· · · · · · · · · · · ·

. . . he is of an imperfectly formed mind.
—*Mina Harker,* Dracula, *chapter 25*

Ask ten *Dracula* fans to name their favorite screen count and you might get ten different answers. It's possible. Count Dracula Fan Club founder Jeanne Keyes Youngson champions Bela Lugosi's portrayal. Others prefer the quiet strength of Christopher Lee. J. Gordon Melton, author of *The Vampire Book*, has noted that he "was much more partial to Lee's victims than Lee's portrayal . . . I prefer Frank Langella's performance."

Lugosi? Lee? Langella? You'll also find those under the spell of Dracula as portrayed by John Carradine, Gary Oldman, Jack Palance, and Max Schreck. But in the final analysis it must be conceded that there has been no definitive portrayal of the count, just as there has been no definite film version of Bram Stoker's novel. The truth is, you could take all of the best elements of the many screen adaptations, jam them together, and you still wouldn't have the book.

The best moment of opportunity was in the 1980s, when the American TV miniseries was at the height of its power. With that kind of budget and that kind of time, a producer might have delivered a definitive version. It could have been done in three nights: the first night, Harker in Transylvania; the second night, Dracula in England; the third night, the hunt for Dracula and the race back to the castle. So the BBC television version had the right idea. "The Louis Jourdan version is the closest in terms of plot, but Louis Jourdan is not Dracula," comments *Dracula* expert Elizabeth Miller. "You need a strong, commanding presence, like Christopher Lee."

Well, you could also take the best elements of all screen portrayals of Dracula, jam them together, and—well, you'd get awfully close to the definitive interpretation. Each actor brought something to the role, and nobody brought everything. Elusive as ever, Dracula is not captured that easily. It's as if the count were looking down from the broken battlements of his Transylvania castle, laughing at he who would be vampire king.

CAPSULE

The Ten Best Dracula Movies

· · · · · · · · · · · ·

*He so crowded on my mind his list of nature's eccentricities and
possible impossibilities that my imagination was getting fired.*
—Dr. John Seward, **Dracula**, *chapter 19*

The essential Dracula film library
should include:

Nosferatu, Eine Symphonie des Grauens
(1922): German director F. W. Murnau's
silent classic, with Max Schreck as the
Dracula character Graf Orlok.

Dracula (1931): The second half of Tod
Browning's film is a letdown, but Bela
Lugosi gives the most famous vampire
performance in screen history.

Drácula (1931; Spanish-language version): Carlos Villerias is no Lugosi, but
George Melford's direction is consistently more imaginative than that of his
American counterpart, Browning.

Abbott and Costello Meet Frankenstein
(1948; directed by Charles Barton):
This was only the second time Lugosi
actually played Dracula in a movie,
and, in some ways, his portrayal is even
better than in the 1931 film.

Horror of Dracula (1958; directed by
Terence Fisher): Christopher Lee takes the
role and audiences by the throat in his first
Hammer Studios appearance as the count.

The Return of Dracula (1958): Francis
Lederer as a Cold War Count in this
extremely moody American movie
directed by Paul Landres.

Bram Stoker's Dracula (1974; directed
by Dan Curtis): This TV movie established Jack Palance as the Dracula you
most feared meeting in a dark alley.

Count Dracula (1977): The three-part
miniseries directed by Philip Saville hews
closest to Stoker, but Louis Jourdan's
Dracula is not what you'd call Stokerian.

Dracula (1979; directed by John
Badham): Frank Langella stars as the
screen's sexiest Dracula.

Bram Stoker's Dracula (1992): Gary
Oldman was the count in director
Francis Ford Coppola's version, which
owed as much to the 1974 TV movie as
it did to Stoker's book.

*Dracula (Gary
Oldman) sets his
undead sights on
Mina (Winona
Ryder) in the
1992 version of
Dracula.*

I realize there's no John Carradine
film on this list, but the actor had very
little to work with in Erle C. Kenton's
monster rallies *House of Frankenstein*
(1944) and *House of Dracula* (1945). His
performance is worth noting, however.
He made the most of his screen time,
making a very un-Lugosi-like Dracula.

Puzzle: Putting the Cross in Crossword

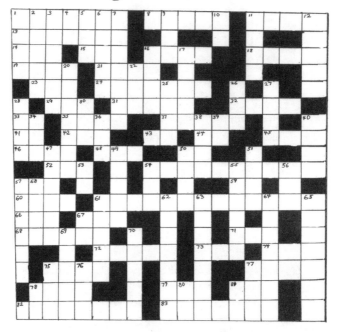

Across

1. He played Dracula in the 1974 TV movie.
8. The count's liquid diet.
11. Bela's count never drinks this.
13. *Son of Dracula* pseudonym.
14. Record kept by *Demeter* captain.
15. "How dare _____ touch him?"
16. Dracula boasts of fighting the _____.
18. Carfax is a Dracula _____.
19. This is found around Castle Dracula in the final chapters.
21. The shovel leaves one on Dracula.
23. Direction taken by vampire hunters from England.
24. Lee film: The _____ Rites of Dracula.
29. Arthur's father is very _____.
31. 32-across was known as this.
32. The historical Dracula was _____ the Impaler.
33. "Children _____ the night."
35. Dracula's wives beckon Mina to "_____ to us."
37. With the day, Dracula's powers _____.
41. Charlotte Stoker, to Bram.
42. Harker reaches Transylvania in chapter _____.
43. Initials of actor who played both Dracula and Renfield.
44. "Listen _____ them!"
45. Seward: "the instant we _____ we all recognized the Count."
46. He wrote Dracula.
48. Hammer Studios' Count Dracula.
50. Old woman to Harker: "Must you _____?"
52. Dracula attacks Mina and Jonathan in their _____.
54. Count Dracula, for one.
57. The *Czarina Catherine* sails at the _____ tide.
59. Stoker clipped an article about a vampire scare in this state (initials).
60. Mina and Seward see a great bat by the light of the _____.
61. Dracula is this, too.
66. Dracula frequently takes the form of a _____.
67. Arthur, to Van Helsing, "my dear _____."
68. Mina witnesses Dracula's _____ on Lucy.
71. Actor Peter who met Carradine's Dracula in *House of Frankenstein*.
72. Lugosi's Dracula at night.

73. Make the Sign of the Cross and point two fingers to ward off the evil _____.
74. Lugosi's fourth wife, for short.
75. Dracula insists that Harker _____ at the castle for a month.
77. Dracula's carriage meets Harker at the Borgo _____.

78. Dracula leaves Harker after hearing the _____ of a cock.
79. Responding to this was vital to Henry Irving's craft.
81. Possible lifetime for a vampire.
82. Wife of 46-across.
83. Dracula's state upon finding wives with Harker.

Down

1. Art Holmwood and Jack Seward to Quincey Morris.
2. Lucy finds herself "_____ with the dead."
3. He played Dracula on Broadway and in the 1931 film.
4. Initials of comedians who met Dracula in 1948: _____ and _____.
5. Dracula, carrying Harker's bags: "_____, sir, you are my guest."
6. This can be used to repel a vampire.
7. Van Helsing must _____ his friends on vampires.
9. First name of comedian who met Frankenstein, the Wolf Man, and Dracula.
10. Title for Seward and Van Helsing.
11. Dracula leaves the *Demeter* in the form of a _____.
12. Prevailing mood at Castle Dracula.
16. Van Helsing and his team hope to _____ Dracula.
17. At sunset, Dracula must _____ the coffin lid.
20. "I bid you _____."
22. Vampire verb after neck has been bitten.
25. Where Dracula likes to dine.
26. Harker is warned of the _____ of St. George's Day.
27. Dracula can travel on moonlight _____.
28. Homey place for Dracula.
30. First name of silent-screen star considered for a film version of Dracula.
34. Van Helsing, in chapter 14, says the news is "_____worse."
36. First name of *Dracula: Dead and Loving It* director.
38. In the final chapter, Harker jumps _____ the cart bearing Dracula's earth box.
39. Dracula: "Yes, I too can love . . . Is it not _____?"

40. The 1931 *Dracula* film opens with a theme from _____ Lake.
47. Partner Bud of 9-down.
49. Mina often makes an _____ in her diary.
50. Lucy's house is invaded by a big _____ wolf.
51. Dracula is described as tall and _____.
53. Van Helsing says, "_____ not thwart me."
54. Harker determines to learn all he _____ about Dracula.
55. Dracula can put victims in a _____.
56. Exclamation of vampire hunter upon finding the undead's lair.
57. For ship travel, Dracula must _____ in an earth box.
58. Arthur and Jonathan hire one for river travel.
61. Dracula serves this wine to Harker.
62. Van Helsing and Seward are men of _____.
63. He played the count in *Return of Dracula*.
64. Bram Stoker's native soil.
65. He played Dracula in *Dracula: Dead and Loving It*.
67. Initials of vampire on *Dark Shadows*.
69. Henry Irving's profession.
70. The carriage to Borgo Pass flies with great _____.
75. Desired show-biz initials for Stoker's Lyceum boss.
76. Seward confesses to feeling "_____ and vague terror."
77. Stoker predecessor in the horror field.
78. Initials of actor who played the count the greatest number of times onscreen.
80. Not dead, but _____dead.
81. Initials of famed illustrator who designed the sets for the 1977 *Dracula* revival.

Classical Drac

· · · · · · · · · · ·

. . . something fluttering from them like the dresses in a ballet. . . .
—*Jonathan Harker,* Dracula, *chapter 1*

Dracula *inspiring ballets and operas? This opera guy is all right with that (Lon Chaney, considered for the first talkie version of* Dracula *in the silent classic* The Phantom of the Opera*).*

Dance with the devil? From pas de deux to pas de death? Dracula in tights? Believe it. Dracula has also gone classical; his batlike movements, flowing black cape, and seductive presence are all naturals for the ballet. And if you remove the third, fourth and fifth letters from *ballet,* you've got *bat.*

The Royal Winnipeg Ballet's acclaimed version of *Dracula,* which had its world premiere in 1998, was turned into a 2002 film by director Guy Maddin. It was aired by CBC Television in Canada and released theatrically in the United States, where several other *Dracula* ballets had been and would be produced.

The Columbia City (South Carolina) Ballet has staged its *Dracula: Ballet with a Bite* since 1991. The Houston Ballet debuted its *Dracula* in 1997. Columbus, Ohio's BalletMet has been performing its *Dracula* since 1999. The Northern Plains Ballet, a regional troupe based in Bismarck, North Dakota, performed a *Dracula* ballet based on Francis Ford Coppola's 1992 film in 2001 and 2006. The Metropolitan Ballet of Minneapolis–St. Paul premiered its *Dracula* in 2006. The Nashville (Tennessee) Ballet treated audiences to a *Dracula* dance in 2007. And *Dracula* is an October favorite with the Colorado Ballet of Denver, and many other companies.

"It's remarkable how well suited it is for ballet," observes *Dracula* expert Elizabeth Miller, who frequently lectures before performances by the Royal Winnipeg Ballet. "I've seen two ballets based on *Dracula,* and I'm about to see two more. It sounds wild when you first hear of a *Dracula* ballet, but then you see how splendidly it can be interpreted through dance. It's just marvelous how well it works."

On the music side of the theatrical street, the Broadway production of *Dracula, The Musical* opened at the Belasco Theatre in August 2004 (with music by Frank Wildhorn, book and lyrics by Don Black and Christopher Hampton). Director Des

McAnuff's cast included Tom Hewitt as Dracula, Melissa Errico as Mina, Don Stephenson as Renfield, Darren Ritchie as Jonathan, Kelli O'Hara as Lucy, Chris Hoch as Arthur, Bart Shatto as Quincey, Shonn Wiley as Seward, and Stephen McKinley Henderson as Van Helsing. Audiences didn't find this a show to die for, however, and it closed after a five-month run.

A concept album for another *Dracula* musical play (by Gareth Evans and Christopher J. Orton, with orchestration by Ian Lynn) was recorded in England in 2006. These two attempts were preceded by *Dracul—The Dracula Musical*, which had its world premiere at the San Diego Repertory's Lyceum Theatre in July 1995 (a recording was released on CD in 1998). And a Canadian musical adaptation (with book and lyrics by Richard Ouzounian and music by Marek Norman) was staged at the Stratford Festival in Stratford, Ontario, in 1999 (a video version was shown in Canada by CBC Television in 2000).

A *Dracula* opera by composer Hectro Fabio Torres Cardona premiered in Colombia in 2005. *Dracula* was also turned into a rock opera in Italy, with music written and performed by the Italian rock band Premiata Forneria Marconi, or PFM (Franco Mussida, Franz di Cioccio, Flavio Premoli, and Patrick Djivas). It was released on CD—that's compact disc, not Count Dracula—in 2005.

· · · · · · · · · · ·

SIDEBAR

Dracula Comic Books: Something to Marvel At

· · · · · · · · · · ·

". . . and that will paint his dreams with horrors. . . ."
—*Professor Van Helsing,* Dracula, *chapter 15*

For more than half of a century, the comic book industry has been, well, drawn by Count Dracula's hypnotic power.

In his delightful and comprehensive essay "Fangs for the Funny Books: Or, Dracula in the Comics" (published in Bob Madison's *Dracula: The First Hundred Years*), author Rickey L. Shanklin notes that Count Dracula made his first comic book appearance in a 1951 issue of the Atlas Comics series *Suspense*. Vampire authority J. Gordon Melton relates that the first comic book adaptation of *Dracula* appeared in August 1953 (the eighth edition of Avon's *Eerie* series).

Faster than a silver bullet, the Comics Code of 1954 put a stop to stories about vampires, werewolves, and ghouls. This didn't stop *Famous Monsters of Filmland* from publishing a comic-book version of Christopher Lee's *Horror of Dracula*. And, in the mid-1960s, the guardians of the Comics Code also didn't seem to mind a Gold Key series of comics featuring *The Munsters* (with Grandpa, of course—a character also known as Sam Dracula in the TV series). Ballantine Books published a comic book *Dracula* adaptation in 1966 as a paperback, a form not regulated by the Comics Code. Gold Key followed this with a series of comic books based on vampire Barnabas Collins and TV's *Dark Shadows*.

Dell Publishing, which didn't subscribe to the Comics Code, tried a *Dracula* comic in 1962, but it only lasted one issue. Dell tried again in 1966, this time with Dracula as a superhero. That lasted three issues. Then Dell tried yet again, briefly, in 1972.

Dracula truly emerged as a comic book star after the Comics Code was revamped in the early 1970s. Marvel Comics launched *The Tomb of Dracula*, a series that ultimately ran seven years (April 1972–August 1979) and seventy issues (with writer Marv Wolfman and artist Gene Colan as principal contributors for much of its run). It pitted a revived Dracula against Frank Drake (a Dracula descendant), Quincy Harker (son of Jonathan and Mina Harker), Rachel Van Helsing (the crossbow-toting granddaughter of the vampire-hunting professor), and, later, vampire-slaying Blade.

The Tomb of Dracula spawned a magazine, *Dracula Lives!* Marvel attempted to revive *The Tomb of Dracula* in 1979, as did Epic Comics in 1991 (with Wolfman and Colan). Marvel's revival lasted six issues; Epic's lasted four.

Dracula met Jack the Ripper in the four-issue *Blood of the Innocent* miniseries published by Warp Graphics. Shanklin, later the author of the *Blood of Dracula* series published by Apple Press, expanded an original story submitted to *Dracula Lives!* with artists Marc Hempel and Mark Wheatley.

Dracula Lives!—as a comic book star.

Topps Comics got into the *Dracula* business with a four-part 1992 adaptation of the Francis Ford Coppola film *Bram Stoker's Dracula*. Topps followed that in 1993 with a three-part *Vlad the Impaler* series.

Thanks to comics, Dracula has encountered everyone from Sherlock Holmes and Jack the Ripper to Zorro and Spider-Man. One of his most intriguing meetings was in the 1991 DC graphic novel *Red Rain*. It pitted bat creature against bat creature: Dracula and Batman. Holy crossover! When does the bug-eating Renfield square off against Robin?

Dracula Goes Pop

· · · · · · · · · · ·

"You are strong in your numbers . . . "
—*Mina Harker,* Dracula, *chapter 24*

On February 21, 2000, thin and weak after a quintuple bypass operation, David Letterman returned to the set of his late-night CBS show. During a taped video gag, the Dracula-like Count from *Sesame Street* appeared as a surgeon in an operating room. "One! One bypass . . . Ah! Ha! Ha!" he bellowed in Lugosi-like tones. "Two! Two bypass. . . ." Letterman and his team had no doubt that, because of the round-the-world influence of *Sesame Street*, everyone would get the joke. And the producers behind *Sesame Street* had no doubt that, because of the universal impact of Tod Browning's *Dracula* (1931), everyone would get that the Count was modeled on the Lugosi image.

Making his debut during the PBS show's 1972–73 season, the number-loving Count von Count sports a goatee and a monocle. But with his cape, accent, fangs, and widow's peak, there's little doubt about the resemblance to the popular image of Dracula. The Spanish version of *Sesame Street* cuts right to the chase, calling him Conde Draco.

Impressions of *Sesame Street*'s Count are not uncommon in movies and sketch comedy, which becomes a bit mind-boggling when you trace it back to Bram Stoker's novel. A comedian impersonating Count von Count is doing an impression of a Lugosi impression, which is based on a film portrayal, which is drawn from a stage play, which has only a slight resemblance to the Count Dracula of the book.

Dracula's goal in the novel is to invade and infiltrate London. By the early 1970s, he had successfully infiltrated the pop culture. "Dracula is everywhere," declares *Dracula* authority Elizabeth Miller. "Everywhere you look, you can find him." This was evident in the addition of the Count to the *Sesame Street* cast. And it was evident on cereal boxes when General Mills introduced Count Chocula in 1971. His original tagline was, "I vant to eat your cereal!"

A chocolate-flavored breakfast treat with marshmallows, Count Chocula was one of two monster-themed cereals launched that year. The other was Frankenberry, a strawberry flavored corn cereal with a Frankenstein-like mascot. Boo Berry, a blueberry cereal with a Peter Lorre–like ghost as its cartoon representative, joined the monster mix in 1973. They were followed by the less successful Fruit Brute in 1974 and Yummy Mummy in 1988.

Sesame Street *counts on the Count to teach kids numbers.*

Frankenberry and Boo Berry are still produced, but they're more easily found during the Halloween season. Count Chocula, though, continues to be a steady seller, available on most supermarket shelves throughout the year, making the vampire the king of the monsters and the king of the monster cereals.

Taking on a pop-culture life of his own, Count Chocula has been referenced in everything from novelist Thomas Pynchon's *Vineland* to episodes of TV's *South Park* and *The Sopranos*. Mixing the three monster cereals Count Chocula, Frankenberry, and Boo Berry into one bowl is called—what else?—the Monster Mash.

Count von Count and Count Chocula also set in motion a rather fascinating American domestication of the Dracula figure—the marketing of the ultimate undead creature to children. A vampire bunny that drains vegetables white was introduced in James and Deborah Howe's 1979 novel for young readers, *Bunnicula*. The title character has red eyes, front teeth that look like fangs, and markings that resemble a widow's peak and a cape. The success of the book spawned several sequels, including *Howliday Inn*, *The Celery Stalks at Midnight*, and *Bunnicula Meets Edgar Allan Crow*. In 1988, British television debuted the cartoon program *Count Duckula*. In 1991, Fox premiered *Little Dracula*, an animated series about a young vampire hoping to grow up to be like Daddy Dracula (voice provided by *SCTV's* Count Floyd himself, Joe Flaherty).

Played by Judd Hirsch, Dracula also appeared in the family friendly *The Halloween that Almost Wasn't*, an October 1979 ABC special. Played by Duncan Regehr, Dracula appeared in *Monster Squad* (1987), a kid-oriented comedy-horror spoof. Played by Keith-Lee Castle, he appears in *Young Dracula*, a children's series that airs on British and Canadian television.

SIDEBAR

The Dracula Tours: Trips to Transylvania

· · · · · · · · · · · ·

All at once the wolves began to howl as though the moonlight
had some peculiar effect on them.
—*Jonathan Harker,* **Dracula,** *chapter 1*

Dracula travel tours have become extremely popular, particularly around
Halloween. Several companies offer travel packages to Romania, some concentrating on Bram Stoker's novel, some on the historical figure of Vlad the Impaler.
Some cover both aspects of Dracula lore.

You can follow Jonathan Harker's route, for instance, eating at the Golden Krone
Hotel in Bistritz, Romania, before traveling on to the Borgo Pass. While in
Transylvania, you can visit Vlad the Impaler's birthplace in Sighisoara or the sites
of his legendary deeds (and misdeeds) in Brasov.

Many tours stop at Castle Bran, often billed (wrongly) as Dracula's castle. Vlad the
Impaler may have visited this impressive fortress (or spent a couple of days there
as a prisoner), but it most decidedly was not his castle. Built by Teutonic knights
in the thirteenth century near the town of Campalung to secure the Bran Pass, it
was later used to protect the merchant center of Brasov. Located on the mountain-pass border between Transylvania and Wallachia, Castle Bran was also said (again
wrongly) to be the model for the fictional castle in Stoker's book. When the castle
was put up for sale in July 2007 at an asking price of $78 million, headlines wondered who might "Buy Dracula's Castle."

More intrepid travelers can make the pilgrimage south, into Wallachia, the actual
district ruled by Vlad. Here, on the River Arges, you'll find the crumbling ruins
of Poenari Castle. Although never known as Castle Dracula, it was built by Vlad
Tepes. The Romanian government constructed a 1,850-step walkway in the 1970s
for those curious enough to climb the riverside hill and seek out Dracula's real
castle.

Another regular stop on the Dracula tours is the island monastery of Snagov,
believed to be the burial place of Vlad Tepes. In May 2001, a group of American
businessmen announced plans to locate the body at Snagov and use genetic
material to clone Vlad. The unnamed businessmen said they had approached the
Scottish research center at Roslin, home of Dolly the cloned sheep. There's no
word yet on whether Dracula has returned from the grave.

That same year, Romania's tourism minister said that the country was planning a $35 million Disney-style Count Dracula theme park "in honor of a national hero." To be built by an American company with German investment dollars, Dracula Land was supposed to open in the summer of 2003 near Sighisoara. Designs called for horror rides, labyrinths, catacombs, a Gothic castle, hotels, restaurants, shops, a golf course, horseback riding, and a Dracula Institute that would coordinate with the thousands of Vlad, vampire, Bela Lugosi, and Dracula clubs around the world. It was expected to cost $60 million and provide a major boost to Romanian tourism. "There are some voices in Romania who accuse me of selling a false legend," the Romanian tourism minister said in March 2001. "But I am a pragmatic man and these critics do not put me off. . . . This is a fantastic project." The government predicted that the park would bring 3,000 jobs to Sighisoara.

In 2002, however, local opposition was building. In early 2003, Romania's prime minister, Adrian Nastase, reassured German investors that he would "fight for this project to be accomplished." The government hired the firm of PriceWaterhouseCoopers to conduct a feasibility study, and by October 2003, the proposed site for the theme park had shifted from Sighisoara to the Snagov Lake region. In the summer of 2006, with several investors giving up on the enterprise, the Romanian government withdrew its support and state funds. The minister of transportation announced that the park was not dead, but admitted it no longer was a top priority.

Those interested in Stoker can stop by the Bram Stoker Dracula Experience in Clontarf, Ireland. Those strictly interested in Stoker's novel can also make a Dracula tour of England, visiting the ruins of Whitby Abbey and enjoying the view of Whitby Harbor described by Mina; taking in the bustle of London's Piccadilly, where Dracula had one of his houses; eating at London's Jack Straw Castle, where Van Helsing had a meal; wandering through Highgate Cemetery, the burial place of Lucy Westenra; or strolling past the Chelsea home of Bram Stoker.

Dracula *fans can follow the route of Jonathan Harker (played here by Keanu Reeves to Gary Oldman's count) on one of the many Transylvania tours that emphasize both Bram Stoker's novel and the historical Vlad the Impaler.*

"The Dracula Industry": Merchandising

· · · · · · · · · · ·

We are bringing a good deal of ready money, as we are to buy. . . .
—*Mina Harker,* Dracula, *chapter 26*

The eye-catching advertising insert appeared in several national magazines, including *TV Guide.* And it sure caught the eyes of many Dracula fans in the fall of 1998. The Franklin Mint was introducing a Dracula collector knife licensed through Universal Studios. For fifty-five bucks, you could own this dandy little item, which featured a four-inch handle shaped like a coffin. Not only that, this coffin was "emblazoned with sculpted bats accented in silver" and "embellished in 24-karat gold accents with the name that struck fear in mortal hearts." More? The coffin handle had a hinged lid that could swing open "to reveal original art depicting the terrifying vampire, awaking to a night of terror. . . . You'll shudder as Dracula's coffin actually opens up!" Fangs bared, Dracula cut quite a figure in this fiery picture.

Such tantalizing terror trinkets were nothing new to a gener-

On the button, this item promoted a Universal Studio tour attraction.

ation of horror fans that cut its fangs on *Famous Monsters of Filmland* magazine. The back pages of those issues were filled with advertisements for a wide variety of mail-order delights: Dracula's own rubber bat (only seventy-five cents, plus twenty-five cents for postage and handling); 160 feet of 8-millimeter film footage of Bela Lugosi as Dracula; the *Famous Monsters Speak* LP album ("50 minutes of sheer terror"); the striking Dracula mask from Don Post Studios; a Dracula iron-on transfer suitable for shirts, bedspreads,

This button, on the other hand, dates back to the 1960s, adding fangs to the Lugosi image of Dracula (Bela never wore them on film)

or notebooks; the Dracula model kit (first the regular, then the glow-in-the-dark version); Dracula posters.

Universal Studios licensed several Dracula items in the 1960s, including puzzles, buttons, and the cherished Aurora model kit. In his 1975 biography of Bram Stoker, an amused Daniel Farson refers to this merchandising boom as "the Dracula Industry." Stoker, Farson notes, "struck a chord that vibrates even more strongly today."

Al Jolson might have told him, "You ain't seen nuthin' yet!" The boom turned into a full-fledged explosion over the next thirty years. Surf the Internet and you'll find a staggering array of Dracula items, both used and new. You'll find replicas of the Dracula ring worn by Lugosi. You'll find vintage recordings and comic books from decades past. You'll find busts, statuettes, and models.

When Francis Ford Coppola's film *Bram Stoker's Dracula* hit theaters in 1992, a company marketed a sword-cane version of the dragon-headed walking stick carried by Dracula portrayer Gary Oldman. When the US Postal Service issued the Lugosi Dracula stamp in 1997, the campaign was supported with several Universal-licensed goodies. When Halloween rolls around each year, Dracula merchandise can be found in almost any store. If he had a slice of "the Dracula Industry," the count would need an accountant to count the profits. There would be enough money to pay for Renfield's psychiatric bills, with sufficient funds left over to fix those broken battlements of Castle Dracula.

Complete with his own coffin, this Dracula figure was served up one Halloween with Burger King meals.

The Transylvania Society of Dracula

· · · · · · · · · · · ·

> *I soon lost sight and recollection of ghostly fears in the*
> *beauty of the scene as we drove along. . . .*
> —*Jonathan Harker,* **Dracula,** *chapter 1*

Dozens upon dozens of clubs and organizations devoted to vampires have come
and gone, like bats peeping through night-shrouded windows. A select few,
like the Count Dracula Fan Club (founded in the mid-1960s by Jeanne Keyes
Youngson) and the United Kingdom's Dracula Society (founded in 1973 by
Bernard Davies and Bruce Wightman), take their cue from the vampire king, surviving through the decades. Others disappear like Graf Orlok at the conclusion of
F. W. Murnau's 1922 film, *Nosferatu.* Some are devoted to Bram Stoker's book,
others to actor Bela Lugosi and all things Dracula. Some stake their claim on the
historical figure of Vlad the Impaler, while others pursue a real kind of blood-
drinking vampire nightlife.

One of the most intriguing is the Transylvania Society of Dracula, which its
founder, Nicolae Paduraru, describes as "a scholarly watchdog in Dracula studies." "The TSD was established in 1991 at my initiative," Paduraru explains. "Its
founder-members are fellows of the academy—university professors, researchers,
and writers in folklore, history, anthropology, comparative religions, literature, eso-
terica. The first chapters appeared in Canada, the United States, Italy, Germany,
Spain, Switzerland, and Japan, each contributing its share to the understanding of
the nature and role of the vampire, of other supernatural categories in the folklore
of peoples. The TSD set out to create an alternative to the mass of preconceived
ideas, downright inventions, and wrong historical and folkloric data."

The Transylvania Society of Dracula summoned the first World Dracula Congress in
May 1995, which, in Paduraru's words, "heralded the arrival of a scholarly watchdog in
Dracula studies. Ever since, the TSD organizes yearly conferences on either the supernatural or on the historical Dracula." One of the society's goals is to clear up confusion
between Stoker's fictional character and the historical figure of Vlad Tepes.

To help set the record straight on all things Dracula, Paduraru strongly recommends *Dracula: Sense and Nonsense,* the book published in 2000 by Elizabeth
Miller, president of the society's Canadian chapter. "So much wrong information is
taken as fact," Miller notes. "So much that is wrong has been endlessly repeated.
There are so many widespread assumptions that are just wrong."

Novel Ideas: Dracula Pastiche

· · · · · · · · · · ·

"You must be scribe and write him all down. . . . "
—*Professor Van Helsing,* Dracula, *chapter 25*

Just as Count Dracula and Sherlock Holmes have become the two characters most frequently portrayed on screen, they have also become two of the most-used literary stars in the world of pastiche fiction. Robert Edward Lory really got things rolling with *Dracula Returns*, the 1973 paperback novel that introduced the count as a reluctant crime fighter. Eight sequels followed in 1973 and 1974.

Fred Saberhagen, who died at age seventy-seven in June 2007, took matters in a different direction with his 1975 novel, *The Dracula Tape.* Then known primarily as a science fiction author, Saberhagen retold the Bram Stoker novel, this time from Dracula's point of view. Count Vlad gives his side of the events, talking into a tape recorder, depicting Van Helsing as an ignorant fanatic and himself as a romantic hero.

Arriving after the success of Barnabas Collins on the TV series *Dark Shadows* but a year before Anne Rice's *Interview with the Vampire*, Saberhagen's Dracula was a sympathetic vampire with a conscience. Expanding on this theme, Saberhagen gave fans ten *Dracula* books between 1975 and 2002. In 1978, the second book teamed Vlad with Sherlock Holmes in a pastiche summit of sorts.

In 1977, vampire expert Donald Glut blended two great interests in a novel, *Frankenstein Meets Dracula.* The work of Lory, Saberhagen, and Glut lit the fuse for a pastiche explosion in the 1990s.

The Ultimate Dracula (1991), edited by Byron Preiss, was a collection of Dracula-inspired short stories by Philip José Farmer, Ed Gorman, John Lutz, Anne Rice, Dan Simmons, and others. Kim Newman's *Anno-Dracula* (1992) and its two sequels, *The Bloody Red Baron* and *Judgment of Tears,* were based on the premise that Dracula was not defeated at the conclusion of Stoker's 1897 novel. Simmons used the historical Vlad Tepes for his

1992 novel *Children of the Night*. Jeanne Kalogridis combined Stoker's vampire and Vlad the Impaler, expanding on the novel in *Covenant with the Vampire* (1994) and the other two books in her *Diaries of the Family Dracul* trilogy: *Children of the Vampire* (1995) and *Lord of the Vampires* (1996). Elaine Bergstrom's *Mina* (1994) and *Blood to Blood* (2000) continued the story of Mina Harker. Freda Warrington's *Dracula the Undead* (1997) was a centennial-year sequel to Stoker's novel. Nancy Kilpatrick's *Dracul: An Eternal Love Story* (1998) was a novelization of the musical first staged in San Diego. *Dracula in London* (2001), a short-story anthology edited by vampire specialist P. N. Elrod, featured tales by Bergstrom, Kilpatrick,

Saberhagen, Chelsea Quinn Yarbro, and others.

Mind you, this is just a sampling of what's available in the *Dracula* pastiche parade. By the time Elizabeth Kostova's *The Historian* became the hot summer best-seller in 2005, *Dracula* fiction had been built up into something of a cottage (or castle) industry. Kostova's novel invited the reader along on a search for Vlad the Impaler. That same year, Tim Lucas focused on one of the book's best-known characters in his *Dracula* prequel *The Book of Renfield: A Gospel of Dracula*.

It's just one more way the count's life has been unnaturally prolonged. Pastiche keeps him from slipping into the past tense.

SIDEBAR

The Dracula Stamp of Approval

· · · · · · · · · · · ·

He took up the letters on the table and stamped them carefully. . . .
—*Jonathan Harker,* Dracula, *chapter 3*

A Dracula pen, pencil, and eraser set was one of the merchandising items issued by the United States Postal Service in conjunction with the 1997 release of the "Classic Movie Monsters" stamps.

It only took a century—a mere trifle to an immortal character like the count. Bram Stoker's *Dracula* was published in 1897. Fast-forward a hundred years: in October 1997, the U.S. Postal Service issued its series of five 32-cent "Classic Movie Monsters" stamps. The stamps featured the faces of Lon Chaney as the Phantom of the Opera; Boris Karloff as the Frankenstein monster and the Mummy; Lon Chaney Jr. as the Wolf Man; and, of course, Bela Lugsoi as Dracula.

The Postal Service was honoring four beloved horror stars. It was paying tribute to five classic Universal Studios horror films. But arriving in the year of the *Dracula* centennial, the Lugosi stamp seemed even more supernaturally special.

Having learned a thing or two from the Hollywood studios, the Postal Service unveiled an extensive merchandising line around the "Movie Monsters" stamps. You could get the image of your favorite horror stamp on a T-shirt, a mouse pad, a postcard, a lapel pin, a magnet, or a collectible pen, pencil, and eraser set. The Dracula portrait was based on the 1931 still of Lugosi's count raising his cape as a shield against Van Helsing's crucifix.

But the Postal Service's Lugosi tribute wasn't the only stamp sought by Dracula fans and collectors in 1997. Earlier that year, closer to the time of the actual *Dracula* centennial, the United Kingdom issued a series of four-stamp series featuring Count Dracula, Frankenstein's monster, Dr. Jekyll and Mr. Hyde, and a red-eyed Hound of the Baskervilles. This portrayal of Dracula was drawn from the description in Stoker's book, with a white mustache, red eyes and lips, white hair, fangs, bushy eyebrows, and pointed ears.

Ireland, paying tribute to the novel and a native son, issued its own four-stamp set, each one with a Dracula image (not of Lugosi, but still of the popular movie conception, with cape, evening clothes, black hair, and a widow's peak). Canada also got into the monster-stamp act in 1997, issuing a set that included a werewolf and a white-faced Dracula with bared fangs and Lugosi-like widow's peak.

Romania responded that year with a four-stamp "stories and legends" Dracula set featuring Vlad the Impaler as a national hero and as a more vampiric figure; the series, recognizing the interests of foreign tourists, included renderings of two spooky castles, one overshadowed by bat wings. Romanian stamps bearing the likeness of Vlad Tepes had already been circulated in 1959 and 1996.

Commemorative stamps featuring Lugosi as Dracula were also issued by Chad, Sierra Leone, and other countries. Talk about going postal!

The Undying Count

. . . .

*"However, he means to succeed, and a man who has
centuries before him can afford to wait. . . ."*
—*Professor Van Helsing,* Dracula, *chapter 23*

The delightful Jeanne Keyes Youngson is the founder of the Count Dracula Fan Club, one of the oldest and largest organizations devoted to Dracula research. She is the author of books on Dracula, and has edited collections of vampire stories. So what does she think of how Stoker finished off the Count at the end of the novel?

"To tell you the truth, I've never read the last chapter," she confesses.

What? Never?

"Never," she confirms. "I can't bring myself to read it. And I don't want to. The character just means too much to me to go through that. So I've never read it. But no matter what Bram Stoker says, Dracula doesn't really die at the end of the book, does he? He is the ultimate survivor, continuing through the ages. He's timeless, taking on different forms to be contemporary."

Stoker merely put a note at the end of chapter 27. In truth, there is no final chapter. The count does go on because, as Youngson aptly puts it, he is timeless. And the themes of the book are not only timeless but adaptable to each new generation working through old and new sets of fears, anxieties, and insecurities. *Dracula,* like Mary Wollstonecraft Shelley's *Frankenstein* (1818) and Robert Louis Stevenson's *The Strange Case of Dr. Jekyll and Mr. Hyde* (1886), catches something of the eternal. It seems relevant today, about 110 years after its publication. It will still seem relevant more than a thousand years from now, when humans carry their fears and ambitions into the Alpha Centauri star system. Through *Dracula,* Stoker both challenges us and warns us, taking his cue from the Wiliam Shakespeare play he knew so well, *Hamlet.* He dares us to ponder the wondrous thought we all face alone, in darkness and in light: what dreams may come . . . and what nightmares.

Acknowledgments

"Come in. My work is finished, and I am free."
—Dr. John Seward, Dracula, *chapter 19*

The *Dracula* experts are quick to welcome new blood into the family. They are eager to bid you welcome. David J. Skal, the leading authority on *Dracula* stage and film adaptations, put me in touch with Elizabeth Miller, the genial Canadian professor who has brought so much sense and dispelled so much nonsense about the historic and literary Draculas. I am indebted to both of them, not only for their indispensable guidance but for their acres of incredible, indispensable research.

Elizabeth, in turn, put me in touch with vampire chronicler J. Gordon Melton, Transylvania Society of Dracula founder Nicolae Paduraru, and Count Dracula Fan Club founder Jeanne Keyes Youngson. As vampire hunters go, you can't do much better than Skal, Miller, Melton, Paduraru, and Youngson. And who's playing on your team? Their shrewd observations are scattered throughout this book.

My deepest thanks go also to Michael J. Barsanti, the curator who guided me through the boxes containing Bram Stoker's *Dracula* notes at the Rosenbach Museum and Library in Philadelphia. Michael, Greg Giuliano, and the entire staff at the Rosenbach couldn't have been more genial or generous.

I am grateful to *Dracula* actors Frank Langella, Christopher Lee, and Michael Nouri for sharing thoughts on the appeal of the count. Invaluable insight was also provided by actors David Boreanaz and Martin Landau, Hollywood collector Ronald V. Borst, film critic and historian Leonard Maltin, author Richard Matheson, and a trio of witty director-producers with heavyweight vampire credits: Wes Craven, the late Dan Curtis, and *Buffy the Vampire Slayer* creator Joss Whedon.

Anyone venturing into the realm of *Dracula* must acknowledge the paths blazed by two landmark books published in 1972: Raymond T. McNally and Radu Florescu's *In Search of Dracula* and Leonard Wolf's *A Dream of Dracula*. It also would be unthinkable to proceed without consulting the four major Stoker biographies: Harry Ludlam's *A Biography of Dracula: The Life Story of Bram Stoker* (1962), Daniel Farson's *The Man Who Wrote Dracula: A Biography of Bram Stoker* (1975), Barbara Belford's *Bram Stoker: A Biography of the Author of Dracula* (1996), and Paul Murray's *From the Shadow of Dracula: A Life of Bram Stoker* (2004).

Also staking out the *Dracula* territory are the scholarly and annotated editions of Stoker's novel. The best of these, to my mind, are the Norton Critical Edition (edited by Nina Auerbach and David J. Skal, 1997), *The Annotated Dracula* (edited by Leonard Wolf, 1975, and later republished as *The Essential Dracula*), and *Dracula: The Definitive Edition* (with introductions and appendices by Marvin Kaye, and illustrations by Edward Gorey, 1996).

For their help in rounding up pictures, books, and research materials, a tip of the coffin lid to the "James" boys: Jim Benson, Jim Perkowski, and Jim Pierson (who also shared the tape of his interview with *Dracula* star Jack Palance). Fraternal help came early and often by way of the Dawidziak boys, brothers Joe and Michael, as well as from Paul Bauer and Drew White, who are like brothers (although more soft-spoken than the, um, blood relations). And there is no adequate way to express my gratitude to artist Joseph Vargo, who gave free reign to use his wonderfully atmospheric depictions of Dracula and vampires.

Thanks also go to Evander Lomke, who, after more than a decade of talking *Dracula* with me, got the idea that I should write this book.

And though named last here, Sara and Becky are first in my heart. This is not written for their benefit: they already know this. It is so that whoever chances upon these words will know of their—to borrow Van Helsing's phrase—"sweetness and loving care."

Answers to Puzzle:
Putting the Cross in Crossword

1 P	2 A	3 L	4 A	5 N	6 C	7 E	■	8 B	9 L	O	10 O	D	■	11 W	I	N	12 E
13 A	L	U	C	A	R	D	■	■	O	■	■	R	■	O	■	■	E
14 L	O	G	■	15 Y	O	U	16 T	U	R	K	17	■	18 L	A	I	R
19 S	N	O	20 W	■	21 S	C	A	R	22 A	■	■	F	■	I
■	23 E	S	E	■	24 S	A	T	A	N	25 I	C	■	26 E	■	27 R	■	E
28 T	■	29 I	L	30 L	■	31 T	E	P	E	S	■	32 V	L	A	D
33 O	34 F	■	35 C	O	36 M	E	■	37 C	E	38 A	39 S	E	■	Y	■	40 S
41 M	A	■	42 O	N	E	■	43 K	K	44 T	O	■	45 S	A	W
46 B	47 R	A	M	■	48 L	49 E	E	■	50 G	O	■	51 T	■	A
■	52 B	E	D	■	N	■	54 C	A	R	P	A	55 T	H	56 I	A	N
57 E	58 B	B	■	O	■	T	A	A	■	59 R	I	■	H
60 M	O	O	N	■	61 T	R	A	N	62 S	63 Y	L	V	A	64 N	I	A	65 N
66 B	A	T	■	67 B	O	Y	■	C	E	N	R	■	I
68 A	T	T	A	C	K	■	70 H	I	D	71 C	O	E	■	E
R	■	72 C	A	W	A	K	E	73 E	Y	E	74 L	i	L
K	75 S	76 T	A	Y	S	N	R	77 P	A	S	S
■	78 C	R	O	W	■	79 T	80 C	U	E	81 E	O	N	E
82 F	L	O	R	E	N	C	E	■	83 E	N	R	A	G	E	D	N

Drawing by Mark Dawidziak

About the Author

Mark Dawidziak has been a theater, film, and television critic for almost thirty years. Since July 1999, he has been the TV critic at Cleveland's daily newspaper, *The Plain Dealer*. During his fifteen years at the *Akron Beacon Journal*, he held such posts as TV columnist, movie critic, and critic at large.

Dawidziak's many books include a horror novel, *Grave Secrets* (1994), and such non-fiction works as *The Barter Theatre Story: Love Made Visible* (1982); *The Columbo Phile: A Casebook* (1989); *Mark My Words: Mark Twain on Writing* (1996); *The Night Stalker Companion: A 25th Anniversary Tribute* (1997), and *Horton Foote's The Shape of the River: The Lost Teleplay about Mark Twain* (2003). Several of his essays and introductions appear in *Richard Matheson's Kolchak Scripts* (2003) and *Bloodlines: Richard Matheson's Dracula, I Am Legend, and Other Vampire Stories* (2006), books he edited for Gauntlet Press. He is currently collaborating with Paul Bauer on a biography of "hobo writer" Jim Tully, a forgotten author who was hailed as "America's Gorky" and acclaimed as a literary superstar in the 1920s and '30s.

Dawidziak has also been a regular contributor to such magazines as *Cinefantastique*, *Commonwealth*, *Mystery Scene*, *Parent's Choice*, *Scarlet Street*, *Sci-Fi Universe*, and *TV Guide*.

In 2001, Dawidziak and his wife, actress Sara Showman, founded the Largely Literary Theater Company. Dedicated to promoting literacy and literature, the company has toured Dawidziak's three-person version of Charles Dickens's A Christmas Carol, *The Tell-Tale Play* (stories and poems by Edgar Allan Poe), and *The Reports of My Death Are Greatly Exaggerated* (humorous sketches by Mark Twain).

Born in Huntington, New York, Dawidziak is a journalism graduate of George Washington University. He lives in Cuyahoga Falls, Ohio, with Sara and their daughter, Rebecca "Becky" Claire.